EPIGRAPHY AND THE GREEK HISTORIAN

Epigraphy is the study of inscriptions found on ancient artefacts such as stones, coins, and statues and the attempt to infer historical data from these inscrip-tions. It is an indispensable tool for archaeologists and classicists, and has considerable potential to enrich the study of ancient history at the undergradu-ate and graduate levels. *Epigraphy and the Greek Historian* is a unified collec-tion of essays that explore various ways in which inscriptions can help students reconstruct and understand Greek history.

The volume is divided into two parts: Athens, and the wider Greek world. The contributors convincingly demonstrate the value of epigraphy for history, arguing that in many cases inscriptions are the only data we have from which to recover the local history of places that were not the main focus of ancient literary sources, which are often frustratingly Athenocentric. Ideally, the histo-rian uses both inscriptions and literary sources to propose plausible recon-structions and thereby weave together the disconnected threads of the past into a connected and persuasive narrative. *Epigraphy and the Greek Historian* is a comprehensive examination of epigraphy and a timely resource for students and scholars involved in the study of ancient history.

(Phoenix Supplementary Volumes)

CRAIG COOPER is dean of Arts and Science at Nipissing University.

PHOENIX

Journal of the Classical Association of Canada
Revue de la Société canadienne des études classiques
Supplementary Volume XLVII
Tome supplémentaire XLVII

EDITED BY CRAIG COOPER

Epigraphy and the Greek Historian

UNIVERSITY OF TORONTO PRESS
Toronto Buffalo London

Toronto Buffalo London
Reprinted in paperback 2014

ISBN 978-0-8020-9069-0 (cloth)
ISBN 978-1-4426-5248-4 (paper)

Printed on acid-free paper

Library and Archives Canada Cataloguing in Publication

Epigraphy and the Greek historian / edited by Craig Cooper.

(Phoenix supplementary ; volumes XLVII)
Includes index.
ISBN 978-0-8020-9069-0 (bound)
ISBN 978-1-4426-5248-4 (pbk.)

1. Inscriptions, Greek. 2. Greece – History – Sources.
I. Cooper, Craig Richard, 1960– I. Series: Phoenix. Supplementary volume (Toronto , Ont.) ; XLVII.

CN350.E65 2008 938 C2007-907112-0

University of Toronto Press acknowledges the financial assistance to its publishing program of the Canada Council for the Arts and the Ontario Arts Council.

University of Toronto Press acknowledges the financial support for its publishing activities of the Government of Canada through the Book Publishing Industry Development Program (BPIDP).

Contents

Part Two: Athens from the Outside: The Wider Greek World

Contributors

Sheila Ager is associate professor of Classical Studies and associate dean of Arts, University of Waterloo.

Craig Cooper is professor of Classics and dean of Arts and Science, Nipissing University.

David Mirhady is associate professor of Humanities, Simon Fraser University.

Frances Pownall is associate professor of History and Classics, University of Alberta.

Bruce Robertson is associate professor of Classics, Mount Allison University.

Gordon Shrimpton is professor emeritus of Greek and Roman Studies, University of Victoria.

Kathryn Simonsen is assistant professor of Classics, Memorial University of Newfoundland.

David Whitehead is professor of Ancient History, Queen's University Belfast.

Abbreviations

Except for very familiar names like Aeschylus, Aristotle, Plutarch, Socrates and Thucydides, and common place names like Corinth, Cyclades, and Cyprus, names and place names are directly transliterated from the Greek. The letter χ, however, is rendered as *ch* and not *kh*. Abbreviations of works of individual authors follows the *OCD*.

Ancient Authors

Aes.	Aeschylus
Aisch.	Aischines
And.	Andokides
Ant.	Antiphon
Ar.	Aristophanes
Arist.	Aristotle
Ath. Pol.	*Athenaion Politeia*
Ath.	Athenaios
Dein.	Deinarchos
Dem.	Demosthenes
Diod.	Diodoros
Eur.	Euripides
Harp.	Harpokration
Hdt.	Herodotos
Hom.	Homer
Hyp.	Hypereides
Is.	Isaios
Isok.	Isokrates
Lyk.	Lykourgos

Lys.	Lysias
Men.	Menandros (Menander)
Nep.	Nepos
Philoch.	Philochoros
Pl.	Plato
Plut.	Plutarchos (Plutarch)
Soph.	Sophokles (Sophocles)
Theophr.	Theophrastos
Thuc.	Thucydides
Xen.	Xenophon

Academic Journals

ABSA	*Annual of the British School at Athens*
AE	*Arkhaiologikè Ephemeris*
AHB	*Ancient History Bulletin*
AJA	*American Journal of Archaeology*
AJAH	*American Journal of Ancient History*
AJP	*American Journal of Philology*
AM	*Mitteilungen des Deutschen Archäologischen Instituts: Athenische Abteilung*
APAW	*Abhandlungen der Preussischen Akademie der Wissenschaften*
ASAA	*Annuario della Scuola Archeologica di Atene e delle Missioni Italiane in Oriente*
ASNP	*Annali della Scuola Normale Superiore di Pisa, Classe di Lettere e Filosofia*
BCH	*Bulletin de correspondance hellénique*
C&M	*Classica et mediaevalia*
ClAnt	*Classical Antiquity*
CP	*Classical Philology*
CQ	*Classical Quarterly*
CR	*Classical Review*
EMC/CV	*Échos du monde classique/Classical Views*
GRBS	*Greek, Roman, and Byzantine Studies*
JdI	*Jahrbuch des Deutschen Archäologischen Instituts*
JHS	*Journal of Hellenic Studies*
PP	*La Parola del passato*
QAL	*Quaderni di archeologia della Libia*
REA	*Revue des études anciennes*

REG	*Revue des études grecques*
RFIC	*Rivista di filoligia e di istruzione classica*
RhM	*Rheinisches Museum für Philologie*
RIDA	*Revue internationale des droits de l'antiquité*
RPh	*Revue de philologie*
TAPA	*Transactions of the American Philological Association*
ZPE	*Zeitschrift für Papyrologie und Epigraphik*
ZSS	*Zeitschrift der Savigny-Stiftung für Rechtsgeschichte*

Epigraphic Collections and Reference Works

APF	J.K. Davies. *Athenian Propertied Families, 600–300 BC*. Oxford, 1971.
ATL	B.D. Meritt, H.T. Wade-Gery, and M.F. McGregor. *The Athenian Tribute Lists*, 4 vols. Princeton, 1939–50.
EM	Epigraphic Museum, Athens.
FGrHist	F. Jacoby. *Die Fragmente der griechischen Historiker*. Berlin, 1923–.
Fornara	C.W. Fornara, ed. and trans. *Archaic Times to the End of the Peloponnesian War*. Vol. 1 of *Translated Documents of Greece and Rome*, ed. E. Badian and R.K. Sherk. Cambridge, 1983.
Harding	P. Harding, ed. and trans. *From the End of the Peloponnesian War to the Battle of Ipsus*. Vol. 2 of *Translated Documents of Greece and Rome*, ed. E. Badian and R.K. Sherk. Cambridge, 1985.
IG	*Inscriptiones Graecae*. Berlin, 1903– .
LGPN I	P.M. Fraser and E. Matthews, eds. *A Lexicon of Greek Personal Names*. Vol. 1, *The Aegean Islands, Cyprus, Cyrenaica*. Oxford, 1987.
LGPN II	M.J. Osborne and S.G. Byrne, eds. *A Lexicon of Greek Personal Names*. Vol. 2, *Attica*. Oxford, 1994.
LSJ	H.G. Liddell and R. Scott. *A Greek-English Lexicon*. Rev. H.S. Jones. Oxford, 1968.

Maier	F.G. Maier. *Griechische Mauerbauinschriften*, vol. 1. Heidelberg, 1959.
Meiggs-Lewis	R. Meiggs and D. Lewis. *A Selection of Greek Historical Inscriptions*². Oxford, 1988.
OCD	S. Hornblower and A. Spawforth. *The Oxford Classical Dictionary*³. Oxford, 1996.
Rhodes-Osborne	P.J. Rhodes and R. Osborne. *Greek Historical Inscriptions 404–323 BC*. Oxford, 2003.
Tod	M. Tod. *Greek Historical Inscriptions*², two volumes in one. Chicago, 1985.
SEG	*Supplementum Epigraphicum Graecum*, vols 1–25.
SV	H. Bengston. *Die Staatsverträge des Altertums*, vol. 2. Munich/Berlin, 1962.
*Syll*³	W. Dittenberger. *Sylloge Inscriptionum Graecarum*³, vol. 4. Index by R.F. Hiller von Gaertringen. Leipzig, 1915–24.
Wickersham-Verbrugghe	J. Wickersham and G. Verbrugghe. *Greek Historical Documents*. Toronto, 1973.

Epigraphical *Sigla*

α̣ε̣	The letters are partially visible but the reading is uncertain.
α̲ε̲	The letters seen by a previous editor are no longer visible.
[αε]	The letters are no longer preserved but supplied by the editor.
<αε>	Letters that were accidentally omitted by engraver are supplied by the editor.
(αε)	Letters are supplied by the editor to complete an abbreviation.
{αε}	The letters inscribed in error are removed by the editor.
[. . .]	Lost or illegible letters for which no restoration is offered; in smaller gaps the number of dots represent the number of lost letters; in larger gaps by a number [. . . . ⁸ . . .].
[– – – –]	A gap of an uncertain number of lost or illegible letters.

Phillip Edward Harding: List of Publications

1972

Review of *Heraclidis Lembi Excerpta Politiarum*, by M.R. Dilts. *Phoenix* 26: 414–15.

1973

'The Purpose of Isokrates' *Archidamos* and *On the Peace*.' *California Studies in Classical Antiquity* 6: 137–49.

Review of *Ancient History Atlas*, by M. Grant. *Classical News and Views* 17: 30–1.

1974

'The Theramenes Myth.' *Phoenix* 28: 101–11.

'Androtion's View of Solon's *Seisachtheia*.' *Phoenix* 28: 282–9.

Review of *Thucydides: The Artful Reporter*, by V. Hunter. *Classical News and Views* 18: 93–4.

1976

'Androtion's Political Career.' *Historia* 25: 186–200.

1977

'Atthis and Politeia.' *Historia* 26: 148–60.

Review of *Das Geschaft mit dem Staat*, by D. Brown. *Phoenix* 31: 268–71.

1978

'O Androtion, You Fool.' *AJAH* 3: 179–83.

Review of *Translated Documents of Greece and Rome*, vol. 1, by C.W. Fornara. *Phoenix* 32: 86–9.

1979

'Orations ... most nedeful to be redde in these daungerous dayes: A Chapter in the *Nachleben* of Demosthenes.' *Classical News and Views* 23: 51–63.

Review of G.L. Cawkwell, *Philip of Macedon*. *Phoenix* 33: 173–8.

1981

'In Search of a Polypragmatist,' in G.S. Shrimpton and D.J. McCargar (eds.), *Classical Contributions: Studies in Honour of Malcolm Francis McGregor*, 41–50. Locust Valley, NY.

1984

Review of *The Thirty at Athens*, by P. Krentz. *EMC/CV* 28: 99–102.

1985

From the End of the Peloponnesian War to the Battle of Ipsus. Vol. 2 of *Translated Documents of Greece and Rome*. Cambridge.

Review of *A Commentary on the Aristotelian Athenaion Politeia*, by P.J. Rhodes. *Phoenix* 39: 389–92.

1986

'An Education to All.' *Liverpool Classical Monthly* 11: 134–6.

Review of *The Way to Chaeronea*, by H. Montgomery. *EMC/CV* 30: 68–9.

1987

'Metics, Foreigners or Slaves? The Recipients of Honours in *IG* II^2 10.' *ZPE* 67: 176–82.

'Rhetoric and Politics in Fourth-Century Athens.' *Phoenix* 41: 125–39.

'The Authorship of the Hellenika Oxyrhynchia.' *AHB* 1: 101–4.

Review of *Focione tra storia e trasfigurazione ideale*, by C. Bearzot. *JHS* 107: 233–4.

Review of *Demography and Democracy*, by M.H. Hansen. *Liverpool Classical Monthly* 12: 159–60.

1988

'King Pausanias and the Restoration of Democracy at Athens.' *Hermes* 116: 185–93.

'Athenian Defensive Strategy in the Fourth Century BC.' *Phoenix* 42: 61–78.

'Laughing at Isokrates: Humour in the Areopagitikos?' *Liverpool Classical Monthly* 13: 18–23.

Review of *Politics of the Archaic Peloponnese*, by K. Adshead. *Liverpool Classical Monthly* 13: XX–XX.

1990

'Athenian Defensive Strategy Again.' *Phoenix* 44: 377–80.

Review of *The Athenian Assembly*, by M.H. Hansen. *Phoenix* 44: 199–200.

1991

'All Pigs Are Animals, but Are All Animals Pigs?' *AHB* 5: 145–8.

1992

'Funerary Monuments from Stymphalos.' *ZPE* 93: 57–66 (with H. Williams).

1993

Review of *Philip II of Macedon: A Life from Ancient Sources*, by A.S. Bradford. *Canadian Journal of History* 28: 321–3.

1994

Androtion and the Atthis. Oxford.

'Comedy and Rhetoric,' in I. Worthington (ed.), *Persuasion: Greek Rhetoric in Action*, 196–221. London.

1995

Review of *Die athenische Demokratie*, by J. Bleicken. *CR* 45: 315–17.

Review of S. Lambert, *The Phratries of Attica*, by S. Lambert. *Ancient History Review* X: 1539–40.

Review of *The Humanity of Thucydides*, by C. Orwin. *EMC/CV* 14: 280–4.

1996

Articles in S. Hornblower and A. Spawforth, eds., *The Oxford Classical Dictionary*, 3rd ed. Oxford. 'Andron'; 'Androtion'; 'Atthis'; 'Cleidemos'; 'Hellanikos'; 'Ister'; 'Melanthios'; 'Phanodemos'; 'Philokhoros.'

Review of *The Fourth Century BC*, by D.M. Lewis et al. Vol. 6 of *The Cambridge Ancient History*, 2nd ed. *CR* 46: 91–3.

Review of *Financing the Athenian Fleet: Public Taxation and Sacred Relations*, by V. Gabrielsen. *CR* 46: 96–8.

2000

'Demosthenes in the Underworld. The *Nachleben* of a Rhetor,' in I. Worthington, ed., *Demosthenes*, 246–71. London.

2006

Didymos on Demosthenes: Introduction, Text, Translation, and Commentary. Oxford.

Introduction

CRAIG COOPER

Malcolm McGregor, former head of the Department of Classics at the University of British Columbia, is reported once to have said that epigraphy was the handmaiden of history. This epigrammatic statement, I think, captures the essence of the traditional approach to the study of epigraphy and its relative importance to history. For scholars like McGregor who worked on the *Athenian Tribute Lists (ATL)*, itself an invaluable work of scholarship for those constructing fifth-century Athenian history, inscriptions were important mainly for what they told us about political history; that is to say, how they served our understanding of Thucydidean history. Though the present volume deals with political history, it also, I hope, does more than this and suggests a much broader use and value for Greek inscriptions. The handmaiden has been set free, so to speak, but like any freed slave must remain under obligation to its former mistress.

The present collection of essays is not a tribute to Malcolm McGregor but to his successor at the University of British Columbia, Professor Phillip Harding, who has done more perhaps than any other Greek historian in Canada to advance the discipline by introducing many of the current generation of Canadian scholars to the Attic orators, Athenian history, and Greek epigraphy. Several contributors to this volume are in fact former graduate students who had their first taste of epigraphy in Phillip Harding's seminar, where he elucidated what seemed to the uninitiated like mysterious texts. Here students handled and studied the squeezes, impressions taken from stones now tucked away in obscure corners of museums. Here too the strange acronyms like *Syll, SEG, IG* i^2 (as opposed to *IG* i^3) were explained. For graduate students fresh from their undergraduate studies these were indeed exotic symbols, representing Sibylline-like books that contained fragmentary texts transcribed from ancient stones and encoded with mysterious markings around their letters: α̣[-----]α̣ by scholars like Dittenberger and Boeckh. After our initiation, we were ready to delve deeper into the study of Greek history and epigraphy. These essays, we hope, reflect our maturation under Phillip Harding's tutelage.

The term epigraphy can cover various forms of writing on a wide range of permanent media, from inscriptions on stone, scratches on *ostraka,* to graffiti on walls.[1] This volume, though, has restricted itself to inscriptions, which were the public face of written documents, particularly in Athens. Usually laws and decrees of Athens were inscribed on stone stelai, after being authorized by the *dēmos* and *boulē*. An inscribed stele thus represented the permanent and public version of the official decree,[2] and as such would be set up in a public place where they could be seen, if not necessarily read, by all.[3] Often in the preamble to a decree the *boulē* would instruct magistrates on how and where to publish a decree. The placement of a decree was as important as its content, a fact not lost on ancient Greeks. Anaximenes of Lampsakos, the fourth-century rhetorician, reports how Ephialtes, the fifth-century BC Athenian reformer, moved the *axones* and *kyrbeis,* objects on which the laws of Drakon and Solon had been inscribed, down from the Acropolis to the Council Chamber and Agora (*FGrHist* 72 F 13). The move physically symbolized the link between the laws and the democratic government that operated in the Agora, where the people themselves shopped and worked. It has been suggested that the Stoa Basileios, which formed part of a series of government buildings on the west side of the Agora, was refurbished shortly after the time of Ephialtes' reforms, perhaps to accommodate these very laws.[4] Indeed, when *anagrapheis* were commissioned in 409 to republish the homicide laws of Drakon, a copy was to be obtained from the *Basileus* in the Stoa Basileios (*IG* i^{3} 104). At the end of the century the stoa again underwent renovations with the addition of two side annexes that would hold the revised code of the restored democracy of 403. Ephialtes' reforms, which led to greater transparency and accountability in government, were aimed in part at stripping the Council of the Areiopagos of its old constitutional powers and transferring these powers to democratic organs of government; it is no surprise that one of the first acts of the Thirty, who overthrew the democracy under the guise of restoring the ancestral constitution of Athens, was to remove from the Areiopagos Ephialtes' laws reforming the Council (*Ath. Pol.* 35.1–2). Democracy had symbolically as well as literally been undone.

When studying the details of an inscribed text we can sometimes forget the monumental aspect of the inscription whose position of prominence in the Agora or on the Acropolis sent a message of its own that resonated beyond the content of the decree itself.[5] *IG* i^{3} 1453 (Meiggs-Lewis no. 45), preserving the decree that enforced the use of Attic coinage throughout the Athenian empire, records (lines 10–12) how the decree is to be set up in the agora of each city by the *archontes*, Athenian governors found throughout the various cites of the empire, and how a herald is to proceed announcing the Athenian orders to comply. This verbal message, combined with the visual image of the decree's erection, would have served as a powerful reminder to the inhabitants of each city that Athens was indeed sovereign. How the decree was viewed or received no doubt varied; it may have been welcomed by traders and democrats sympathetic to Athens but viewed with derision by those who resented Athenian infringement of their autonomy. At any rate the physical presence of a stele spoke loudly; in Thomas' words, it served as a 'symbolic memorial,' and it is not surprising that one of the first acts of rebellion was to overturn or destroy that memorial.[6] More work needs to be done by scholars on the monumental significance of inscriptions and what they came to symbolize to various audiences; though the present volume gives some consideration to this, most of the papers have taken the more modest task of exploring what the actual texts of inscriptions can tell us about history.

The volume itself is divided into two parts: 'Athens' and 'Athens from the Outside: The Wider Greek World.' In Part One, five essays are devoted to exploring what inscriptions can tell us about Athenian history. Most deal with the fourth century BC. In the first paper, David Mirhady examines closely the text of *IG* i^3 104, which preserves the decree authorizing the republication of Drakon's homicide law in 409/08. According to Mirhady, the various procedural terms, φεύγεν, δικάζεν, διαγνôναι, αἰδέσασθαι (lines 11–12) of Drakon's law originally prescribed a step-by-step procedural order that led from assignation of guilt to reconciliation. In particular, Mirhady takes issue with the traditional interpretation of φεύγεν, 'flee,' as referring to the punishment of exile, and suggests rather that the term refers to the killer becoming a defendant that is fleeing from the proclamation and prosecution of the deceased family. This interpretation is consistent with Attic legal idiom. Mirhady points specifically to Demosthenes 23.25–6, a passage that seems to suggest that Drakon's homicide law dictated a trial and not punishment. Indeed, Mirhady draws extensively on the Attic orators to support his various arguments; the role of the *Basileus*, for instance, is to judge (δικάζεν) causation (αἰτία), and in Attic idiom the defendant can be spoken of as 'the one having αἰτία.' But these same sources also show how the homicide law came to be applied differently in fourth-century Athens than it had been in the seventh century, though the law itself had undergone little change. In the fourth century the *Basileus* no longer judged but introduced the case; it was the *Ephetai*, like the democratic courts, who now assumed that role, and the only vestige of the King's former power was to judge in perfunctory fashion unknown killers in the Prytaneion. Under the original terms of Drakon's homicide law the *Ephetai* were in actual fact a court of appeal that would evaluate the King's judgment, should it be appealed. This conclusion has two very important implications: first, it suggests that Solon's important legal innovation, ἔφεσις, was not profoundly innovative but much more incremental; and secondly, it reveals great flexibility in Athenian law, which could be adapted over time to changing political circumstances with out necessarily being changed itself.

The second paper had a curious beginning as a seminar paper in Professor Harding's course on fourth-century Greek history. In this paper Craig Cooper examines *IG* ii^2 111 (Harding no. 55) for what it can tell us about Athenian politics. The inscription, discovered on the south slope of the Athenian Acropolis, preserves a decree, dated to 363/2, authorizing Aristophon's settlement of affairs of Ioulis on the island of Keos. Although Chabrias had just put down an island-wide revolt on Keos, the Athenians were forced to dispatch a second force under Aristophon's command to quell renewed unrest in Ioulis. In the wake of his success there, Aristophon proposed a decree in the assembly that incorporated portions of Chabrias' previous settlement. Soon after, Aristophon was indicted for his proposal by the young orator Hypereides. Cooper cautiously follows Dreher's suggestion that *IG* ii^2 404 preserves the actual provisions of the decree that authorized Chabrias' original settlement of Keos and argues that Aristophon's punitive treatment of Ioulis, in contrast to Chabrias' generous amnesty, may have provided ammunition for Hypereides' attack against Aristophon. Further, the prosecution of Aristophon should be seen in a wider political context, as one of many trials that were brought forward at this time by younger politicians like Hypereides and Apollodoros in an attempt to discredit the old guard who had dominated politics for the last decade or so.

In the study of Greek history, there can at times be 'a pleasing conjunction of literary and documentary evidence,' as David Whitehead notes. Whitehead is thinking of Demosthenes 20.42 and *IG* i^3 125, both of which commemorate the generosity of Epikerdes of Kyrene. He accepts Pritchett's arguments that what Epikerdes did in 413 was not ransom Athenian citizens taken captive in Sicily but provide money to feed these prisoners. But the concern of his paper is not with this particular episode of Athenian history but to test Pritchett's assertion that there was another expedition to Sicily in the mid-360s that ended in failure and did involve ransoming. As Whitehead clearly argues, Isaios 6.1, which mentions Chairestratos' syntrierarchy to Sicily, and *IG* ii^2 283, which preserves a decree honouring a certain Ph [- -] of Cypriot Salamis for ransoming Athenian citizens taken captive in

Sicily, cannot be made to show a pleasing conjunction that would prove Pritchett's assertion that such a naval expedition did in fact take place. *IG* ii^2 283 may instead refer to the ransoming of merchants taken captive by pirates, a suggestion that finds a parallel in *IG* ii^2 284. Isaios 6.1, on the other hand, can perhaps be brought into conjunction with *IG* ii^2 1609, which has been restored to read [Χαιρέστρ]ατος Κηφι(σιεύς) as syntrierarch in the year 366/5. But Whitehead is right to caution that this is only a possibility, as the restoration and the date are far from certain. Whitehead's paper stands as a salutary caution to historians not to proceed too far in searching for agreement between literary and documentary sources, particularly when that search might lead to creating 'history from square brackets.'

'History from square brackets' was an expression coined by E. Badian to describe the danger of creating history on the basis of some conjectural restoration to the missing text of a damaged inscription.[7] Part of the task of the epigraphist is to restore missing text; sometimes this can be straightforward, given the formulaic nature of inscriptions; at other times restorations are mere speculation and nothing more. [Χαιρέστρ]ατος is, as Whitehead points out, not the only possible restoration for an -ατος ending name. The restoration of the phrase ὦνος ἐ[ν]άτ[ηι] ('on the ninth day of the month of') to line 1 of *IG* ii^2 404 originally led scholars to conclude that it could not be dated before 338/7, the earliest known date for an inscription to carry such a formula. But Schweigert's restoration of a similar formula to *IG* ii^2 122, which he dates to 357/6, should mean scholars can move the date of *IG* ii^2 404 up to the Social War and see it as one of many decrees passed by Athens infringing on the autonomy of league members. And indeed scholars have. But such a conclusion rests on shaky ground, and the footing can easily slip from underneath it. It hangs rather precariously on two restorations to *IG* ii^2 122: the restored word 'on the sixth day' and the restored archon date. But neither restoration is secure. Schweigert's dating of *IG* ii^2 122 rests on a single fact – that the decree it preserves falls in the same prytany as a decree dealing with ambassadors from Elaious that can be securely dated to 357/6, the archonship of Agathokles. Yet *IG* ii^2 122 preserves only the final sigma of the archon's name and thus cannot be dated with any certainty to that year. Remove that restoration and the whole epigraphic deck of cards begins to fall and with it the dating of *IG* ii^2 404 to the Social War. Cooper has shown that *IG* ii^2 404 can just as easily be dated to the 360s based on other, more convincing considerations.

Damage done to an inscription can thus present difficulties both in restoring the text and assessing the overall dimensions of an inscription. This problem is highlighted by Kathryn Simonsen, who examines the state of *IG* ii^2 1622, which preserves a list of debts collected from naval officials between the years 345 and 342. The stele was damaged when it was reused as a gutter, making it difficult to determine how much of the top portion and left hand side of stele was lost. Simonsen estimates that five columns are missing from the left hand side of the stele, covering entries of tribes I–VII, though it is equally possible that the inscription was originally opisthographic, with five columns on the front and five on the back of the stele. What *IG* ii^2 1622 may represent, then, is the back side of the original inscription. Damage to the surviving part of stele has also erased key details that would have provided important clues to interpreting the inscription. Columns **a–c**, for instance, list repayment of debts of trierarchs by tribe but columns **e–f** do so according to the ship the trierarchs commanded. Because the initial headings, which might have provided an explanation for this change in accounting style, are lost, Simonsen must argue on the basis of the entries themselves – tribal entries list one or two men per ship but ship entries several men – that the change reflects the introduction of the symmory system. In any case the naval inventories, of which *IG* ii^2 1622 is one of many, attest to an ongoing problem of indebtedness, with trierarchs owing debts of long standing, sometimes even from several different ships. One of the main causes of this indebtedness was a misappropriation of equipment. *IG* ii^2 1622.379–579, the main focus of Simonsen's paper, attests to this fact. It is unique among naval inventories, however, in that it concerns only the debts of ταμίαι and νεωρίων ἐπιμεληταί and indicates that between 345 and 343 Athens made a concerted effort to collect on outstanding debts held by these naval officials whereas trierarchs, it seems, remained untouched. Simonsen suggests that this crackdown was the angry response of the assembly over Athens' failed military operations that led to the signing of the peace of Philokrates (346), a peace that soon came to be repudiated by certain politicians. As in the case of the *diapsephismos* of Demophilos (346/5), a scapegoat was sought. The enemy within consisted of naval officials whose mismanagement and misappropriation may have contributed directly to navy's poor performance.

What's in a name? A great deal, it seems. Names reflect societal values and befit the station of the individual. In Athens there was a sharp distinction between citizen-names and slave-names: the former reflect their status as full civic participants; the latter their foreign origin and position as outsiders. Attic inscriptions (*IG* i^3 421–30) bear this out. Of the slaves listed in these inscriptions, the majority had names that were simply ethnic adjectives or Greek names given to them by their owners. Where Bruce Robertson improves on the work of earlier scholars who have catalogued slave-names is in quantifying the difference in naming patterns between slaves and citizens and showing how such findings can inform our understanding of Athenian ideology of slave and citizen. As comparanda, he uses *IG* i^3 1032, a naval list from the beginning of the fourth century that contains 146 slaves' names and a random selection of citizens' names generated from *LGPN II* (Osborne and Bryne 1994). Though many slave-names are composed in a common manner, contain elements common to Greek onomastics, or are identical to citizen-names, there are clear differences. These include the use of non-Greek ethnic adjectives or non-Greek names. Some names, like Manes, are so common that they must represent an ethnic nickname that reflects the racial prejudice of Athenians. As Robertson concludes, the wide use of ethnic adjectives and a few common foreign names indicates that Athens reduced the complexity of barbarian life to a few common labels, a practice intrinsic to systems of racial discrimination. This lack of individualization, reflected in the repetition of a few common names among slaves, is not, however, seen among names of citizens, which show a much greater variety. This difference represents an ideological distinction between slave and citizen. Athenians were seen as distinct individuals with their own personal traits and abilities; slaves were more or less interchangeable, whose only mark of differentiation was found in the labour they provided. Slaves were only suited to work and not to civic duties of peace and war, a reality that is also reflected in their names. Whereas it was common for Athenians to choose names for their children that included some military, civic, or aristocratic element, such elements were far less common among slave-names. The distinction objectified the real social difference between slaves and citizens.

As a source, inscriptions can be invaluable for reconstructing political, social, and legal history, but as with any ancient source they should be treated with caution since they can be misleading. Any restoration to the text of an inscription must be reviewed carefully, since we do not always know the original intent that led to the erection of a particular inscription. What message did it seek to convey? As we noted above, inscriptions were not only documents but monuments that sought to communicate to their target audience a certain message that went well beyond the mere words of the inscription, however important these are to modern historians. Those from outside of Athens would also have viewed an inscription that the Athenians had erected very differently than the Athenians themselves. The three papers in Part Two of this volume explore how Athens was viewed from the outside by the wider Greek world.

Modern historians were certainly not the first to view inscriptions critically; this honour goes to Theopompos. Earlier historians may cite epigraphic evidence, but they do so without questioning their content. Fragments (*FGrHist* 115 FF 153–6) from his digression in book twenty-five of the *Philippika* suggest that Theopompos had consulted and cited several inscriptions in a critical and polemical manner in order to cast doubt on Athens' own claims of achievement in the fifth century. Frances Pownall argues from F 153 that Theopompos actually viewed on public display in the deme Acharnai the inscription that bore a transcription of the Oath of Plataia (Tod no. 204). That inscription simply states that the Athenians swore the oath, whereas we know from literary sources that the oath was taken by the Greeks. Theopompos claims that the Athenians had falsified the oath in some way, and Pownall suggests that what Theopompos objected to was not necessarily the historicity of the oath itself but the exaggerated role Athens claimed for itself in unifying Greek resistance to the Persians. The stele on which the Oath of Plataia was inscribed also records a version of the Ephebic oath and is dedicated to the gods Ares and Athena *Areia*, with a pediment containing a relief sculpture of hoplite armour.[8] The martial message of the monument is unmistakable, and if indeed Theopompos had viewed this stele, it is this message that he was objecting to. Similarly, from F 154 we learn that Theopompos further claimed that the Peace of Kallias had also been falsified by the Athenians, since it was inscribed not in Attic but Ionic, which he knew was adopted by Athens only in 403/2 under the archonship of Eukleides (F 155). Again the implication is that the historian had actually examined the stele, and in this particular case scrutinized it and called its authenticity into question on the basis of other public documentation on display in Athens, Archinos' decree authorizing the adoption of the Ionic alphabet. As Pownall notes, Theopompos was the first ancient historian to draw a connection between Athens' public inscriptions and its imperialism, seeing them simply as imperialistic documents in the service of Athenian propaganda.

Athens inscribed texts more than any other Greek city-state, and its extensive 'epigraphic habit' has led to a certain Athenocentrism in the study of Greek history. As Hedrick notes, 'this extraordinary quantity of preserved texts has given the city of Athens a preeminent position in modern historiography of Classical Greece.'[9] This Athenocentric point of view, which we have inherited from ancient historians like Thucydides and Xenophon, tends to overshadow our discussion of Greek social and political history (this volume is in some ways no different), and hence we tend to forget that there was a vibrant Greek culture out there among the other city-states in the Second Athenian League (*IG* ii^2 43). Gordon Shrimpton attempts to correct this bias by showing that the Ionians were a considerable force in the Eastern Mediterranean and were the true 'education of Hellas.' The Ionians had a different perspective on the Greek world from the Athenians, dividing it into two sacred regions, one in the west around the shrine of Apollo in

Delphi and one in the east around the shrine of Poseidon at Panionion. The island of Delos, with its sacred precinct to Apollo, divided the two worlds, and though Delos increasingly became the sacred focus of Ionia in the face of growing aggression from Lydia and Persia, for easterners it always remained a boundary between east and west and not the centre of Ionia as Athenians wanted to make it. To the Persians, the Greeks whom they mention in inscriptions and depict on tomb reliefs were Ionians; Greek involvement in Egypt largely came from Ionia. Moreover, the Ionians led the way in cultural development: from Ionia emanated philosophy, poetry, and every form of history. There is the distinct possibility that democracy was not an Athenian invention but was a concept known first to the Ionians; a fragmentary inscription (Meiggs-Lewis no. 8) indicates that Chios already had a popular council from the second quarter of the sixth century, and Herodotos indicates that the Samians entertained *isonomia* twenty years before Kleisthenes introduced it to Athens. The watershed moment in Ionian history that led to Ionia's decline as the cultural, intellectual, and political leader was Lade. After this Ionia fell increasingly under Athens' shadow. Some of its own writers were accomplices, weaving the Theseus myth to stress Ionia's connection to Athens; though others railed at Athens' demagogues and the imperialism they promoted, these bitter attacks only emphasized Athens' dominance. However much Athenians may have wanted to avoid the abuses of the Athenian empire, in the charter to the Second Athenian League (*IG* ii^2 43) most Ionians were lumped together without distinction, as nonentities in the new league. As Shrimpton notes, inscriptions provide historians the means to recover the contribution of these smaller states that often stand beyond the Athenocentric focus of other ancient sources.

One such smaller city-state was Thera. There is so very little in the literary and historical record about Thera that the only way to recover its local history is through inscriptions. As Sheila Ager notes, 'Inscriptions assist both in rescuing the history of obscure regions and in shedding new light on dark periods in the history of better-known places.' In particular, inscriptions testify to a Ptolemaic presence on the island which would not be otherwise known. Over one thousand inscriptions, stretching over a thousand-year period, have been found so far. Despite this wealth there are obvious gaps, particularly from the Archaic and Classical periods. Inscriptions from these two periods may tell us something about Theraian social and institutional life but little about her broader history; her great expedition that founded Kyrene is nearly invisible in the epigraphic record. Two relevant inscriptions survive: an enigmatic Archaic inscription from Thera itself (*IG* xii.3 762), about which little sense can be made, and a fourth-century one from Kyrene (*SEG* ix 3), which contains a decree of the Kyrenean people granting isopolity to citizens of Thera and purportedly preserves the oath taken by the founding colonists from Thera. As Ager notes, the value of *SEG* ix 3 in contributing to our understanding of Theraian history is complicated by questions of the authenticity and veracity of the oath. In contrast to the Archaic and Classical periods, the Hellenistic period is rich with public inscriptions. They indicate, as we noted, an ongoing Ptolemaic presence on the island which is not attested in our literary sources, but without these 'corresponding literary accounts we are often lacking contextual meaning,' and this can lead to that epigraphic pitfall of creating 'history from square brackets.' In the Classical Period this is an acute problem, particularly when it comes to determining when Thera entered the Athenian Empire. The editors of the *Athenian Tribute Lists* claimed the year 430/29, but their claim was based on the restoration of Thera's name to *IG* i^3 281, which, however, preserves not a single letter of the name. The first indisputable reference to Thera comes from 426/5 in *IG* i^3 68, the decree concerning 'Appointment of Tribute Collectors' (Meiggs-Lewis no. 68), which, as Ager argues, suggests that Thera was condemned to pay a war indemnity. This suggestion makes better sense of Thucydides' grouping (2.9.4) of Thera and Melos as the only two Aegean states to remain outside the Athenian alliance at the beginning of the Peloponnesian War. Perhaps Thera, like Melos, was forced to join after initially refusing. Once again, epigraphy has served as a useful handmaiden to history.

We have come full circle in our introduction and returned to Malcolm McGregor and the *Athenian Tributes Lists*. As I have tried to suggest, epigraphy, though the handmaiden of political history, is also a handmaiden to various other forms of history. From inscriptions we can learn a great deal about legal and social history; in some cases they are the only source we have in recovering local history, particularly of places that stand outside the main focus of ancient literary sources, which at times can be frustratingly Athenocentric. Ideally, all types of sources are needed to create a convincing history. Inscriptions can provide details that literary and historical sources leave out or ignore. Literary sources can provide a meaningful context for an inscription. In all cases, the historian must make plausible inferences when weaving together the disconnected threads into a connected and persuasive narrative. Like a rhetorician, the historian of ancient history uses *eikos* to challenge his opponent's position and persuasively argue his or her own. In the end this is something we learned from Professor Harding himself, who taught us to appreciate ancient Greek rhetoric as much as history and epigraphy.

Notes

1 On the difficulty of categorizing and defining epigraphy, see Bodel 2001: 2–5
2 On inscriptions as public memorial of assembly business, see Thomas 1994: 37–45.
3 On the question of literacy and who could read inscriptions see Bodel 2001: 15–24; Thomas 1992: 65–73; Harris 1989: 47–55, 74–5.
4 Shear 1971: 250; 1975: 369–70; cf. Rhodes 1981: 134–5.
5 On the monumental aspect of inscriptions, see Thomas 1992: 78–88.
6 Thomas 1992: 84.
7 Badian 1989; cf. Bodel 2001: 52–6 for his discussion of this problem.
8 Tod: 303.
9 Hedrick 1999.

References

Badian, E. 1989. 'History from Square Brackets.' *ZPE* 95: 131–9.
Bodel, J., ed. 2001. *Epigraphic Evidence: Ancient History from Inscriptions*. London and New York.
Dreher, M. 1985. 'Zu IG II^2 404, dem athenischen Volksbeschluß über die Eigenstaatlichkeit der keischen Poleis.' *Symposium* 1985: 263–81.
Harris, W.V. 1989. *Ancient Literacy*. Cambridge, MA.
Hedrick, C.W. 1999. 'Democracy and the Athenian Epigraphical Habit.' *Hesperia* 68: 387–439.
Pritchett, W.K. 1991. *The Greek State at War*. Vol. 5. Berkeley and Los Angeles.
Rhodes, P.J. 1981. *A Commentary on the Aristotelian* Athenaion Politeia. Oxford.
Schweigert, E. 1939. 'Greek Inscriptions: 4. A Decree Concerning Elaious 357/6 B.C.' *Hesperia* 8: 12–17.
Shear, L.T. 1971. 'The Athenian Agora: Excavations of 1970.' *Hesperia* 40: 241–79.
– 1975. 'The Athenian Agora: Excavations of 1973–1974.' *Hesperia* 44: 331–74.
Thomas, R. 1992. *Literacy and Orality in Ancient Greece*. Cambridge.
– 1994. 'Literacy and the City-State in Archaic and Classical Greece,' in A.K. Bowman and G. Woolf, eds., *Literacy and Power in the Ancient World*, 33–50. Cambridge.

PART ONE

Athens

Drakonian Procedure

DAVID MIRHADY

IG i^2 115 (i^3 104) lines 11–14:

καὶ ἐὰμ μὲ 'κ[π]ρονοί[α]ς [κ]ṯ[ένει τίς τινα, φεύγ]ε[ν· δ]ικάζεν δὲ τὸς βασιλέας αἴτιο[ν] φόν[ο] ε[ἴτε τὸν αὐτόχειρα εἴτ]ε [β]ολεύσαντα· τὸς δὲ ἐφέτας διαγν[ô]ṿ[α]ι̣, [αἰδέσασθαι δ' ἐὰμ μὲν πατὲ]ρ εἶ ἒ ἀδελφὸ[ς] ἒ hυε̂ς, hάπαντ[α]ς, ἒ τὸν ḳο[λύοντα κρατε̂ν.[1]

Even if someone kills someone not from forethought, he flees, and the Kings judge to be causative of murder the agent or planner, and the *Ephetai* decide, and all reconcile, if there is a father or brother or sons, or the opposer prevails.

In these first lines of the first partially extant Athenian law code, Drakon makes a confusing beginning, elliptically prescribing the same procedures for both intentional and unintentional homicide – at least that seems a cogent understanding based on the limited evidence available.[2] But in the rest of the sentence, he may actually be more straightforward, although there has been much less scholarly clarity about his procedural instructions here than there might have been. Drakon says that the killer 'flees,' and the Kings 'judge,' and the *Ephetai* 'decide,' and the family of the deceased 'reconciles' – each procedure indicated by an infinitive verb conjoined to the sequence by the particle δὲ[3] – yet few scholars have accepted that he is actually prescribing this sequence as a procedural order. It seems plausible that he is prescribing such a step-by-step order, however, which leads to further considerations about the roles to be played by these various groups and the determinations to be made by them at each of the stages of such a procedural order. The six following lines of the code dwell on the two last steps in the procedure, the decision of the *Ephetai* and reconciliation with the family members. Drakon seems to want to move beyond judgment, δικάζεν, and its assignation of causality (αἰτία), the 'etiology' of the homicide. In this complex, elliptical, and fragmentary first sentence, Drakon seems to point the way from causality towards reconciliation.

The preliminary lines of the inscription record the circumstances in 409 BC of the re-inscription of Drakon's law (νόμος) concerning homicide (φόνος). It has been in the keeping of the *Basileus* (line 6) and is to be inscribed on a stone stele (lines 7–8), which is to be set in front of the Stoa Basileios. Then begins the actual law, which refers to itself using the archaic term θεσμός (lines 19–20). It had formerly been inscribed on at least two *axones* (lines 10, 56), though only about thirty of the perhaps 110 lines available on the two *axones* are legible.[4] After the four procedural steps described in the first three lines, the next six are devoted to identifying which family members are to be included in decisions about reconciliation and the procedures to be followed in the absence of family members (lines 13–19). Then follows a provision regarding the law's retroactivity: those who have killed previously are also to be bound by the θεσμός (lines 19–20). At that point, as the text's fragmentation starts to increase beyond reconstruction, the inscription seems to suggest more about the procedures only cursorily listed in the opening lines. In particular, it describes the role of the prosecution rather than that of the killer, about whom it has said only that he 'flees' (φεύγεν, 11). In the case of these previous killers, *and so presumably also in the case of new killers,* relatives (of the deceased) are to make a proclamation (προειπε̂ν, 20) in the Agora and to share in the prosecution (συνδιόκεν, 21). After that, there is again mention of someone being 'causative[5] of murder' (αἴτιος φόνου, 23–4), which is presumably again, as in line 12, a reference to the 'judgment' (δικάζεν) of the Kings, although gaps in the text impede this conclusion. After another gap there is mention of the 'Fifty-One,' the *Ephetai*. Presumably they are again, as in line 13, to make a 'decision' (διαγνο̂ναι, 24–5; cf. lines 29, 35–6). The next legible part of the inscription (26–9) deals with the possibility that someone kills an exiled, convicted killer, an *androphonos,* who keeps away from the proscribed areas, the border markets, and so on. The exile is not referred to here as a φεύγων, but he is afforded the protections of an innocent Athenian abroad. The last legible portion of the inscription (lines 36–8) deals with killing in self-defence.[6]

With the inscription as a whole sketched out, closer analysis of the first, conditional sentence of Drakon's law in context can reveal definite procedural steps. After the elliptical protasis, the first part of the apodosis prescribes 'flight,' φεύγεν, for the killer. This word has been understood to refer to the punishment of exile,[7] but it seems entirely possible (and from my point of view more intelligible) that it refers primarily to the killer's becoming a defendant, a φεύγων in a judicial process.[8] That is, he must stand trial. The use of φεύγειν as the idiom of forensic defence is common in Attic oratory.[9] In Demosthenes 23.66, φεύγων ἁλοὺς is the idiom used for a convicted defendant. Demosthenes 23.45 cites the term ἐξεληλυθότων for exiles for involuntary homicide and says specifically that they are different from φευγόντων.[10] Flight, of course, involves fleeing from something; in this case it seems to be from an accusation to come or from the self-help retribution of an aggrieved family. In Antiphon 5.9 it is a δίκη, but in many passages there is no specification of what is being fled from.[11] In the later iteration of the procedure in Drakon's law, the one directed against earlier killers (lines 20–2), the family of the deceased is to make a proclamation in the Agora and to unite in prosecution (cf. Dem. 47.70). This seems the sort of thing the killer 'flees' from at this point. From other sources we know that once the proclamation is made, the defendant must keep away from the agora and from other proscribed places within the polis (Ant. 6.35–6, 40; Dem. 20.158), just as the convicted killer, a φεύγων ἁλοὺς in external exile must stay clear of the border markets, games, and Amphiktyonic rites (lines 27–8). The accused killer then becomes a sort of internal exile. His flight is from the proscribed places, but it is also to something, not yet necessarily to the safety of external exile but first to that of the judicial process, the intercession of the polis (cf. Aes. *Eum.* 422: τὸ τέρμα τῆς φυγῆς). If we read the law as a chronological sequence, there has not yet been any judicial decision dictating (external) exile. A killer might of course spontaneously head for Athens' borders, but he might not. Some (accused) killers obviously remained to stand trial. Demosthenes 38.22 suggests that reconciliation with an involuntary homicide could be achieved even before a killer went into exile.

It may be objected that without a reference to external exile, Drakon's law does not include a penalty for homicide. After all, exile does seem the common punishment for homicide (see for example Aes. *Ag.* 1412: νῦν μὲν δικάζεις ἐκ πόλεως φυγὴν ἐμοί). But Demosthenes 23.25–6 provides important, though largely neglected,[12] evidence:

καὶ προσειπὼν ὁ θεὶς τὸν νόμον "ἐὰν ἀποκτείνῃ," κρίσιν πεποίηκεν ὅμως, οὐ πρότερον τί χρὴ πάσχειν τὸν δεδρακότ' εἴρηκεν, καλῶς, ὦ ἄνδρες 'Αθηναῖοι, τοῦθ' ὑπὲρ εὐσεβείας ὅλης τῆς πόλεως προϊδών. πῶς; οὐκ ἔνεστιν ἅπαντας ἡμᾶς εἰδέναι τίς ποτ' ἐστὶν ὁ ἀνδροφόνος. τὸ μὲν δὴ τὰ τοιαῦτ' ἄνευ κρίσεως πιστεύειν, ἄν τις ἐπαιτιάσηται, δεινὸν ἡγεῖτο, δεῖν δ' ὑπελάμβανεν, ἐπειδήπερ ἡμεῖς τιμωρήσομεν τῷ πεπονθότι, πεισθῆναι καὶ μαθεῖν ἡμᾶς διδασκομένους ὡς δέδρακεν· τηνικαῦτα γὰρ εὐσεβὲς ἤδη κολάζειν εἰδόσιν εἶναι, πρότερον δ' οὔ. [26] καὶ ἔτι πρὸς τούτῳ διελογίζετο, ὅτι πάντα τὰ τοιαῦτ' ὀνόματα, οἷον ἐάν τις ἀποκτείνῃ, ἐάν τις ἱεροσυλήσῃ, ἐάν τις προδῷ, καὶ τὰ τοιαῦτα πάντα πρὸ μὲν τοῦ κρίσιν γενέσθαι αἰτιῶν ὀνόματ' ἐστίν, ἐπειδὰν δὲ κριθείς τις ἐξελεγχθῇ τηνικαῦτ' ἀδικήματα γίγνεται. οὐ δὴ δεῖν ᾤετο τῷ τῆς αἰτίας ὀνόματι τιμωρίαν προσγράφειν, ἀλλὰ κρίσιν. καὶ διὰ ταῦτα, ἄν τις ἀποκτείνῃ τινά, τὴν βουλὴν δικάζειν ἔγραψεν, καὶ οὐχ ἅπερ, ἂν ἁλῷ, παθεῖν εἶπεν.

The legislator, while he adds the words 'if he kills,' has nevertheless created a trial; he has not said before what the doer must suffer, and thereby has shown fine foresight, men of Athens, for the piety of the whole city. How so? It is impossible that all of us should know whoever the manslayer is. He thought it dangerous, if someone made an accusation, to give credence in such matters without a trial, but he conceived that, inasmuch as we are to avenge the sufferer, we ought to be persuaded and learn by instruction that he has done it, for then it is pious to penalize on the basis of knowledge, but not before. [26] Moreover he reasoned that before the trial occurs, such expressions as 'if someone kills,' 'if someone robs a temple,' 'if someone commits treason,' and the like are all (merely) terms for accusations. But after someone's trial and conviction, then they become acts of injustice. To a term for accusation he thought it proper to ascribe not punishment, but only trial. And therefore he wrote, 'if someone kills someone, the Council judges,' and not what exactly he should suffer if convicted.

What Demosthenes objects to is that his opponent Aristokrates' decree takes the form ἂν ἀποκτείνῃ τις Χαρίδημον ... ἀγώγιμον ἐκ συμμάχων εἶναι, where ἀγώγιμον εἶναι stands as punishment (τιμωρία) and not just arrest before trial (16, cf. 11). Demosthenes' argument speaks for itself, strongly indicating that the legislation for homicide dictated judicial procedure, a trial (κρίσις), not punishment. It seems most unlikely that Demosthenes could have composed this argument if the homicide law of Drakon, with all its prominence – Demosthenes mentions Drakon and his legislation by name at 23.51 – had dictated the punishment of exile with the word in line 11. Demosthenes 23.53 likewise has the passage ἐάν τις ἀποκτείνῃ ἐν ἄθλοις ἄκων ... μὴ φεύγειν (see above, n. 8), where φεύγειν also seems to refer only to standing trial as a defendant.[13] In the case described by that passage there might have been a trial over whether the killer acted involuntarily (ἄκων). But, as Demosthenes puts it, there would seem little for him to be a defendant about – let alone go into exile for – if all conceded that he had acted both involuntarily and in the context of an athletic contest. A point of the legislation seems to be that there are certain contexts in which accidental deaths occur, and no one is to be thought the cause of such deaths, except perhaps the victims themselves.[14]

In Demosthenes 20.158, Demosthenes comments on homicide procedure in a way that is also relevant. There, after a killer has been banned from the sacred places he goes through the judicial process, at the end of which he may be found to be innocent.[15] The process seems to concede that he is the killer and thus in a sense causative of the homicide. It even uses the term *androphonos* ('manslayer'). The judgment of the Kings concerning causation would thus be upheld. But the judicial process, presumably a trial before the *Ephetai*, may find the killer innocent (καθαρός) – the homicide having been allowable – and thus entails lifting the ban from the sacred places. The passage does not set out the punishment but only the conditions of the internal exile undertaken by a killer who has yet to undergo a judicial process.

The foregoing discussion probably sets out too great a dichotomy between φεύγειν as 'go into exile' and 'stand trial.' The way the law expresses the protasis, 'if someone kills someone not from forethought,' rather than 'if someone is accused of killing someone not from forethought,' also allows that exile follows as the punishment. The starting point of the judicial process seems already an assumption that the individual did the killing, rather than simply an accusation, despite Demosthenes 23.25. The Greek conflates the punishment of exile and standing trial. Nevertheless, in the Drakon inscription, the emphasis is on the judicial procedure, in which the punishment of exile is regulated through further steps.

The second part of the apodosis, referring to the Kings' judgment, does not mention any prosecution, though later in the inscription prosecution is mentioned in the case of the earlier killers (lines 20–2), where it is to be pursued by the family of the deceased. The Kings, presumably the *Basileus* and the *Phylobasileis*, are to make a judgment (δικάζεν) of causation (αἰτία).[16] Gerhard Thür has argued that the Homeric meaning of the verb is to prescribe the means of settling a dispute, not to settle it directly.[17] From a practical point of view this seems partly the role for the Kings here also. They make a (preliminary) judgment, which sets the terms for a later trial, if one is needed, before the *Ephetai*. In the classical period a vestige of this procedure seems to occur in the προδικασίαι (Ant. 6.42). There the prosecutors, under the supervision of the *Basileus*, make a claim about the αἰτία of the defendant three times over successive months.[18] At the beginning of the process, they also make a proclamation that the accused person be excluded from many important meeting points.[19] Throughout this process, if what I have argued earlier is correct, the defendant is a φεύγων. One result of the Kings' part in the procedure is, of course, that the defendant, the fleer, the φεύγων now takes on the accusation, the αἰτία, for the homicide. In fact, in Attic idioms the defendant is also referred to as 'the one having the αἰτία,' ὁ τὴν αἰτίαν ἔχων (*Ath. Pol.* 57.4; Dem. 23.36; cf. 58.29; Aes. *Eum.* 579). Unlike in Canadian law, the defendant is thus in a sense presumed guilty when he goes before the larger court of *Ephetai*. He must 'be released' from the αἰτία (Ant. 1.7, 2.2.11, 5.40, 6.15, 32; Lys. 7.8; cf. Aes. *Eum.* 83). The defendant in the *Third Tetralogy* plays on the notion of cause, saying that the man who died was more the cause of his death than the defendant himself and that the deceased was the cause not only of his own misfortune but also of the charge against the defendant (Ant. 4.2.1; cf. 4.4.5, 5.64).

As well as setting out the means of settling the dispute by defining its terms, the Kings' (preliminary) judgment also served as at least a tentative declaration on behalf of the polis about where the cause, the αἰτία, for the pollution of homicide lay, in order that the polis itself did not suffer its ill effects. Ilias Arnaoutoglou argues that the notion of pollution starts with the proclamation.[20] I would argue rather that with the proclamation, the assignation of the pollution to a single individual begins. Until then, the entire polis is tainted. The *First Tetralogy* makes essentially this point and suggests that the assignation of pollution begins already with the initiation of the prosecution (2.1.3: πάσης τῆς πόλεως μιαινομένης ὑπ' αὐτοῦ, ἕως ἂν διωχθῇ).[21] That seems the reason why it is important for the Kings to make their judgment first, even to make it spontaneously – without a prosecution – against an unknown killer and even against an object or animal (*Ath.Pol.* 57.4; Dem. 23.76; Harp. *s.v.* ἐπὶ Πρυτανείωι). The result of a delay in making such an assignation is illustrated forcefully by the plague in *Oedipus the King*: once he hears the reason for the plague, Oedipus as king immediately issues his edict against the as yet unknown killer (223–51).[22] Thus it seems that the public proclamation against the killer by the victim's family and the Kings' judgment occur at the same time, the Kings' 'judgment' being perhaps only a formal consequence of the claim entailed in the family's proclamation. In Antiphon 2.1.3, the speaker claims that the pollution redounds on the prosecution if their prosecution is unjust, the King who oversees the prosecution apparently having no responsibility.[23] In lines 26–9 of the inscription, where the code deals with someone who kills a person who is observing the terms of his exile, the *Ephetai* are again given their role of διαγιγνόσκεν, but the Kings' δικάζεν almost disappears, perhaps being swept into the phrase 'by the same (procedure)s' at line 29 (ἐν τοῖς αὐτοῖς ἐνέχεσθαι· διαγιγνόσκειν δὲ τὸς ἐφέτας; cf. Dem. 23.37). If that is true, the passage gives further evidence that it is now the function of the *Ephetai* that is paramount, the Kings' role becoming only a formality.

The *Athenaion Politeia* makes clear that later terminology has changed. It says that it is the King's role to 'introduce' the case (εἰσάγει), whereupon the *Ephetai* 'judge' it (δικάζουσι).[24] Aeschylus seems to describe a mythological charter for this change in terminology. In response to Orestes' demand that she try his case (κρῖνον δίκην), whether or not he acted (ἔρξαιμι) justly, Athena invokes an a fortiori argument: the matter is so great that it would not be right (θέμις) even for *her* to discern (διαιρεῖν) cases of murder; let alone that any single mortal judge (δικάζειν) them (*Eum.* 468–71). In the place of the 'Kings,' Athena passes the function of judging to a court of sworn *dikastai* (lines 483–4). As Apollo says later, she is to 'introduce' the case (εἴσαγε, 581), but of course she retains a vote to break a tie (lines 741, 754). Indeed, by the time of Solon, not long after Drakon, the Areiopagos Council is said to 'judge' (δικάζειν, Dem. 23.22). However, according to the *Athenaion Politeia,* when the King does not know who did it, he and the tribal kings themselves 'judge' (δικάζει).[25] So it seems that the Kings of the classical period still have some vestigial function as judges.[26]

The third part of the apodosis dictates the role of the *Ephetai,* who seem to appear now as an appeal court. Since their name seems associated with ἔφεσις, appeal/referral, it would seem entirely appropriate for us to refer to them as 'Appellate Judges,' but the confusions this might cause make the use of the Greek term preferable.[27] Many judgments of the Kings would presumably not be appealed; the killer would simply head for the border, content to live as an exile if he could, and the matter would be finished. But it seems that the function of the *Ephetai,* if there was an appeal, was to evaluate the preliminary assignation of αἰτία by the Kings. Two decisions seem necessary: first, whether the αἰτία is correct (in some cases it will be conceded by the defendant); and second, concerning the defendant's volition. The *Ephetai* do not judge, δικάζειν; the action Drakon assigns them is rather 'to decide,' διαγνῶναι.[28] In later Athenian law vestiges of this distinction occur in several passages. Public arbitrators, for instance, are said to render a γνῶσις.[29] As in the Drakon law, if one of the parties objects to the decision, he prevails and the decision does not stand. That is, even if the *Ephetai* decide that the homicide was involuntary, a member of the victim's family may block reconciliation. The implication of a decision that the homicide was involuntary seems to be that reconciliation is expected to take place (cf. Eur. *Hipp.* 1325, 1335, 1406). In democratic Athens, the *dikastērion,* the popular court, became the great appellate court; an appealed arbitrator's decision went to it.[30] However, in Demosthenes 23.71, where the Palladion (which is staffed by the *Ephetai* and whose area was principally involuntary homicide; cf. And. 1.78; Dem. 23.38, 43.57) is referred to as a *dikasterion,* it is also said to render a decision, a γνῶσις.[31] Not only in Drakon's law, but also in other passages, decisions or determinations of motive seem to be referred to using the verb διαγιγνώσκειν (Lys. 3.43, cf. 3.28). Likewise, in their oath the *dikastai* swore that they would judge (δικάζειν) according to the laws and by their 'most just decision,' γνώμῃ τῇ δικαιοτάτῃ (cf. Aes. *Eum.* 674–5: ἀπὸ γνώμης φέρειν ψῆφον δικαίας).[32] The implication seems to be again that the γνώμη or γνῶσις engages somehow a freer form of decision, one not bound by formal procedures or laws.[33]

A few lines later in the inscription (17), we learn that in the absence of surviving relatives of the deceased, the *Ephetai* decide whether or not the killing was unintentional and, if so, select members of the phratry to admit the killer (cf. Aes. *Eum.* 656: ποία δὲ χέρνιψ φρατέρων προσδέξεται;).[34] Such a readmission seems to annul the proclamation debarring the killer from public places; it releases the defendant, the φεύγων, from internal exile. Given the importance for the Athenian democracy of Solon's law of ἔφεσις to the *dikastērion* (*Ath. Pol.* 9.1), it should not be surprising that ἔφεσις already had precedent in Drakon's law, which itself seems to assume the office and function of the *Ephetai.* If we can posit a trajectory in Athens from the rule (and judicial authority) of the Kings to the rule of the *dêmos* and judgment of the popular court, then it seems that homicide procedure consistently maintains an aspect of archaism. In the fifth century, Ephialtes stripped the once-powerful Areiopagos of many of its political functions, but left it with homicide jurisdiction (*Ath. Pol.* 25.2; Philoch. F 64). In Drakon's law, the judgment of the presumably once-powerful Kings, while maintaining a place in the judicial procedure, is checked by a mechanism for appeal and qualification, if not reversal.

The last part of the first sentence of Drakon's law deals with reconciliation (αἰδέσασθαι), which includes not only the polis but in particular the family of the deceased, the prosecution. In *Eumenides* 600–2, Orestes explains that Klytaimnestra faced two counts of pollution, the first because she killed her husband and the second because she killed Orestes' father. Only the second count (προσβολή) actually involves Orestes, but a similar pattern may follow for Athenian homicide law in general; namely, that there is a twofold wrong, one from the perspective of the killer and the other from the perspective of the family of the victim. That is why they in particular take on the role of prosecution. Attention to the killer dominates the first sentence of Drakon's law: he flees, is judged, and is finally 'decided' upon. But his perspective then gives way to that of his victim's family. Of course they have taken part in prosecuting the killer, but it seems likely that they do so out of obligation.[35] Now, once the killer has been convicted, they must consider whether or not to reconcile.

Αἰδέσασθαι (literally 'to have αἰδῶς "modesty," "respect," with regard to someone') is a challenging word and concept. It reflects on the part of the prosecution a need to have modesty, to set a limit to their demands against the killer. It seems akin to the notion of ἐπιείκεια ('fair-mindedness') outlined by Aristotle (*Eth. Nic.* 5.10), by which a prosecutor or court limits the demands to which the laws – if strictly interpreted – give a right, in order to achieve a finer sense of justice. Ernst Heitsch notes the connection of αἰδέσασθαι to pity in Homer (*Il.* 21.74, 22.123–4, 419, 24.207; *Od.* 3.96, 22.312).[36] Demosthenes associates reconciliation with φιλανθρωπία (21.43). Reconciliation, however, also seems to have involved a consideration, a payment, which entailed a sort of binding contract preventing the prosecuting family from taking up their vendetta/prosecution again (Dem. 37.59; 38.22).

If no member of the family of the deceased survives, either of the immediate family or of cousins, then there come into play first the decision of the *Ephetai* whether or not the killing was intentional, and second, admission of the killer by ten phratry members (lines 16–18). These two acts must substitute for the reconciliation by the family. (Drakon uses the imperative mood, rather than a jussive infinitive, for the admission; perhaps the phratry members are to have no discretion about the readmission.) One thing that distinguishes the *Ephetai* and phratry members from the family is that they are in no position, as disinterested groups, to accept a payment (a ποινή or ἄποινα) to facilitate reconciliation. It seems to have been common practice for the families of the killer and the deceased to make and receive such payments after the judicial process and presumably usually, but not always, after a period of external exile. (To make or receive them before the process would have been a subversion of justice.) Although the circumstances are different, the advice given to Agamemnon to respect (αἰδεῖσθαι) the priest of Apollo and accept payment for the release of his daughter follows a similar pattern of respect for the person combined with acceptance of a consideration (Hom. *Il.* 1.33, 377: αἰδεῖσθαι θ' ἱερῆα καὶ ἀγλαὰ δέχθαι ἄποινα; cf. Aes. *Eum.* 475). Since in the absence of family members the readmission seems to follow as a matter of course after the decision regarding volition, it seems to follow that the payment to the family of the deceased would have been largely influenced by their view, and the *Ephetai's*, of the volition of the killing. If the *Ephetai* decide that the killing was not voluntary, readmission of the killer follows, apparently without concern for there being no payment, which in any case would presumably have been quite low, especially after a lapse of time in which the deceased's family members have died out. If the *Ephetai* decide (or have decided), however, that the killing was voluntary, then in the absence of the deceased's family members no one is in a position to decide what amount of payment would be sufficient or to receive it. But there seems an implication that surviving members of the deceased's family would have been in such a position.[37]

The re-inscription in 409 BC of Drakon's law reveals one of the first attempts to regulate homicide in Athens. Carawan has argued that the word '*aitios* ... looks to the consequences of guilt – liability – rather than to the initial cause.'[38] The results of this analysis suggest that there may indeed have been a time when αἰτία and liability, and so the suitability for punishment, were identified, that there was an automatic penalty attached to a judgment of αἰτία. But Drakon's law in fact goes two steps beyond this judgment: first, a decision of the *Ephetai* determines both whether the judgment is correct and also, if it is, whether the αἰτία was voluntary or not; second, it formulates grounds for achieving, not punishment, but reconciliation. In some passages of Homer, likewise, it seems that there are some more primitive notions of justice at work, whereby the person who is the cause of some wrong should suffer for it, by a sort of fiction of judicial necessity (*Il.* 1.153–7, 2.87, 15.137, 21.370; *Od.* 22.49–50). Sometimes, however, the point is made that it is the gods who are the 'cause' of human troubles (*Il.* 3.164, 13.222–7, 19.86–8, 410; *Od.* 11.559; at *Od.* 1.32–4 Zeus explicitly rejects the notion). There are also suggestions that good men ought to move beyond an assignation of cause (e.g. *Il.* 13.111–15).

Homer famously describes a scene from the shield of Hephaistos in which disputants in a homicide case come before a circle of elders in the agora (*Il.* 18.497–508). The starting point of the dispute is not an accusation, but rather simply strife (νεῖκος). With the crowds of the *dēmos* demonstrating partisan support for each side, the elders each propose a δίκη as a basis for ending the strife, for settling the dispute, for achieving reconciliation. Likewise, in the *Homeric Hymn to Hermes*, although the babe Hermes protests that he is not the cause (αἴτιος, 4.275, 383) for Apollo's cattle being missing, when the strife between him and Apollo is resolved by the arbitration of Zeus, the father largely disregards the issue of cause and directs Hermes to show his brother where he had hidden the missing animals. Zeus moves beyond αἰτία to a basis for reconciliation, to find resolution or, as the hymnist puts it, ὁμόφρονα θυμόν (4.391).

Notes

1 The text printed here is essentially that of Stroud 1968: 5. There are many gaps in the text, but Stroud's restorations (like that proposed in his commentary, p. 47, for the 17-letter gap in line 12) have received widespread acceptance. I have included Stroud's restoration in line 12 with his text.

2 In his lucid and comprehensive discussion, Gagarin (1981: 96–110) has championed this interpretation, which I find the most plausible. Against, see the bibliography of Carawan 1998: 35 n. 4.

3 Note that in the last clause, [αἰδέσασθαι δ' ἐάμ πατὲ]ρ, there may be a bigger break, a new complete sentence with a new protasis, indicated by ἐὰμ μὲν, but there seems no interruption in the paratactic sequence. See Gagarin (1981: 146), who sketches how each procedure begins with an infinitive.

4 Regarding the law's authenticity and the circumstances of its re-inscription, see most recently Sickinger 1999: 14–24.

5 This translation of the adjective αἴτιος will seem awkward, but I have found none better. 'Responsible' and other translations that suggest liability to further action seem to beg the question whether or not such liability is implied. Note that the noun αἰτία can refer either to a 'cause' or to an attribution of cause, that is, an 'accusation.' In line 27 (cf. Dem. 23.38 ἐάν τις ἀποκτείνῃ τὸν ἀνδροφόνον ... ἢ αἴτιος ᾖ φόνου), αἴτιος seems to stand in for [β]ολεύσαντα (12–13), denoting not the person who actually kills but the one who plans and thus causes a killing indirectly. Cf. Ant. 6.17: αἰτιῶνται δὲ οὗτοι μὲν ἐκ τούτων, ὡς αἴτιος ὅς ἐκέλευσε πιεῖν, and 1.20.

6 The inscription does not give any indication of how it may have dealt with other cases of justifiable homicide, like that of Orestes in the *Eumenides*. *Eum.* 586–93 suggests that there was a preliminary process, like an *anakrisis*, in which the defendant (Orestes) had to answer questions from the prosecution (the Chorus of Furies), regarding the three issues of fact, means, and motive: did he kill, how, and why? Sommerstein (1989: 192) argues that the Chorus 'does not ask him why; that issue, crucial to his plea of justification, is raised by Orestes himself (600) ...' Strictly speaking, Sommerstein is right: the Chorus asks only by whose advice he killed his mother. But that question does address the issue of motive, of why he killed. It may, however, also touch on the issue of planning, of identifying who the βουλεύων is, in this case Apollo (cf. Ant. 6.17; Lys. 13.87; and n. 4 above). At any rate, these questions would need to be answered before a determination of the appropriate court could be made.

7 Stroud 1968: 7; Gagarin 1981: xvi; Carawan 1998: 33.

8 Tsantsanoglou (1972: 173, cited by Gagarin 1981: 30 n. 1) reads the inscription somewhat differently but also with the understanding that φεύγειν refers to the killer standing trial. Treston (1923: 195) supplies the translation 'let him be put on trial,' without comment.

9 E.g. Ant. 5.9: πρῶτον μὲν γὰρ κακοῦργος ἐνδεδειγμένος φόνου δίκην φεύγω. ('Although charged as a malfeasant, I am fleeing an action for murder.') Cf. Dem. 23.69: τῷ δὲ φεύγοντι τὰ μὲν τῆς διωμοσίας ταὐτά, τὸν πρότερον δ' ἔξεστιν εἰπόντα λόγον μεταστῆναι, καὶ οὔθ' ὁ διώκων οὔθ' οἱ δικάζοντες οὔτ' ἄλλος ἀνθρώπων οὐδεὶς κύριος κωλῦσαι. ('As for the defendant [fleer], the rules for his oath are the same, but he is free to withdraw after making his first speech, and neither the prosecutor, nor the judges, nor any other man, has authority to stop him.'); 23.53: ἐάν τις ἀποκτείνῃ ἐν ἄθλοις ἄκων, ἢ ἐν ὁδῷ καθελὼν ἢ ἐν πολέμῳ ἀγνοήσας, ἢ ἐπὶ δάμαρτι ἢ ἐπὶ μητρὶ ἢ ἐπ' ἀδελφῇ ἢ ἐπὶ θυγατρί, ἢ ἐπὶ παλλακῇ

ἣν ἂ ἐπ' ἐλευθέροις παισὶν ἔχῃ, τούτων ἕνεκα μὴ φεύγειν κτείναντα. ('If someone kill involuntarily in an athletic contest, or overcoming him in a fight on a road, or unwittingly in battle, or in intercourse with his wife, or mother, or sister, or daughter, or concubine kept for procreation of free children, he does not flee [or, he does not stand trial] for having killed for these reasons.'); Lys. 10.31: τῇ δ' αὐτῇ ψήφῳ φόνου φεύγω τοῦ πατρός. ('In the same vote I am fleeing [an accusation] of murdering my father.')

10 In Dem. 23.45, those in exile as a result of involuntary homicide are referred to in fact both as ἐξεληλυθότων and μεθεστηκότων. However, the φευγόντων seem to be those exiled for more serious crimes, those whose property has been confiscated. In 23.77, the exile is a πεφευγώς, one who has fled.

11 Cf. Lys. 4.4: περὶ τῆς αἰτίας ἧς ἐγὼ φεύγω; cf. Hdt. 7.214.2: φεύγοντα 'Επιάλτην ταύτην τὴν αἰτίην οἴδαμεν. Ant. 5.10: τοῖς τοῦ φόνου φεύγουσι τὰς δίκας; cf. e.g. Dem. 21.91; 30.5, 9, 16; Aes. *Eum.* 753. In *Ath. Pol.* 57.3 there is the idiom ἐὰν δὲ φεύγων φυγὴν ὧν αἴδεσίς ἐστιν, which refers to exile. Cf. Dem. 23.38: τὸν πεφευγότ' ἐπ' αἰτίᾳ φόνου καὶ εαλωκότα, ἐάνπερ ἅπαξ ἐκφύγῃ καὶ σωθῇ. φεύγειν is certainly used of exile in Dem. 22.66; 23. 31, 38, 42, 51–2, 72–3, 85; 24.149, 153; 50.48.

12 See, however, Tsantsanoglou 1972: 172.

13 A brief survey of passages using the phrase ἐάν τις shows that many in fact refer only to procedure and not to punishment. But the survey is not as decisive as Demosthenes would suggest. For procedure, see Dem. 20.156; 21.47; 23.22, 30, 36, 37, 51, 53, 66, 77, 83; 24.50; Lyk. 1.121; Lys. 10.9; 14.5; for punishment, see And. 1.96, 116; Dem. 20.40, 100; 21.47, 113; 23.44; 24.110, 212; 26.24; Lyk. 1.20; Lys. 1.32; 14.8. Dem. 21.47 can be counted in both lists. An analogous expression for φεύγειν in these procedural contexts is ὑπόδικος (cf. Lys. 10.9).

14 In the second of the Antiphon *Tetralogies*, the prosecution is aimed precisely at a boy who allegedly killed another involuntarily in the context of athletics (3.1.2). No mention is made there, however, of the exclusion of athletics in the law. Of course, throwing javelins *at each other* is not part of the competition in the way that punching is part of boxing. Lysias 1 also involves a situation that might be covered by the legislation cited in Dem. 23.53. Certainly it would be from the speaker's point of view. He is the defendant and argues, presumably in the Delphinion, that he had killed Eratosthenes (as Eratosthenes was lying) 'upon' his wife. But the prosecution seems to argue that the case was premeditated homicide, a case of entrapment (Lys. 1.37).

15 Dem. 20.158: ἐν τοίνυν τοῖς περὶ τούτων νόμοις ὁ Δράκων φοβερὸν κατασκευάζων καὶ δεινὸν τό τιν' αὐτόχειρ' ἄλλον ἄλλου γίγνεσθαι, καὶ γράφων χέρνιβος εἴργεσθαι τὸν ἀνδροφόνον, σπονδῶν, κρατήρων, ἱερῶν, ἀγορᾶς, πάντα τἄλλα διελθὼν οἷς μάλιστ' ἄν τινας ᾤετ' ἐπισχεῖν τοῦ τοιοῦτόν τι ποιεῖν, ὅμως οὐκ ἀφείλετο τὴν τοῦ δικαίου τάξιν, ἀλλ' ἔθηκεν ἐφ' οἷς

ἐξεῖναι ἀποκτιννύναι, κἂν οὕτω τις δράσῃ, καθαρὸν διώρισεν εἶναι. ('Now Drakon, in the laws about these things, marked being a [hands-on] killer as fearsome and terrible by banning the manslayer from the lustral water, the libations, the loving-cup, the sacrifices and the market-place; although he enumerated everything that he thought likely to deter from doing such a thing, he never robbed him of the process of justice; but he defined the circumstances that make homicide possible [licit] and defined the killer free from taint if he acts in these ways.')

16 Carawan (1998: 33–4) puts in a period: 'and the kings shall give judgement (δικάζειν). Guilty of homicide [is either the perpetrator] or the planner.' The passage is admittedly very fragmentary, but Carawan makes no claim that there is a missing δέ, which might indicate a new sentence.

17 Thür 1970.

18 There is actually very little evidence of what occurred at the προδικασίαι. But cf. Thür 1990: 151. Although the prosecution and defence had to swear oaths to their claims and to their relationship to the victim at the actual trial (Ant. 6.6; Dem. 23.67–8; 47.72), they may not have had to do so at the προδικασίαι. Likewise, their claims may not have used the actual language of attributing αἰτία, but they will have attributed it implicitly.

19 MacDowell (1963: 24–5) points out that altogether three proclamations are made: one at the tomb of the killed person, though it had only religious and not legal force (Dem. 47.69); a second in the Agora by the prosecution (Ant. 6.35); and a third by the *Basileus* (*Ath. Pol.* 57.2). My suspicion is that the second and third are almost synonymous. The *Ath. Pol.* seems to make a point of saying that it is the *Basileus* who makes the proclamation: καὶ ὁ προαγορεύων εἴργεσθαι τῶν νομίμων οὗτός ἐστιν. Cf. Lys. 6.9.

20 Arnaoutoglou (1993: 129) argues against legal implications for the notion of pollution, arguing instead that the exclusionary protocols served rather as means of social exclusion and thus deterrence.

21 *Eum.* 448–52 raises the issue of the killer being purified elsewhere. It is unclear what consequence that could have for an Athenian court or why Aeschylus makes such a point of it.

22 See Carawan 1999. Cf. Dem. 47.69.

23 The Lawcode of Gortyn also makes of δικάζειν (δικάδδεν, δικαδδέτο) a fairly formal process governed by the presence of witnesses (cols. 1.21, 9.30, 38, 50, 11.27–8). Cf. Carawan 1998: 59.

24 *Ath. Pol.* 57.4: δικάζουσι δ' οἱ λαχόντες ταῦτ' ἐφέται πλὴν τῶν Ἀρείῳ πάγῳ γιγνομένων, εἰσάγει δ' ὁ βασιλεύς, καὶ δικάζουσιν ἐν ἱερῷ καὶ ὑπαίθριοι. ἐφέται is the supplement of Kenyon 1920. While his reading may not be correct, it seems certain that it is the *Ephetai* to whom the text is referring. In the next sentence, the *Basileus* is said to remove his crown when he 'judges.' The

implication seems to be that he judges as one among the *Ephetai*. Cf. 3.5 referring to the Archons: κύριοι δ' ἦσαν καὶ τὰς δίκας αὐτοτελεῖς [κρίν]ειν, καὶ οὐχ ὥσπερ νῦν προανακρίνειν. Cf. also Ant. 6.42.

25 *Ath. Pol.* 57.4: ὅταν δὲ μὴ εἰδῇ τὸν ποιήσαντα, τῷ δράσαντι λαγχάνει, δικάζει δ' ὁ βασιλεὺς καὶ οἱ φυλοβασιλεῖς, καὶ τὰς τῶν ἀψύχων καὶ τῶν ἄλλων ζῴων.

26 Cf. Dem. 23.28: εἰσφέρειν δ' ἐ⟨ς⟩ τοὺς ἄρχοντας, ὧν ἕκαστοι δικασταί εἰσι, τῷ βουλομένῳ. τὴν δ' ἡλιαίαν διαγιγνώσκειν. ('The Archons shall bring cases into court, of which each is severally a judge for the volunteer [prosecutor], and the Heliaea decides.')

27 MacDowell (1963: 48) notes that although Harpokration and Pollux give similar explanations, some modern scholars have seen others. Like most scholars now, he himself is not committed. If the interpretation of this paper is correct, then the origin of the term may in fact lie in an appeal of the Kings' *dikazein*. Later changes in terminology and procedure take the emphasis off the notion of 'appeal.'

28 'Decide' seems the best translation for διαγνῶναι, but it is far from adequate. The verb seems to be used because the *Ephetai* must not simply follow the claims of the prosecution (and their witnesses), which formally dictate the Kings' judgment, but must also come to understand and evaluate certain facts of the case. Their 'understanding' of it at the same time entails a legally binding determination of, for instance, whether the killing actually was committed by the accused killer and whether his action was voluntary. This combination of 'diagnosis' and 'decision' is difficult to render in English.

29 *Ath. Pol.* 53.1–2: καὶ τὰ μὲν μέχρι δέκα δραχμῶν αὐτοτελεῖς εἰσι δ[ικά]ζε[ι]ν, τὰ δ' ὑπὲρ τοῦτο τὸ τίμημα τοῖς διαιτηταῖς παραδιδόασιν· οἱ δὲ παραλαβόντες, [2] ἐὰν μὴ δύνωνται διαλῦσαι, γιγνώσκουσι, κἂν μὲν ἀμφοτέροις ἀρέσκῃ τὰ γνωσθέντα καὶ ἐμμένωσιν, ἔχει τέλος ἡ δίκη. ἂν δ' ὁ ἕτερος ἐφῇ τῶν ἀντιδίκων εἰς τὸ δικαστήριον, ἐμβαλόντες τὰς μαρτυρίας καὶ τὰς προκλήσεις καὶ τοὺς νόμους εἰς ἐχίνους, χωρὶς μὲν τὰς τοῦ διώκοντος, χωρὶς δὲ τὰς τοῦ φεύγοντος, καὶ τούτους κατασημηνάμενοι, καὶ τὴν γνῶσιν τοῦ διαιτητοῦ γεγραμμένην ἐν γραμματείῳ προσαρτήσαντες, παραδιδοασι τοῖς δ' τοῖς τὴν φυλὴν τοῦ φεύγοντος δικάζουσιν. ('[The Forty] have independence to judge claims not exceeding ten drachmas, but suits above that value they pass on to the Arbitrators. These take over the cases, and if they are unable to effect a compromise, they *give a decision*, and if both parties are satisfied with their decisions and abide by them, that ends the suit. But if one of the two parties appeals to the popular court, they put the witnesses' testimony and the challenges and the laws concerned into deed-boxes, those of the prosecutor and those of the defendant separately, and seal them up, and attach to them a copy of the Arbitrator's *verdict* written on a tablet, and hand them over to the four judges taking the cases of the defendant's tribe.') Thür (1990: 150) suggests that

διαγιγνώσκειν indicates a formal vote. While the arbitrators, acting individually, clearly did not vote, Thür must be right that the fifty-one *Ephetai*, with their large, uneven number, did.

30 Admittedly, not all cases went to an arbitrator.

31 In Dem. 23.71, the γνῶσις τοῦ δικαστηρίου follows oath swearing and arguments; cf. Ant. 6.3.

32 Dem. 20.118; 23.96; 39.40; 57.63; Aisch. 3.6. See Mirhady 2007: 231, n. 42 and Sommerstein 1989: 212.

33 The *Eumenides* offers several more passages that echo the idiom of deciding a case on the basis of γνῶσις: καταγνωσθῇ δίκη, 573; καὶ ψῆφον αἴρειν καὶ διαγνῶναι δίκην αἰδουμένους τὸν ὅρκον, 709–10; cf. διαιρεῖν, 488.

34 Both Podlecki (1989: 178) and Sommerstein (1989: 206) interpret this passage of the *Eumenides* to refer only to ongoing rites of the phratries rather than as a purificatory rite done in the absence of family members. To me the verb προσδέξεται suggests rather a one-time readmission rite. Cf. Eur., *Phoen.* 1706: τίς σε πύργος Ἀτθίδος προσδέξεται; and Soph., *OT* 1428.

35 The obligation was probably not legal. Cf. Gagarin 1981: 138–9. But if there was to be a prosecution, it seems that the family of the deceased was the party in a legal position to pursue it.

36 Heitsch (1984: 9) also notes the occurrence of a payment (*Il.* 9.632–6).

37 Note that Demosthenes 21.43 points out that killing from forethought was punished with death, perpetual exile, and confiscation of goods. The passage would seem to rule out reconciliation by the family of the deceased (ἔπειθ' οἱ φονικοὶ τοὺς μὲν ἐκ προνοίας ἀποκτιννύντας θανάτῳ καὶ ἀειφυγίᾳ καὶ δημεύσει τῶν ὑπαρχόντων ζημιοῦσι, τοὺς δ' ἀκουσίως αἰδέσεως καὶ φιλανθρωπίας πολλῆς ἠξίωσαν. ('Again, the murder laws punish those killing from forethought with death, perpetual exile, and confiscation of goods, but [those killing] involuntarily they treat with reconciliation and much philanthropy.') If these inferences are correct, then there seems a substantial difference between killing 'from forethought' and killing 'voluntarily.' Only the former is punished with death, etc.; the latter leaves open the possibility of reconciliation by the family. But the passage may also be simply rhetorical exaggeration. Perhaps no such conclusions should be drawn from it.

38 Carawan 1998: 42.

References

Arnaoutoglou, I. 1993. 'Pollution in the Athenian Homicide Law.' *RIDA* 40: 109–37.

Carawan, E. 1998. *Rhetoric and the Law of Draco*. Oxford.

– 1999. 'The Edict of Oedipus (*Oedipus Tyrannus* 223–51).' *AJP* 120: 187–222.
Gagarin, M. 1981. *Drakon and Early Athenian Homicide Law*. New Haven, CT.
Kenyon, F.G. 1920. *Atheniensium Respublica.* Oxford.
Heitsch, E. 1984. *Aidesis im attischen Straftrecht*. Mainz.
MacDowell, D.M. 1963. *Athenian Homicide Law in the Age of the Orators.* Manchester.
Mirhady, D.C. 2007. 'The Dikasts' Oath and the Question of Fact,' in A. Sommerstein and J. Fletcher (eds.), *Horkos: The Oath in Greek Society*, 48–59. Exeter.
Podlecki, A.J. 1989. *Aeschylus: Eumenides*. Warminster.
Sickinger, J. 1999. *Public Records and Archives in Classical Athens*. Chapel Hill, NC.
Sommerstein, A. 1989. *Aeschylus: Eumenides*. Cambridge.
Stroud, R. 1968. *Drakon's Law on Homicide*. Berkeley.
Thür, G. 1970. 'Zum δικάζειν bei Homer.' *ZSS* 87: 426–44.
– 1990. 'Die Todesstrafe im Blutprozess Athens.' *Journal of Juristic Papyrology* 20: 143–56.
Treston, H.J. 1923. *Poine: A Study in Ancient Greek Blood-Vengeance*. London.
Tsantsanoglou, K. 1972. '*Phonou pheugein* (I.G. i^2 115. 11–13),' in G. Bakalakes and M. Andronikos (eds.), *Kernos*, 170–9. Thessaloniki.

Hypereides, Aristophon, and the Settlement of Keos

CRAIG COOPER

In 363/2 BC Aristophon of Azenia, a prominent politician of long standing, was sent as general to the island of Keos to quell a revolt. In the wake of his success there he proposed a decree to settle affairs, but his settlement soon came under attack. In 362/1, at the relatively young age of twenty-eight and perhaps to make a name for himself, Hypereides (frs. 40–4) prosecuted Aristophon, charging that his settlement was harmful and motivated by greed. Hypereides conducted a vigorous prosecution of the wily old politician, who was acquitted, it seems, by only two votes (Hyp. 3.28). Shortly thereafter Hypereides assisted Apollodoros in his prosecution of the general Autokles (Dem. 36.53) over his failed activities in the Hellespontos (Dem. 23.104). The attack was again directed against Aristophon, who in 362/1 had persuaded the Athenians to pass a decree dispatching an expedition to the region under Autokles' command (Dem. 50.6). Since the one-year limit for indicting the proposer of the decree had passed, the prosecution went after his associate: Autokles was suspended from office (Dem. 50.12) and at the trial Hypereides spoke in support of Apollodoros, who had served as trierarch on the campaign.

A number of fragmentary inscriptions survive (*IG* ii^2 111; *IG* ii^2 404; *IG* xii.5 594; *SEG* xiv 530) relating to Keos and to Aristophon's settlement of the island. In this paper I explore Hypereides' motivation for prosecuting Aristophon and consider what in that settlement could be deemed harmful and what implications these two factors have for our understanding of Athenian politics and foreign policy during the period.

Aristophon's Settlement of Keos

IG ii^2 111 (Harding no. 55)[1] records a treaty between Athens and Ioulis[2] that dates to the year 363/2 (the Archonship of Charikleides), passed on the motion of Aristophon. According to the terms of this decree, in the month of Skirophorion Ioulis must repay three talents of the money reported by the restored exiles of Ioulis that was due under the terms of an earlier decree passed by the Athenian *dēmos* on the motion of Menexenos (lines 1–11). Should the debt remain unpaid by the appointed time, the task of collecting the money would fall to those appointed by the *dēmos* to collect money from the islanders, assisted by the five generals of Ioulis (lines 11–17). The decree also sets out to validate oaths and agreements that had been previously concluded by Chabrias, who had served as general in 363/2, the same year as Aristophon:[3] 'In order that both the oaths and the treaty that the general Chabrias concluded and sworn with the Keans on behalf of the Athenians and the Keans whom the Athenians restored, these same generals are to have them (oaths and the treaty) inscribed on a stele and set up in the temple of Pythian Apollo, as they were in Karthaia' (Harding).[4] The secretary of the Athenian *boulē* is to do the same on the Acropolis (lines 17–25). We further learn from the decree (lines 27–45) that these new arrangements proposed by Aristophon were made necessary, since certain Ioulietai – who had transgressed the oaths and the agreements by making war against the Athenian *dēmos*, the Keans, and the other allies – had returned to Keos, though they had been condemned to death (presumably by the terms of Chabrias' agreement); had removed the stelai on which were inscribed the agreements (of Chabrias) with Athens and the names of those who had transgressed the oaths and the agreements; had killed certain pro-Athenians restored by the *dēmos*; and had in contravention of the oaths and agreements condemned to death and confiscated the property of Satyrides, Timoxenos, and Miltiades, because they had accused Antipatros before the Athenian *boulē* when it condemned him to death for killing the Athenian *proxenos* and for transgressing the oaths and the agreements. These Ioulietai, we are told, are to be exiled from Keos and Athens, their property is to become the public property of the *dēmos* of Ioulis, and their names are to be registered in the assembly with the secretary by the generals of the Ioulietai presently in Athens, namely Heracleides and Echetimos (cf. line 52). Further, (lines 45–9) legal recourse is to be made available to those who claim to be falsely accused: if any of those whose names have been registered dispute the charge of belonging to the condemned group, after providing guarantors to generals of the Ioulietai within thirty days, they can stand trial according to the oaths and agreements first in Keos and then upon appeal in Athens, which is ἔκκλητος. We are next told (lines 49–51) that Satyrides, Timoxenos, and Miltiades are to return to their property on Keos and are to receive commendation, as are the four envoys from Ioulis now in Athens: Demetrios, Herakleides, Echetimos, and Kalliphantos; commendation is also to be extended to the city of Karthaia and to Aglokritos. What follows in the decree (lines 57–85) are the agreements that were sworn by the Athenian generals (Chabrias?) and their allies to the cities on Keos (lines 57–69), and the oaths and agreements of the Kean cities sworn to the Athenian generals, the allies, and those Keans restored by the Athenians (lines 69–81). What are not preserved in the inscription are the oaths sworn by the restored Keans with the Athenians (lines 82–5).

From this inscription we can reconstruct to some degree the sequence of events of the revolt. It began, perhaps in 364, with the assassination of the Athenian *proxenos* by Antipatros (lines 38–9), who headed an anti-Athenian faction that seems to have had its core strength in Ioulis;[6] the assassination was followed by the exile of a number Keans loyal to Athens (lines 19, 34) and open war against Athens (lines 28–9). It was likely at this time that the Keans concluded treaties of isopolity with Histiaia (*IG* xii.5 594) and Eretria (*SEG* xiv 530), perhaps to gain the protection of Thebes, who was an ally of the two Euboian cities (more below).[7] At some point Chabrias was sent to deal with the revolt but his settlement, which included trial(s) before the Athenian *boulē* of Antipatros and his fellow conspirators that resulted in their conviction and condemnation to death, was short lived.[8] Soon after Chabrias' departure, the conspirators from the city of Ioulis, who obviously had not awaited trial but went into exile, returned, overturned the stelai on which had been inscribed the agreements and the names of the conspirators,[9] and killed some loyalists while condemning to death and confiscating the property of others, including Satyrides, Timoxenos, and Militades, who had accused Antipatros before the *boulē*. It seems that this fresh insurrection was limited to Ioulis, since Karthaia appears not to have been implicated in the renewed unrest, as it is specifically singled out for commendation in the decree (line 54).[10] Moreover, the decree indicates that stelai set up in Karthaia, on which were inscribed the oaths and agreements of Chabrias, were not overturned as they had been in Ioulis. No mention is made of the other two cities on the island (Koresia and Poiessa), and the fact that only Ioulis and Karthaia are singled out in the decree may suggest that the initial revolt, which Chabrias was sent to quell, was restricted to or had its main support in these two cities alone.

In response to the renewed unrest the Athenians sent Aristophon, who was also serving as general for 363/2, and in the aftermath of his success in Keos he was made *proxenos* of Karthaia (*IG* xii.5 542.43). According to Tod, the reference at line 10 of *IG* ii² 111 (Harding no. 55) to Skirophorion, the last month of the Attic year, suggests that Aristophon's motion dates to late spring or early summer of 362.[11] This should mean that his intervention on the island of Keos came early in the campaigning season of 362, still providing enough time for him to quell the revolt, for envoys from Ioulis (lines 51–2) to be dispatched to Athens and negotiate a final settlement, and for Aristophon himself to return and see his motion pass through the assembly.[12] Hypereides' prosecution would have followed sometime in late 362 or early 361.

As the inscription makes clear, Aristophon's intervention was not the first; his settlement of affairs, which he proposed in the assembly, was based on an early settlement reached by Chabrias, who was serving as *stratēgos* in that same year (363/2), and also on the motion of Menexenos. The inscription does not make clear the exact relationship between Menexenos' proposal, which is also incorporated into Aristophon's decree, and Chabrias' settlement. Menexenos was either the one who proposed the initial adoption of Chabrias' settlement of Keos, acting as *rhētōr* for the general, who was still out campaigning and rarely addressed the assembly himself, or he proposed a separate motion dealing only with arrears of reparation owed by Ioulis.[13] If we are right in placing Aristophon's activities in the spring of 362, Chabrias' intervention, which ended in the defeat of the rebels, the restoration of the pro-Athenian exiles, and a provisional settlement, probably dates to the late summer or early fall of 363, towards the end of the campaigning season of that year. In quick succession would have followed Menexenos' proposal in the Athenian assembly formally ratifying Chabrias' settlement, the administration of the oaths on Keos by Chabrias, and the publication of the treaty in the cities of Keos (lines 18–24), thus officially putting the agreement into force.[14] The trials of Antipatros and the other rebels before the Athenian *boulē*, which were perhaps a condition of Chabrias' agreement or an additional measure called for by the Athenian assembly, would have followed in the late fall of that year or early winter of 362. Perhaps when Chabrias left Keos, the three Keans – Satyrides, Timoxenos, and Militades – made their way to Athens to prosecute Antipatros; their absence from Keos would explain why they were not killed by the rebel exiles who had returned to Ioulis after Chabrias and the Athenian fleet had departed.

The most common reading of the inscription,[15] which I have followed above, has Chabrias' activities preceding those of Aristophon, a point not accepted, however, by Laqueur, who instead suggests that Chabrias' settlement was made after Aristophon's motion and partly abrogated the terms of that motion.[16] The generals of Ioulis, who are ordered at line 20 to publish the oaths and agreements of Chabrias, are identified as 'the ones who are instructed in the decree to help in exacting the money' (ὃς εἴρηται ἐν τῶι ψηφίσματι συνεισπράττεν τὰ χρήματα). The reference is to lines 4–17, where the five generals are specifically named in Aristophon's motion to assist those commissioned by the *dēmos* to exact money due from the islanders.

Assuming that τῶι ψηφίσματι refers not to this decree but to an earlier one, Laqueur suggests that lines 17–27, which call for the validation of oaths and agreements concluded by Chabrias, are part of a later amendment that abrogated Aristophon's earlier motion but was nonetheless incorporated into that earlier motion.[17] Thus lines 5–17 (calling for the payment of three talents), lines 27–36 and 41–5 (calling for the exile of Ioulietan rebels), lines 45–9 (granting judicial protection for those Ioulietai falsely accused), and lines 51–2 (calling for the commendation of envoys of the Ioulietai) all belong to Aristophon's earlier motion, which has now been superseded by Chabrias' settlement; whereas lines 17–27 (calling for the validation of Chabrias' oaths and agreements), lines 36–41, 48–51 and 52–3 (all of which refer to Satyrides, Timoxenos, and Miltiades),[18] and finally lines 57 to the end (giving the text of the oaths and agreements sworn by the Athenian generals to the Kean cities and by the Keans to the Athenians) are all later additions.

Further, Laqueur argues that there is an essential contradiction between Aristophon's motion and Chabrias' settlement that is avoided if we accept that Chabrias' arrangement came later. Whereas Aristophon's motion calls for punitive measures in the exile and confiscation of property of the Ioulietan rebels, Chabrias' agreements (lines 58–61) grant a general amnesty by which the Athenians pledge not to hold a grudge against any Keans for past wrongs, nor to kill or exile any Kean who abides by the oaths and the agreements. According to Laqueur's reconstruction the scope of negotiations, limited under Aristophon to Ioulis, was broadened by Chabrias to include all cities. In Aristophon's motion the phrase Ἰουλιῆται οὓς κατήγαγον Ἀθηναῖοι (line 5) was replaced by Κείων ὃς κα[τή]γαγον [Ἀ]θηναῖοι (lines 19, 70) of Chabrias' agreements.[19] As Billheimer points out, however, the more natural interpretation of the text of the inscription is that the sphere of operations had narrowed rather than widened. Aristophon was dealing with an isolated group who had subsequently revolted after Chabrias had settled affairs on Keos. His motion to publish the agreements and oaths concluded by Chabrias 'implies their previous adoption,' something confirmed by lines 22–3, which indicate that they had already been published in Karthaia.[20] And as for the alleged contradiction between Aristophon's proposed punishments and Chabrias' amnesty, again Billheimer rightly points out that the amnesty only applied to 'those who abide by the oaths and this treaty' (lines 60–1). Anyone who rebelled placed himself outside the protection of the amnesty and could thus be punished.[21] Although Billheimer is right on this point, Laqueur's concern about the contradiction in the two settlements may provide a clue to understanding Hypereides' accusation that Aristophon's motion was harmful: it proposed punitive measures that violated the generous spirit of Chabrias' agreements.

The problem with Laqueur's reconstruction is that it creates more difficulties than it resolves. It adds an additional phase to the unrest on Keos that seems unnecessary. According to Laqueur, Ioulis revolted from the league in 364/3; peace was soon restored to Ioulis (the occasion of Menexenos' motion?) but was short lived. The Ioulietan rebels returned, killing and condemning those loyal to Athens; Aristophon was then sent to deal with matters. His proposal, which called for punitive measures against Ioulis alone in the form of repayment of the three talents and the banishment of the rebels, was amended to include all of Keos after Chabrias' subsequent intervention, presumably because the unrest had spread to the rest of the island. If that is the case an amnesty seems an inappropriate response to renewed unrest on a much wider scale.[22] But the addition of punitive measures restricted only to those in Ioulis, who had refused to abide by the generous terms of Chabrias' settlement, makes more sense. Moreover, as Billheimer points out, the greatest weakness in Laqueur's reconstruction is that it requires us to accept that Aristophon's original motion, though overturned, was nonetheless published with Chabrias' new agreement incorporated into it under the date and mover of the original motion that had now been abrogated.[23] In the end it is better to accept that Chabrias' settlement came first and that Aristophon was later sent to deal with renewed unrest that remained localized in Ioulis, something that his motion reflected when it called for the punishment of Ioulietan rebels while still confirming the general terms of Chabrias' settlement.

IG ii^2 404

Before proceeding to discuss the wider context of the revolt on Keos, one other inscription needs to be examined for its relevance, *IG* ii^2 404:[24]

ΣΤΟΙΧ . . . .^{15}. . . . . ΤΟΔΕ -
. . . .^{14}. . . . . . ῶνος ἐ[ν]άτ[ηι - - - - - - - - - - - - - - - - - - -]
[. . . . τῆς πρυτα]νείας· τῶν π̣ρο[έδρων ἐπεψήφιζε - - - - - - - - - - - - - -]
. . . .^{9}. . . ΑΣ· ἔδοξεν τῶι δήμ[ωι -]
[. . . . . . .εἶπεν· π[ερὶ ὧν ἔδοξεν ἔννο[μα ἱκετεύειν - - - - - - - - - - - - - -]
. . . .^{9}. . . .καὶ Σίμαλος καὶ -
[. . . . .^{7}. . . ὅ]πως ἂν σᾶ ἦι Κέως τῶ[ι δήμωι τῶι Ἀθηναίων - - - - - - - -]
. . . .^{8}. . αἱ πόλεις αἱ ἐγ Κέω[ι -]
. . . .^{8}. . ἦλθον εἰς τὸ συνέδρι[ον. . . . .^{9}. . . . . τ]ῷ̣ι δήμω[ι . . . .^{7}.]
. . . .^{8}. . π]όλεις καὶ ἀνεγράφη [τῶν πόλ]εων ἑκάστης τὰ ὀ[νόματα ἐ]-
[ν τῆι στή]ληι καὶ σύνταξιν συντ[εταγμέ]ναι εἰσίν· δεδόχθ[αι τῶι δ]-
[ήμωι κυ]ρίους μὲγ εἶν[α]ι τοὺς ὅρκ[ους κ]αὶ τὰς συνθήκας τῶ[ι δήμωι]

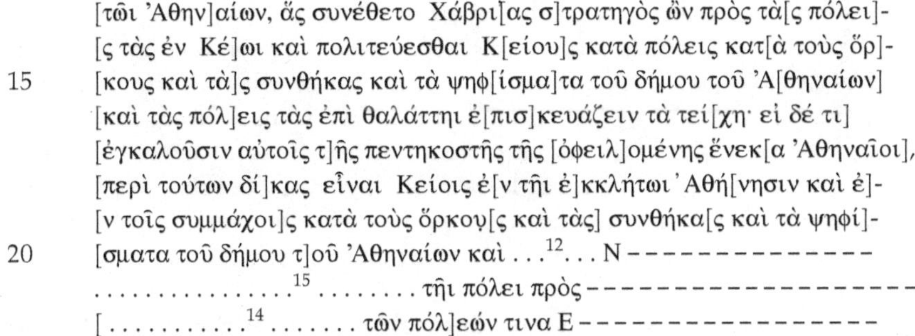

[τῶι Ἀθην]αίων, ἅς συνέθετο Χάβρι[ας σ]τρατηγὸς ὢν πρὸς τὰ[ς πόλει]-
[ς τὰς ἐν Κέ]ωι καὶ πολιτεύεσθαι Κ[είου]ς κατὰ πόλεις κατ[ὰ τοὺς ὅρ]-
[κους καὶ τὰ]ς συνθήκας καὶ τὰ ψηφ[ίσμα]τα τοῦ δήμου τοῦ Ἀ[θηναίων]
[καὶ τὰς πόλ]εις τὰς ἐπὶ θαλάττηι ἐ[πισ]κευάζειν τὰ τεί[χη· εἰ δέ τι]
[ἐγκαλοῦσιν αὐτοῖς τ]ῆς πεντηκοστῆς τῆς [ὀφειλ]ομένης ἕνεκ[α Ἀθηναῖοι],
[περὶ τούτων δί]κας εἶναι Κείοις ἐ[ν τῆι ἐ]κκλήτωι Ἀθή[νησιν καὶ ἐ]-
[ν τοῖς συμμάχοι]ς κατὰ τοὺς ὅρκου[ς καὶ τὰς] συνθήκα[ς καὶ τὰ ψηφί]-
[σματα τοῦ δήμου τ]οῦ Ἀθηναίων καὶ ...[12]... Ν --------------
................[15]........ τῆι πόλει πρὸς -------------------
[...........[14]....... τῶν πόλ]εών τινα Ε -----------------

IG ii² 404 preserves a decree passed by the Athenian *dēmos* that adopted a settlement concluded by Chabrias with the cities of Keos (lines 11–13). According to this settlement the cities of Keos are to exercise their political rights 'city by city'; that is, independently of one another. The first nine lines of the inscription are badly damaged, not preserving the archon date (line 1), the name of the tribe in prytany (line 1), or the particular day of that prytany and the name of the *proedroi* who put the motion to a vote (line 2), as we find in *IG* ii² 123 (Harding no. 69), the Andros decree to which *IG* ii² 404 is often compared.[25] Consequently the inscription has been variously dated. Based on the restoration in line 1 of the phrase ὦνος ἐ[ν]άτ[ηι ('on the ninth day of the month of'), Koehler (*IG* ii.5 135f.) concluded that the decree could not be dated before 338/7, the earliest known date for an inscription to carry such a formula. But Schweigert's restoration of a similar formula to *IG* ii² 122, so he claims, 'removes the last objection to dating *IG* ii² 404 ... in 356 BC.'[26] Lewis, who accepts Schweigert's arguments, also sees the Social War (357/6) as the appropriate context for the inscription and suggests that Chabrias' settlement, which called for the Keans to govern themselves by *poleis* (line 14), dissolved the Kean federation which had until now been tolerated by the Athenians (more below).[27] Kirchner (*IG* ii² 404) likewise suggests the context of the Social War, based on line 6 ('in order that Keos be safe for the Athenian demos ...'), which finds a parallel in lines 8–9 of *IG* ii² 123 (ὅπως [ἂ]ν Ἄνδ[ρος] ε[ἶ] σ[ᾶ] τῶι δ[ή]μωι τῶι Ἀθη[να]ίων),the decree that led to the installation of a garrison on Andros in 357/6. We do not know the particular safeguards that the decree of *IG* ii² 404 called for to ensure Keos' safety, but such a response would have been as appropriate to the unrest of 364, when we know Chabrias intervened on the island, as to the Social War. Indeed, governors and garrisons are attested for Amorgas and Andros in the same period (363/2).[28] As Cawkwell argues, Androtion's involvement in ransoming prisoners while governor of Arkesine (*IG* xii.7 5.15)[29] suggests the period of Alexander of Pherai's activities in the Aegean in 362, and Timarchos was likely governor of Andros (Aisch. 1.107) in the same year (363/2).[30] Thus the introduction of a garrison and governor on Andros in 357/6 was not an innovation of the Social War but simply a reaffirmation of an existing practice, and cannot then be used as conclusive evidence for dating *IG* ii^2 404 to that period. Rather, the safeguards envisioned for Keos in *IG* ii^2 404 may in fact have formed part of Chabrias' original settlement of 363/2, which the decree of *IG* ii^2 404 either seeks to confirm or reaffirm, in much the same way as Aristophon's motion reaffirms Chabrias' settlement.

In fact, Cargill himself suggests but quickly dismisses the possibility that *IG* ii^2 404 refers to Chabrias' settlement of 363/2. Instead he suggests that if not the original membership treaty in the Second Athenian League, *IG* ii^2 404 may have at least incorporated certain phrases from that treaty, including the provision of lines 14–15 that the Keans govern themselves by cities.[31] Even if this is true, it need not, however, restrict the decree of *IG* ii^2 404 to the 370s, when Chabrias was actively recruiting members for the league, but could be equally appropriate to any later settlement by Chabrias that sought to reaffirm and define more clearly the Kean cities' position within the league. Again, the unrest of 364 and Chabrias' settlement of 363/2, which brought Keos back into the league, would be an appropriate context.

Maier dates the decree of *IG* ii^2 404 between 362 and 350;[32] in his mind the decree does two things: first, it reaffirms the validity of the agreement concluded by Chabrias in 363/2; and second, it dissolves the sympolity of the Kean federation. It belongs, he argues, to a series of Athenian decrees passed since 364 aimed at curtailing the legal sovereignty of smaller league states. At lines 16–20 we are told that cases between the Athenians and the Keans involving the import tax in the Peiraieus are to be heard in the appellate city of Athens.[33] A similar appeal provision for suits over 100 drachmai is found in *IG* ii^2 111 (lines 73–5), granted under the terms of Chabrias' agreement sworn to by the Kean cities.[34] It is possible that other appeal provisions were provided for under the terms of oaths sworn by the restored Keans (lines 82–4), no longer preserved on the inscription. Further, the decree of *IG* ii^2 404 authorized the *poleis* on the sea to build walls; according to Maier, in Koresia and Karthaia there is evidence that the walls were rebuilt around this time according to a uniform plan but on a smaller scale than the older walls that they replaced. He suggests that the fortifications were destroyed by Chabrias when he suppressed the revolt in 364 and that sometime later, perhaps in response to the activities of Alexander of Pherai in 362, this decree was passed authorizing the rebuilding of the walls.[35]

Maier's suggestion that the decree of *IG* ii^2 404 reaffirms the validity of Chabrias' settlement of 363/2 is most attractive. I have even hinted above that *IG* ii^2 404 preserves, if not the actual settlement itself, at least provisions of that settlement, which the decree of *IG* ii^2 404 seeks to build on. Dreher goes even further, arguing that the inscription preserves the actual decree that authorized Chabrias' original settlement of 363/2.[36] He points to the verbal parallel between *IG* ii^2 404.12–14 (κυ]ρίους μὲṿ εἶν[α]ι τοὺς ὅρκ[ους κ]αὶ τὰς συνθήκας τῶ[ι δήμωι]| [τῶι 'Αθην]αίων, ἃς συνέθετο Χάβρι[ας σ]τρατηγὸς ὢν πρὸς τὰ||[ς πόλει][ς τὰς ἐν Κέ]ωι) and *IG* ii^2 111.17–18 (ὅπως δ' [ἃ]ν κ[αὶ] οἱ ὅρκοι καὶ αἱ συνθῆκαι ἃς συνέθ|ετο Χαβρίας ὁ στ[ρ]ατηγὸς κα[ὶ] ὤμοσε Κείοις ὑπὲρ 'Αθηναίων). Though one should not press such parallels, which are largely formulaic, Dreher's other arguments are more convincing. Aristophon's settlement, which is based on Chabrias' own, treats Ioulis as an independent city with its own financial administration (lines 5–11), generals (lines 15, 20, 44, 47), and legal jurisdiction (lines 45–9), and thus presumes the kind of political autonomy laid down in *IG* ii^2 404.[37] A lot depends on how one interprets lines 10–18 of *IG* ii^2 404:

> ... the cities and the name of each of the cites was inscribed on the stele and they paid *suntaxis*. It has been resolved by the *dēmos* that binding are the oaths and agreements with the *dēmos* of the Athenians, which were arranged by Chabrias while general with the cities on Keos, and that the Keans govern themselves by cities according to the oaths and agreements and decree of the *dēmos* of the Athenians, and the cities on the sea build their walls.

The author of this decree speciously implies that since the names of each of the four Kean cities were listed on the stele of the league treaty, something which was indeed true, and paid tribute (the implication here is separately),[38] something which may not have been true, they must govern themselves independently in accordance with the oaths and agreements of Chabrias. The question is whether the infinitive πολιτεύεσθαι is governed by δεδόχθ[αι or in apposition to κυρ]ίους μὲν εἶν[α]ι τοὺς ὅρκ[ους κ]αὶ τὰς συνθήκας. Are we to read 'be it resolved by the *dēmos* that the oaths and agreements which Chabrias made are binding and further the Keans govern themselves by cities' or 'that the oaths and agreements which Chabrias made are binding, namely that the Keans govern themselves by cities'? In other words, did Chabrias insist as part of his settlement of 363/2 that the Kean cities govern themselves independently, or was this the provision of some later decree whose author sought to justify it by appealing to Chabrias' settlement? Throughout *IG* ii^2 404 there are repeated references to the cities on Keos as if they were treated as independent entities (lines 8,

10, 14, 22), and as we have seen, Maier and others, including Dreher, have argued that the decree dissolves the Kean federation (on which more below). But was this actually true of Chabrias' agreement of 363/2 that was adopted by Aristophon? If it was, then we can possibly conclude with Dreher that *IG* ii^2 404 predates *IG* ii^2 111 (Harding no. 55) and preserves the actual decree that ratified Chabrias' settlement. But before we can properly answer this question, we must look at the nature of the Kean federation.

The Kean Federation

On the island of Keos were four cities: Karthaia, Koresia, and Poiessa on the coast and Ioulis inland. It has been argued that at some time prior to Chabrias' settlement, at least three of the cities formed some kind a federation, perhaps modeled after Euboia.[39] *SEG* xiv 530 records an isopolity treaty between Keos and Eretria that parallels the isopolity between Keos and Histiaia of *IG* xii.5 594.[40] Both inscriptions were found in Ioulis. The letter forms of *SEG* xiv 530, according to Lewis, can hardly fix the date closer than 390–340; I would suggest with others a date around 364 for both inscriptions and place the context of such isopolities in the context of the revolt of Keos from the Second Athenian League.[41] What we learn from the inscriptions is that Keos had a three-tier system based on tribes, *trittyes*, and *choroi* (demes), the latter occurring only in one other place – Eretria. Lewis suggests that such a system is better suited to a federation of three cities, with each tribe drawing a *trittys* from each of the three cities involved in federation. That the federation was made up of three rather than the four cities of Keos is perhaps suggested by *IG* ii^2 43, which records the charter of the Second Athenian League (377/6).[42] Poiessa is listed on the front face of the stele separately (line 82), squeezed between the left and right columns that list the names of those who entered the league either at its inception or soon after, while the names of other three cites appear on the left side of the stele listed collectively as Κείων Ἰουλιῆται, Καρθαιε͂ς, Κορήσιοι (lines 119–22). This should mean that Poiessa entered the league earlier, on its own, followed sometime later by the three cities of the Kean federation.[43] Thus before 375, the year in which they entered the Second Athenian League, these three cites were somehow associated and collectively know as the Keans.[44] That the islanders were acting in some kind of federated structure before this date is, according to Lewis, also suggested by the 'Sandwich decree' (*IG* ii^2 1635.113),[45] which records the Κεῖοι borrowing money collectively. The inspiration for the federated constitution of Keos was Eretria, and Lewis argues that the federation was formed when Euboia revolted from Athens in 411 during the Peloponnesian War. To guard her southern approaches, Eretria set up a federal structure in Keos modeled on her own institutions. And it may be significant that both known isopolity treaties are with Eretria and Histiaia. If Lewis is correct, the Kean federation existed from the late fifth century. But how long it existed into the fourth century is an open question.

IG ii^2 43 may indicate tacit if not wholehearted recognition by Athens of a Kean federation of Koresia, Ioulis, and Karthaia.[46] But it is not clear whether the federation continued to be recognized after the revolt of Keos in 364. Chabrias' settlement, which forms part of Aristophon's motion (*IG* ii^2 111), is ambiguous. The oaths sworn by Chabrias on behalf of the Athenians are with Κεῖοι (line 18) but were to be set up in the individual cities of Karthaia (line 23), Ioulis (line 31), and presumably Koresia. The text of the oath is introduced by the statement (lines 57–8) that the Athenian generals and the allies concluded the following agreement and swore the following oaths with the cities of Keos (πρὸς τὰς πόλες τ[ὰ]ς ἐν Κέωι); that is, with each individual city. This is precisely the formulation we find in *IG* ii^2 404, which calls for the Keans to govern themselves by cities. Further, Ioulis has its own *stratēgoi,* who are to assist in various ways in implementing the agreement by exacting the money that is due (line 15), registering the names of those whose property is to be confiscated (line 45), and accepting guarantors from those appealing the registration of their names (line 47). Moreover, Karthaia is called a polis (line 54), perhaps again in recognition of its separate identity.

Thus *IG* ii^2 111 (Harding no. 55) may indicate that Keos had only a very loose federation, in which each city retained a certain autonomy, appointing its own generals and having treaties set up in each polis rather than in a central location. Alternatively, it could indicate that Athens had now dissolved the federation that had posed a threat to her when it revolted in 364. If the latter interpretation is true, it strengthens Dreher's view that *IG* ii^2 404 predates *IG* ii^2 111 and in fact preserves the actual decree authorizing Chabrias' settlement of 363/2, which called on the Kean cities to govern themselves independently. The isopolity treaties with Eretria (*SEG* xiv 530) and Histiaia (*IG* xii.5 594), which I have suggested were entered into at the time of the revolt, speak only in terms of Keos and not of individual cities and suggest that certain offices were held collectively. Anyone from Histiaia or Eretria who wants to exercise citizenship in Keos (presumably in any one of the three cities, not just in Ioulis where the two inscriptions were found) must apply to the *Thesmophylakes* ('Guardians of the laws'), joint magistrates of the three cities,[47] who will assign a tribe, *trittys,* and deme to the applicant.[48] Tod's edition of *IG* xii.5 594.18–21 also indicates that there were a number of other joint bodies who were to look after the interests of the Histiaians, including a *boulē, probouloi,* and *astynomoi.*[49] No doubt each of the three cities contributed to these bodies. The two inscriptions clearly suggest a federal structure with shared offices and legal responsibilities among the three cities of the federation. This does not mean, however, that each city of the federation did not elect its own officials in other capacities, like *stratēgoi,* or insist that treaties be posted in each polis rather than at some central location, although some such location must have existed where federal bodies met to discuss collective concerns. Both the isopolities were found in Ioulis and presumably copies of the treaties were also set up in Koresia and Karthaia, as was the case with Aristophon's settlement. But in the case of the latter there is, as I have suggested, a strong possibility that Aristophon's settlement, which incorporated the agreements of Chabrias, no longer recognized the federal structure at Keos. This is certainly true of the decree of *IG* ii^2 404, which at the very least preserves provisions of Chabrias' settlement if not the actual settlement itself.

The Context of the Revolt

The revolt of Keos has been connected with Thebes' naval activities in the Aegean under Epameinondas.[50] According to Diodoros (15.78.4–79.1; cf. Aisch. 2.105; Isok. 5.54), at Epameinondas' prompting and perhaps with the help of Persian money, Thebes embarked on an ambitious naval program that called for the building of 100 triremes and dockyards to house the ships.[51] To assist his plans he made diplomatic overtures to Rhodes, Chios, and Byzantion.[52] The program dates to 367/6 and was completed with great speed, for by 365/4 Epameinondas was operating in the Aegean with a fleet. The involvement of Persian money was perhaps prompted by the aggressive activities of the Athenians in the Aegean in the 360s, which were no doubt troubling to the Great King. In 366 the satrap Ariobarzanes revolted and sought aid from Athens. The Athenians dispatched Timotheos (*stratēgos* in 366/5) with thirty triremes and 8000 peltasts, with orders to support Ariobarzanes but without violating the King's peace (Dem. 15.9, 23.141; Isok. 15.108; Nep. *Timoth.* 1.3). Timotheos opened operations by attacking Samos, which had a Persian garrison under the authority of the Persian satrap Tigranes. After laying siege to the island for ten months, Timotheos starved the Samians into submission; not only was the Persian garrison expelled but so were the Samians (Diod. 18.18.9). Athenian kleruchies were sent to settle the island in 365/4.[53] The dispatch of these colonists may not have violated the exact terms of the charter of the Second Athenian League since Samos was not an ally, but it did violate the spirit of the treaty and may have been viewed by Athens' allies as an indication of her growing aggression (Isok. 15.112; Dein. 1.14) and must have led some to look for an opportunity to revolt, which presented itself in the presence of a Theban fleet operating in the Aegean.

Timotheos maintained his aggressive posture. In 364 he sailed northward to relieve Iphikrates as *stratēgos* of Amphipolis and the Chersonesos (Dem. 23.149). There is some debate whether he first made a brief excursion to the Thermaic Gulf, where he conducted successful operations against Pydna and Methone but failed to take Amphipolis (Dein. 1.14; Dem. 23.150) before sailing to the Hellespontos, returning only in the following year to the Chalkidike to continue operations there;[54] or whether he sailed directly to the Hellespontos (Isok. 15.112), where he first captured Sestos from the Thracian king Kotys and then Krithote.[55] In any case, while still in the Propontis he captured Kyzikos, which was under Persian control. From there he sailed into the Black Sea and intervened in the internal affairs of Herakleia, where civil strife had broken out (Justin 16.4). After concluding his activities in the Black Sea, Timotheos (re)turned to the Chalkidike. By this point we are at the year 363 and affairs in Keos would have already or nearly been settled, but Timotheos' activities first in Samos and then later in the Hellespontos may have caused additional concerns for the islanders and, more importantly, fueled and hardened opposition to Athens by those who led the two revolts.

It is within the context of these aggressive activities on the part of Athens that we find Epameinondas setting sail with his fleet in 364. The Athenians responded by dispatching a squadron of ships under Laches' command, who, however, broke off his pursuit when confronted by the size of the Boiotian fleet (Diod. 15.79.1). This allowed Epameinondas to sail unopposed to Byzantion (Isok. 5.54), which defected from Athens.[56] It seems, however, that Epameinondas could not entice the Chians or the Rhodians to join the Boiotian alliance (Plut. *Phil.* 14.2). But the fact that the Athenian fleet was so easily cowed and Byzantion so readily responded to Theban overtures may have encouraged Keos to revolt. The Keans at this time probably concluded the treaties of isopolity with Eretria and Histiaia, both of whom were allied with Thebes, a fact that may have assured them of Theban help.[57] But such help never materialized, and Athens quickly put an end to the revolt, first through the intervention of Chabrias and then through that of Aristophon.

The Trials

Soon after Aristophon proposed his decree to settle the affairs of Keos he was indicted by Hypereides, apparently for making an illegal proposal (fr. 40), either late in the fall of 362 or early in 361. The trial itself coincided with a number of high-profile impeachment suits against a number of generals who had failed in their operations in the Aegean: Timomachos, Leosthenes, Kallistratos, Philon, and Theotimos (Hyp. 3.1).[58] All these trials seem to date to 361/0.[59] Hypereides himself makes reference to these cases at the beginning of his defence of Euxenippos, and as Whitehead plausibly notes, such trials may have left a vivid impression on Hypereides, who was just starting his political career;[60] more so if he himself had a hand in any of these trials or was involved in other political prosecutions of his own at the time. The trial of Autokles for treason dates to the same year, and Hypereides (frs. 55–65) seems to have assisted in the prosecution conducted by Apollodoros, who is also known (Dem. 36.53) to have prosecuted several other generals at this time, including some (Timomachos) in Hypereides' list.

This leads directly to the question of the nature of the prosecution against Aristophon. Little is known of the case, since only a few scrappy fragments remain (frs. 40–44). Fragment 40 (Σ Aisch. 1.64) suggests a *graphē paranomōn* but surprisingly notes that Hypereides secured a conviction: ὡς στρατηγήσας ἐν Κέῳ διὰ φιλοχρηματίαν πολλὰ κακὰ ἐργασάμενος τοὺς ἐνοικοῦντας, ἐφ' ᾧ γραφεὶς ὑπὸ Ὑπερείδου παρανόμων ἑάλω. Yet the fact that Aristophon's motion was published should confirm that Hypereides failed in his prosecution.[61] In his defence speech for Euxenippos (Hyp. 3.28), Hypereides himself seems to make reference to his prosecution, claiming, however, that Aristophon, who had become extremely powerful politically, was acquitted by only two votes. In the same breath he boasts about his prosecutions of Diopeithes and Philokrates, the latter of whom he impeached. The context, an enumeration of *eisangelia* suits conducted by Hypereides, has suggested to some that Aristophon was also impeached by *eisangelia*.[62] And this in fact is how the suit is characterized by Hansen, who also refuses to identify it with Hypereides' *graphē paranomōn* of fr. 40.[63] But in fact the only case which Hypereides clearly identifies at 3.28 as an impeachment (τοῦτον εἰσαγγείλας ἐγὼ κτλ.) is his prosecution of Philokrates, and Whitehead's arguments against concluding from association that Aristophon's case (and for that matter that of Diopeithes) was an *eisangelia* are cogent.[64] Moreover, Hansen's reluctance, shared to some extant by Whitehead, to conflate the two prosecutions seems also unwarranted; Hypereides is only known to have prosecuted Aristophon once, and as we shall see below, only on the occasion of the Keos affair. Further, the context of the scholiast's discussion of Hypereides' prosecution may be a reference to Aristophon's alleged acquittal in seventy-five *graphai paranomōn* (cf. Aisch. 3.198), which would make Hypereides' successful conviction all the more remarkable, although this is not emphasized by the scholiast.[65]

If, however, we identify the two prosecutions and accept that Hypereides failed, then either the text of the scholia needs to be emended, as Meier suggests, to παρ' ὀλίγον ἑάλω ('he was almost convicted'), or the fragments refer not to Hypereides' prosecution of Aristophon over his Keos settlement but to a different motion proposed by Aristophon; perhaps, as Trevett suggests, to appoint Autokles as *stratēgos* in command of the Hellespontos in the fall of 362 (Dem. 50.4–6, 12).[66] But this cannot be right for two reasons: first, the scholiast makes clear that Hypereides' prosecution concerned Aristophon's generalship in Keos; and second, as Demosthenes (23.104) indicates, when Autokles was tried for destroying Miltokythes, the time for indicting the proposer of the decree had already passed.[67] As Hansen notes, the connection suggested by Demosthenes between the trial of Autokles and the decree, which was proposed and carried by an unnamed *rhētōr* just before Autokles' departure (Dem. 23.104), is made clear in Hypereides fr. 55, where we are informed that at the trial Hypereides argued that Autokles should be punished like Socrates for his words.[68] This suggests that Autokles spoke in favour of the motion that would directly bear on his treatment of Miltokythes; the decree itself perhaps addressed Miltokythes' request for aid from the Athenians in his revolt against Kotys, which he made just before Autokles' departure to take over command of the Hellespontos (Dem. 50.5).[69] But that request seems to have fallen on deaf ears. According to Demosthenes (23.104) the decree was couched in such terms that Miltokythes withdrew in fright and as a consequence, Kotys gained control of the Sacred Mountain and its treasures, and Autokles was condemned for destroying Miltokythes. The decree, which Autokles supported in the assembly that led to Miltokythes being rebuffed, was presumably the same decree proposed by Aristophon that mobilized the trierarchs and appointed Autokles commander (Dem. 50.5–12). In the meeting of the assembly that led directly to Aristophon's decree to mobilize, ambassadors were present both from Miltokythes, requesting aid against Kotys, and from the Prokonnesians against Kyzikos. There was also much discussion about the ongoing harassment of grain ships from the Pontos. Aristophon's motion, Apollodoros implies, addressed all three issues. If indeed we are right to connect it with Autokles' trial, Hypereides could not then have indicted Aristophon personally under a *graphē paranomōn,* since a year had already lapsed between initial motion to appoint Autokles and the time of his trial. But Trevett perhaps is right to see a close connection between Aristophon's and Autokles' trials. Hypereides may have used the trial of Autokles as another opportunity to attack Aristophon.

Nonetheless, we are left to conclude that fragments 40–5 refer to Hypereides' indictment over Aristophon's handling of Keos. Though Hypereides may have failed in that prosecution, his near conviction suggests that the young orator conducted a vigorous attack against the veteran politician. Indeed, the fragments reveal a speech full of abuse and invective, a strategy that nearly paid off. He alleged that Aristophon was the product of an adulterous affair: 'the *moichidion* born from a *moichos*' (fr. 42). He accused Aristophon of constant perjury, nicknaming him Adrettos (fr. 40).[70] Every virtue that Aristophon boasted of, Hypereides twisted into a vice: Aristophon's wisdom was simply craftiness, his bravery recklessness, his frugality miserliness, and his sternness spite (fr. 44). Hypereides argued (fr. 41) that Aristophon was given complete licence to do and say whatever he wanted, thus indicating that he was attacking Aristophon both for his actions as general and for his proposed settlement of Keos.

In particular, he noted how Aristophon had gained a monopoly (fr. 43). We cannot be sure of the context of this allegation, but it may be connected to the accusation of fragment 40 that Aristophon had done much harm to the inhabitants through greed (διὰ φιλοχρηματίαν). It may also have something to do with Aristophon being made *proxenos* of Karthaia soon after his settlement (*IG* xii.5 542.43). *Proxenia* and other honorary awards could be presented as sources of profit (Aisch. 3.33).[71] Hypereides himself would later accuse both Demades and Demosthenes of profiting by grants of *proxenia* which they secured for others (Hyp. 1.25; cf. Dein. 1.45), and a similar kind of accusation may have been leveled at Aristophon. His grant of *proxenia* could have been presented as evidence that he was or expected to be rewarded financially for his kind treatment of Karthaia, which is singled out in Aristophon's motion for commendation; by contrast, Ioulis and its inhabitants were treated with much greater severity, or so it could have been argued in court. Moreover, a *proxenos* could be expected to speak not in the interests of Athens but of the city he represented (Aisch. 2.141),[72] and this too might lie at the heart of Hypereides' claim (fr. 41) that Aristophon was given licence to do and say whatever he wanted, as if Aristophon assumed the honour of *proxenos* granted him the freedom to act and speak as he liked.

It is hard to see what in Aristophon's motion could be construed as harmful, when in fact it incorporated provisions set down previously by the decree of Menexenos and the settlement of Chabrias. The punitive measures introduced by Aristophon (lines 41–2), exile and the confiscation of property of those conspirators who had returned to Ioulis, are in fact directed at those who had already been tried and condemned to death under the terms of Chabrias' settlement (lines 30–1). It is quite possible that under Aristophon's proposal the net was widened to catch more Ioulietai than were initially tried under Chabrias' agreement, and this may explain why an appeal process was granted under Aristophon's decree, particularly if that provision had been a concession won by Ioulietan negotiators. Indeed, the procedure (lines 42–5) by which the actual names of the conspirators were registered by the generals of Ioulis in the Athenian assembly would have served as a visible reminder of the harsh terms of Aristophon's decree, particularly when contrasted to the amnesty sworn to by Chabrias. We can only surmise about Hypereides' line of attack.

Nonetheless, the trial of Aristophon should been seen in the wider context of Athenian politics of the late 360s. Politicians like Timotheos, Kallistratos, and Aristophon, who had dominated politics for the previous decade or longer,[73] were coming under increasing attack, particularly when recent military operations in the northern Aegean that these men had either sponsored or supported began to unravel.[74] Timotheos, despite his vigorous efforts, had failed in 363/2 to take Amphipolis (Dem. 23.150–2), which Athens had been seeking to recover since 368/7.[75] At one point he even met with defeat there (Σ Aisch. 2.31) and for this was impeached by Apollodoros (Dem. 36.53).[76] Kallistratos and Chabrias had already been prosecuted and acquitted in 366/5 for their handling of Oropos, which ended up in Theban hands (Σ Aisch. 3.85).[77] In 361/0 Kallistratos was again impeached (Hyp. 3.1–2), this time for being bribed to make a proposal contrary to the interest of the people.[78] To avoid trial, he went into exile (Hyp. 3.2) and was condemned in absentia (Lyk. 1.93).[79] The context of Hypereides' reference to Kallistratos' trial, a series of impeachment suits against generals who had failed in the northern Aegean, suggests that Kallistratos' proposal that led to the charge of bribery somehow related to those activities. This was certainly true in the case of Autokles. After eight months of service in the Hellespontos, Autokles was suspended from office (Dem. 50.12), denounced in the assembly by Apollodoros, and later prosecuted for treason (Hyp. fr. 63).[80] Apollodoros led the prosecution, with Hypereides assisting either as logographer or more likely as *synēgoros*.[81] His participation can be accounted for. The trial presented Hypereides with another opportunity to discredit Aristophon further, a chance to capitalize on his recent and nearly successful prosecution of Aristophon.[82] Though Aristophon himself could not be indicted for his proposal to mobilize the trierarchs under Autokles' command, that proposal, which turned aside Miltokythes' request for an alliance and led directly to Kotys' success against Autokles, did play a prominent part at the trial (Dem. 23.104). Hypereides (fr. 55) himself seems to have attacked the general for his vocal support of it in the assembly.

How successful Hypereides was in discrediting Aristophon is questionable. Aristophon himself seems to have been involved in the impeachment of Leosthenes in 361 (Aisch. 2.124) over his failure at Peparethos (Hyp. 3.1; Diod. 15.95.3).[83] This trial occurred right around the same time as Hypereides' prosecution of Aristophon over the Keos affair and came several months before the trial of Autokles, who may in fact have been acquitted.[84] Hypereides' near success thus seems to have had little political effect. Leosthenes' decision not to await trial (Hyp. 3.2), if indeed we are to connect Aristophon to the trial, indicates that he feared his chances in court against the veteran politician. Aristophon continued to remain active into the next decade. In 356/5 he impeached several generals, though his success was less than spectacular: two were acquitted and one had his sentence commuted.[85] But in the years just prior to and following these trials he continued to propose decrees in the assembly, indicating that he had suffered no real political damage from Hypereides' prosecutions.[86] Again in the 340s we find him behind a number of decrees.[87] There is perhaps some merit in Hypereides' boasting over his near conviction of a man who had become extremely powerful politically (3.28). To fall short by just two votes was in fact a real accomplishment against the Teflon man of Athenian politics, one who could dare to boast in court, we are told, that he had been acquitted of seventy-five *graphai paranomōn* (Aisch. 3.194).

Notes

1 *IG* ii^2 111 = Tod no. 142; *Syll*^{3} no. 173; *SV* no. 289; Rhodes-Osborne no. 39. I follow the text of Rhodes-Osborne.

2 Ioulis was one of the four cities on the island of Keos, the others being Karthaia, Koresia, and Poiessa. At some point three of these cities formed a federation, on which see Lewis 1962.

3 Develin 1989: 263.

4 As Thomas (1989: 46) notes concerning these lines, the very act of inscribing the text of the treaty validates it and makes it authoritative.

5 On the argument that the phrase ἔκκλητος πόλις should mean suits can be appealed, see Tod: 131–2; Accame 1941: 140–1; Cargill 1981: 136. A similar phrase (τὰς δίκας ἐκκλήτος) is used at line 74, where we are told that all suits over 100 drachmai can be appealed to Athens.

6 Dreher (1985: 267 and n. 21) suggests 363 for the revolt based on the fact that Aristophon's resolution (lines 23–7) indicates that Chabrias' agreements had not yet been published in Athens. Cawkwell (1961: 84 n. 5) suggests the possibility that the settlement referred to at line 17 was made in early 362.

7 Most editors date the treaty of isopolity between Keos and Histiaia to 364 (*Syll*^{3} no. 172; Tod no. 141; *SV* no. 287). Duant and Thomopoulos (1954: 316-22), who first published the inscription preserving the isopolity treaty between Keos and Eretria, argue that the two isopolity treaties should be dated close together but prior to Keos entering the Second Athenian League. I would agree that the two

decrees date close together but prefer the later date of 364, when Keos was in revolt. Cf. Cargill 1981: 135–6; Rhodes-Osborne: 200.

8 Dreher (1985: 271; cf. 267 and n. 21) argues that though the treaty negotiated by Chabrias had been formally adopted by the Athenian Assembly, and the oaths putting the treaty in force had been subsequently administered by Chabrias and the other generals to the Keans (lines 17–18) and a text of the treaty set up at least in Karthaia and Ioulis, the publication of the treaty in Athens itself was actually never carried out, since Ioulis revolted again soon after.

9 Since stelai were visual markers or memorials of the treaty, the overturning of such stelai was a visual gesture of breaking that treaty. On obliterating inscribed texts, which served more as monuments than documents, see Thomas 1989: 45–60.

10 Tod: 131.

11 Tod: 131; cf. Rhodes-Osborne: 202.

12 *IG* ii^2 404.5, which includes a reference to supplication, indicates that the Keans had sent ambassadors to Athens to negotiate changes to Chabrias' agreements that would form the basis of a decree admitting Keos back into the league. This, as Dreher (1985: 271) argues, led to the appeal provisions found in the decree of *IG* ii^2 404, which he believes preserves Chabrias' settlement of 363/2.

13 On the growing separation in the fourth century in political leadership between *rhētores*, who dominated the assemblies and the courts, and the *stratēgoi* like Chabrias, Iphikrates, and Timotheos, who campaigned and seldom appeared in the assembly, see Hansen 1991: 268–71; 1983a; 1983b; Perlman 1963; 1967; Roberts 1982.

14 According to Dreher (1985: 270–1), once Chabrias had negotiated a provisional settlement but before he administered the oaths, the Keans sent ambassadors to Athens (*IG* ii^2 404.5–6) to negotiate changes to his proposed settlement. The result of this negotiation was the decree of the assembly that formally ratified Chabrias' treaty; once the treaty was ratified, Chabrias then administered the oaths and had copies of the treaty set up in the Kean cities, putting the settlement into force. It is quite possible that Chabrias was not present during the ratification process in Athens but remained on the island supervising the restoration. Once a copy of the treaty had been brought to Keos and he had administered the oaths and made arrangements for the treaty to be set up, he was free to leave.

15 Tod: 131; Buckler 1980: 173; Billheimer 1938: 479–82.

16 Laqueur 1927: 179–83; cf. Billheimer (1938: 479–82) who provides a useful summary of Laqueur's arguments.

17 Likewise, τὸς ὅρκος καὶ τὰς συνθήκας of lines 27–8 refer to another agreement, as they do in line 17; Laqueur 1927: 179.

18 Laqueur sees the loose appositional connection between Σατυρίδο καὶ Τιμοξένο καὶ Μιλτιάδο (lines 36–7) and τῶν δὲ θάνατον κατέγνωσαν (lines 34–5) as evidence of additions. Cf. Billheimer 1938: 479–80.

19 Laqueur 1927: 183.
20 Billheimer 1938: 481; cf. Dreher 1985: 271.
21 Billheimer 1938: 481–2.
22 Billheimer 1938: 480.
23 Billheimer 1938: 481.
24 *IG* ii^2 404 = Maier no. 37; cf. *SEG* xix 50; xxi 254; xxxix 73. For a translation see Wickersham-Verbrugghe no. 56.
25 Wickersham-Verbrugghe no. 56; Kirchner on *IG* ii^2 404.
26 See Schweigert (1939: 14 n. 1), who also believes 'the subject-matter, phraseology and letter forms of *IG* ii^2 404 are eminently suitable to the year 356.' He dates *IG* ii^2 122 to the Social War because the decree falls in the same prytany as the decree concerning Elaious, which was passed in the archonship of Agathokles, the same year (357/6) as *IG* ii^2 123, the Andros decree; but as Cargill points out (1981: 135 n. 123), there is no basis for such a dating.
27 Lewis 1962: 4.
28 Cawkwell 1981: 51–2; cf. Hornblower 1983: 233. See also Dreher (1985: 266) for different arguments against pressing the parallel.
29 *IG* xii.7 5 = Tod no. 152; *Syll*^{3} no. 193; Rhodes-Osborne no. 51.
30 This is based on the assumption that Aischines is describing Timarchos' offices in chronological order. See Cawkwell 1981: 52 and n. 47; Fisher 2001: 244; Develin 1989: 264.
31 Cargill 1981: 134–5 and n. 13. At line 9 there is mention of the league *synedrion*.
32 Maier 1959: 158–9.
33 Lines 16–20: 'If Athenians have any charge against them over the 1/50th being owed, in these matters the Keans are to have their cases heard in the appellate city Athens [and among the allies?] according to the oaths and agreements and the decrees of the Athenian *dēmos* ...' It is possible that such suits could also be appealed to the league *synedrion* but this is based solely on the restoration [καὶ ἐν τοῖς συμμάχοι]ς in lines 18–19. See Cargill's objection to this restoration (1981: 137–8 n. 18). Maier restores the text to read [καὶ ἐν Κέωι κατὰ πόλει]ς ('and in Keos in the cities'), but this restoration seems inconsistent with provisions granting an appeal outside Keos. On the league *synedrion* in general see Cargill 1981: 15–128 and Accame 1941: 107–42.
34 Lines 74–6: 'Private lawsuits and [public indictments against Athenians I shall make] all appealable (to Athens) in accordance with [the treaty, all those that are over] one hundred drachmas' (Harding).
35 Alexander of Pherai had captured Tenos in 362 (Dem. 50.4).
36 Dreher 1985: 265–72.
37 Dreher 1985: 268.
38 Lewis 1962: 4.

39 Lewis 1962.

40 *IG* xii.5 594 = *SEG* xiv 531; Tod no. 141; *Syll*[3] no. 172; *SV* no. 287.

41 Tod: 125; Rhodes-Osborne: 200.

42 *IG* ii[2] 43 = Tod no. 123; Rhodes-Osborne no. 22.

43 On the front face, lines 79–83 list two groups of allies; the first comprises Chios, Mytilene, Methymnos, Rhodes, Byzantion, and Thebes, who were already allies of Athens when Aristoteles proposed the creation of the league. The second group comprises the Euboian cities of Chalkis, Eretria, Arethousa, and Karystos and the neighbouring island of Ikos, all of whom joined shortly thereafter (see Cargill 1981: 38). But see Accame (1941: 72–3), who suggests that Arethousa refers not to a Euboian but Thracian city, which Cawkwell (1981: 42) sees as evidence of voluntary accession to the league. Contrast Cargill 1981: 33. Poiessa is squeezed between Rhodes (on the left column) and Arethousa (on the right column). According to Diodoros (15.30.5), after Chabrias left Euboia, he sailed to the Cyclades where he won over Peparethos and Skiathos and others subject to Sparta. Both Peparethos and Skiathos are listed on the front face with a third group of names (lines 84–90). It is possible that this is the occasion when Poiessa was recruited. One difficulty with this suggestion is that all the cities listed on the left column (Perinthos, Peparethos, Skiathos, Maroneia, Dion) are located on islands north of Euboia, in the Chalkidike, along the Thracian coast, or in the Propontis and were obviously recruited together in a sweep north; but the right column, which no longer preserves names, likely included cities from the central Cyclades (Kos, Syros, Oine, Thermai, Ios, Seriphos, Naxos, or Oreos). See Cargill 1981: 37–8. Poiessa may have been recruited at the same time as these other cities in the central Cyclades. But see Cawkwell's objections (1981: 42–3), at least in terms of the left side, about seeing in the list of names 'the progress of Athenian generals through the waters of the Aegean and Ionian Sea.' Cargill (1981: 38–9) suggests that some of names written between the two columns on the front face, including that of Poiessa, may have been added after Aristoteles' amendment (lines 91–6), which he tentatively dates after the battle of Naxos in the fall of 376.

44 On the dating of the names on the left side to 375 see Cawkwell 1981: 41–7.

45 Lewis 1962: 2; *IG* ii[2] 1635 = Tod no. 125; Rhodes-Osborne no. 28.

46 Lewis: 1962: 3.

47 Tod: 124.

48 *SEG* xiv 530. 5–9: [ἐὰν δὲ ὁ Ἐρετρ]ιεὺς βόληται ἐγ Κέωι πολ[ιτεύεσθαι, ἀπογ]ραψάσθω πρὸς τὸς θεσμοφύλακ[ας τὸ αὐτô ὄ]νομα· οἱ δὲ θεσμοφύλακες δόντω[ν αὐτῶι φυλὴ]ν καὶ τριττὺν καὶ χῶρον. The reference to *thesmophylakes* in *SEG* xiv 530 assures us that the word is the right restoration in *IG* xii.5 594 (Tod no. 141) and not *nomophylakes* printed by Tod. *IG* xii.5 594.6 preserves τριπτύν, which must be a variation of τριττύν of *SEG* xiv 530.9.

49 Tod no. 141.18–21 (= *Syll.*[3] 171): 'Επι]μέλεσθαι δὲ ἐγ Κείωι [μὲν τήν τε βουλὴν καὶ τοὺς πρ]οβούλους καὶ τ[οὺς .....[12]..... καὶ τοὺς ἀσ]τύνμους τῶ[ν 'Ιστιαιέων .... The gap of twelve letters should be filled with θεσμοφύλακας. See Lewis 1962: 1.

50 Tod: 131; Buckler 1980: 173; Cargill 1981: 169; Hornblower 1982: 201; Rhodes-Osborne: 201.

51 See Buckler (1980: 160–1), who argues for Persian financing; but contrast Stylianou (1998: 494–6), who questions the involvement of Persian money or whether Boiotia could build so large a fleet.

52 Diodoros (15.79.1) says that Epameinondas made the cities ἰδίας, 'his own.' On the meaning of this, see Hornblower 1982: 200 n. 137 and Stylainou 1998: 496–7.

53 This is Worthington's date (1992: 151), but a date of 366/5 is possible based on Diod. 18.18.9, who states that in 323 Perdikkas restored the Samian exiles forty-three years after they had been exiled; hence a date of 366/5. See Hornblower 1982: 197 n. 120. Perhaps the kleruchs came in the fall of 365, allowing Timotheos to sail out in the spring of 364 to the Hellespontos.

54 Buckler 1980: 166–8; cf. Develin 1989: 261.

55 Worthington (1992: 149–50) follows Schaefer vol. 1 (1885: 100) in arguing that Timotheos went directly to the Hellespontos before turning his attention to Thrace, which is how it is presented in Isokrates' account of Timotheos' career (15.112). Demosthenes (23.150) indicates that he directed his attention first to Amphipolis before the Chersonesos, so followed by Sealey 1966: 152. Buckler places both his initial operations in the Chalkidike and the beginning of operations in the Hellespontos in 365. This seems unlikely, for as Worthington points out, the ten-month siege meant that Timotheos could not have left Samos before the campaigning season of 364, to which we may add the time needed to settle the colonists. Moreover, as Worthington convincingly argues, that would leave insufficient time for Timotheos to capture all of the cities, allegedly as many as twenty, which occurred during Timotheos' operations in the Chalkidike, before heading to the Hellespontos. These were likely captured after his excursion into the Hellespontos. Sealey (1966: 152) places the capture of Methone, Pydna, and Potidaia in 363/2.

56 Cargill 1981: 169; Hornblower 1982: 200 and 1983: 232; Stylianou 1998: 496–7; but see Buckler 1980: 169–75, who, however, does not believe that Byzantion defected and joined the Boiotian alliance at this time. Both Hornblower and Stylianou point to Dem. 50.6, which indicates that in 362 Byzantion was harassing Athenian grain ships.

57 Buckler 1980: 173.

58 Timomachos (Hansen 1975: no. 91), *stratēgos* in 361/0 (Develin 1989: 267–8), was impeached by Apollodoros (Dem. 36.53) for treason for betraying the Thracian Chersonesos to Kotys (Dem. 19.180; Σ Aisch. 1.56) and for embezzlement

by his treasurer Hegesandros (Aisch. 1.56: Trevett 1992: 134). Leosthenes (Hansen 1975: no. 88), *stratēgos* either in 362/1 or 361/0 (Develin 1989: 268), was impeached, it seems, by Aristophon (Aisch. 2.124) for treason for losing Peparethos to Alexander of Pherai, who had captured five ships and 600 prisoners (Diod. 15.95.1–3). Kallistratos (Hansen 1975: no. 87) was impeached in 361/0 for being bribed to make a proposal contrary to the interests of the people (Hyp. 3.1–2; Whitehead 2000: 172) and was condemned to death in absentia (Hyp. 3.2; Lyk. 1.93). Philon (Hansen 1975: no. 89) was presumably also impeached for treason in 362/1 (Hyp.3.2; cf. Whitehead 1995: 64–7). Theotimos (Hansen 1975: no. 94), *stratēgos* in 361/0 or 360/59 (Develin 1989: 268), was impeached for treason for losing Sestos (Hyp. 3.2).

59 See Whitehead 2000: 172–5; Hansen 1975: 94–8.

60 Whitehead 2000: 171–2.

61 Hansen (1974: 31), who on the basis of the scholiast accepts that the decree was overruled in court, suggests that Hypereides' indictment cannot be aimed at the extant decree relating to Ioulis (*IG* ii^2 111: Harding no. 55).

62 Engels 1993: 36 and n. 43.

63 *Eisangelia*: Hansen 1975 no. 97; *graphē paranomōn*: Hansen 1974 no. 10.

64 Whitehead 2000: 223–4.

65 By ὡς παρανόμων γραφὴν πεφευγώς, the scholiast may be thinking of Aisch. 3.198, and consequently Sauppe amends the text to ὡς παρανόμων γραφὰς οέ πεφευγώς (see Dilts 1992: 29). The scholia reads, 'Aristophon has been ridiculed (κεκωμῴδηται) for speaking for pay on behalf of Chares and for being a defendant (πεφευγώς) in a *graphē paranomōn* and for having served as general on Keos, where he did considerable harm against the inhabitants through greed, for which he was indicted for an illegal proposal and convicted,' as if he, or his source, were thinking of three separate incidents and not one single incident relating to the Keos affair. On the implausibility of Aristophon facing seventy-five *graphai paranomōn* over the course of his career, see Oost 1977 and Whitehead 1986.

66 Trevett 1992: 133, perhaps following the suggestion of Sealey 1966: 147.

67 According to Apollodoros (Dem. 50.4), the assembly that voted to mobilize the trierarchs and appoint Autokles commander met on 24th of Metageitnion, that is, early September of 362. That would mean that his trial occurred sometime after Metageitnion of 361/0. See Hansen 1975: 96.

68 Hansen 1975: 96; cf. Trevett 1992: 132–3; Schaefer vol. 1, 1885: 160 n. 2.

69 See Trevett 1992: 131–2.

70 Adrettos was the hill where jurors annually swore their dikastic oath.

71 Perlman 1958: 186.

72 Perlman 1958: 186.

73 Kallistratos had been active since 392/1, when we find him involved in a series of impeachment suits (Hansen 1975 nos. 69–72). See Hansen 1989: 50–1; Sealey

1966: 133–63. Timotheos was active since 378/7, when he served as *stratēgos* (Hansen 1989: 60), and Aristophon since 403/2, when he proposed a number of measures in the assembly (Hansen 1989: 37–8). On the question of whether there was a forty-year hiatus in Aristophon's career, see Oost 1977 and Whitehead 1986.

74 See Sealey (1966), who presents them as the leaders of three dominant factions in Athens during this period, to which most all other politicians were allied. Most scholars would now modify Sealey's views and see Athenian politics as a much more fluid business. I only use them here as representative figures. See Trevett's arguments (1992: 127–9, 135) against seeing Apollodoros' prosecution of Timotheos in late 370s (Dem. 49) as an attempt by the Kallistratos faction to regain their influence.

75 Iphikrates had been sent as general to Amphipolis in 368/7 (Aisch. 2.27; Dem. 23.149); see Hornblower 1982: 194–5. Cf. Sealey (1966: 147–8), who argues that Kallistratos was behind the policy of reviving claims to Amphipolis based on his friendship with Iphikrates.

76 Hansen 1975 no. 93. The date is possibly 360/59, the archonship of Kallimedes, but Καλλιμήδους is a conjecture for καλαμῖνος or καλμίωνος of Σ Aisch. 2.31. Like Hansen (1975: 97–8), I am inclined to place the trial of Timotheos at the same time as Apollodoros' other prosecutions of 361/0.

77 Kallistratos: Hansen 1975 no. 83; Chabrias: Hansen 1975 no. 84. Sources for the two trials: Arist. *Rhet.* 1.7.13; 3.10.7; Dem. 21.64 and Σ; Plut. *Dem.* 5.1–4. See Sealey 1966: 148–50; Hansen 1975: 92–3; Buckler 1980: 193–5; Cawkwell 1961: 84.

78 Hansen 1975 no. 87; Whitehead 2000: 172–3; Hansen 1975: 94–5.

79 Σ Aisch. 2.124 indicates that Kallistratos went into exile to Byzantion, which had defected from Athens two years earlier.

80 Apollodoros, who was serving as trierarch under Autokles' command, was back in Athens, having been ordered to convey ambassadors there (Dem. 50.12), possibly from Miltokythes. He returned to the Hellespontos with Autokles' replacement Menon, whom he would also impeach (Dem. 36.53; Hansen 1975 no. 95). After serving five extra months into the new year (361/0) as trierarch (Dem. 50.1), Apollodoros returned to Athens and began legal proceedings against Autokles, perhaps early in 360, well over a year after Aristophon's proposal. See Trevett 1992: 131–3; Hansen 1975: 95–6.

81 Hansen 1975: 96; Trevett 1992: 133; Rubinstein 2000: 242 n. 12.

82 Perhaps little less than a year earlier, if Aristophon's trial for the Keos affair occurred in the winter of 361 and Autokles' trial in the winter of 360.

83 Hansen 1975 no. 88. On the basis of the fact that Aristophon prosecuted Leosthenes' trierarchs (Dem. 51. 8–9; Hansen 1975 no. 142), Hansen (1975: 95) assumes that Aristophon also initiated the impeachment against Leosthenes.

84 Hansen 1975: 96 n. 11.

85 Hansen 1975 nos. 100–3.

86 357/6: *IG* ii^2 121; 355/4: *IG* ii^2 130; 354/3: Dem. 24.11. As Whitehead notes (1986: 314 n. 12), the enactment formula of *IG* ii^2 121 and 130 may indicate that Aristophon was serving on the *boulē* in those two years.

87 Two decrees against Philip in the years 346–340 (Dem. 18.70, 75) and *IG* ii^2 224 of 343/2. Hansen 1989: 38.

References

Accame, S. 1941. *La lege ateniese*. Rome.

Billheimer, A. 1938. 'Amendments to Athenian Decrees.' *AJA* 42: 456–85.

Buckler, J. 1980. *The Theban Hegemony*. Cambridge, MA.

Cargill, J. 1981. *The Second Athenian League*. Los Angeles/London.

Cawkwell, G.L. 1961. 'The Common Peace of 366/5 BC.' *CQ* 55: 80–6.

– 1981. 'Notes on the Failure of the Second Athenian Confederacy.' *JHS* 101: 40–55.

Develin, R. 1989. *Athenian Officials 684–321 BC*. Cambridge.

Dilts, M.R. 1992. *Scholia in Aeschinem.* Stuttgart/Leipzig.

Dreher, M. 1985. 'Zu IG II^2 404, dem athenischen Volksbeschluß über die Eigenstaatlichkeit der keischen Poleis.' *Symposium* 1985: 263–81.

Duant, C., and J. Thomopoulos. 1954. 'Inscriptions de Céos.' *BCH* 78: 316–22.

Engels, J. 1993. *Studien zur politischen Biographie des Hypereides: Athen in der Epoche der lykurgischen Reformen und des makedonischen Universalreiches.* Munich.

Fisher, N. 2001. *Aeschines: Against Timarchos.* Oxford.

Hansen, M.H. 1974. *The Sovereignty of the People's Court in Athens in the Fourth Century BC and the Public Action against Unconstitutional Proposals.* Odense.

– 1975. *Eisangelia: The Sovereignty of the People's Court in Athens in the Fourth Century BC and the Impeachment of Generals and Politicians.* Odense.

– 1983a. 'The Athenian "Politicians," 403–322 BC.' *GRBS* 24: 33–55 (reprinted in Hansen 1989: 1–24).

– 1983b. '*Rhetores* and *Strategoi* in Fourth-Century Athens.' *GRBS* 24: 151–80 (reprinted in Hansen 1989: 25–72).

– 1989. *The Athenian Ecclesia II: A Collection of Articles 1983–89.* Cophenhagen.

– 1991. *The Athenian Democracy in the Age of Demosthenes.* Oxford/Cambridge, MA.

Hornblower, S. 1982. *Mausolus.* Oxford.

– 1983. *The Greek World 479–323 BC.* London/New York.

Laqueur, R. 1927 (1979). *Epigraphische Untersuchungen zu den griechischen Volksbeschlüsssen.* Leipzig/Berlin, repr. Rome.

Lewis, D.M. 1962. 'The Federal Constitution of Keos.' *ABSA* 57: 1–4.
Oost, S. 1977. 'Two Notes on Aristophon Azenia,' *CP* 72: 238–42.
Perlman, S. 1958. 'A Note on the Political Implications of *Proxenia* in the Fourth Century BC.' *CQ* n.s. 8: 185–91.
– 1963. 'The Politicians in the Athenian Democracy of the Fourth Century BC.' *Athenaeus* n.s. 41: 327–55.
– 1967. 'Political Leadership in Athens in the Fourth Century BC.' *PP* 22: 161–76.
Roberts, J.T. 1982. 'Athens' So-Called Unofficial Politicians.' *Hermes* 110: 354–62.
Rubinstein, L. 2000. *Litigation and Cooperation*. Stuttgart.
Schaefer, A. 1885–7. *Demosthenes und seine Zeit*², 3 vols. Leipzig.
Schweigert, E. 1939. 'Greek Inscriptions: 4. A Decree Concerning Elaious 357/6 BC.' *Hesperia* 8: 12–17.
Sealey, R. 1956. 'Callistratos of Aphidna and His Contemporaries.' *Historia* 5: 178–203 (reprinted in Sealey 1966: 133–63).
– 1966. *Essays in Greek History*. New York.
Stylianou, P.J. 1998. *A Historical Commentary on Diodorus Siculus Book 15*. Oxford.
Thomas, R. 1989. *Oral Tradition and the Written Record in Classical Athens*. Cambridge.
Trevett, J. 1992. *Apollodoros, the Son of Pasion*. Oxford.
Whitehead, D. 1986. 'The Political Career of Aristophon.' *CP* 81: 313–19.
– 1995. 'The Impeachment of Philon (Hypereides, *Pro Euxenippo* 1).' *AHB* 9: 64–7.
– 2000. *Hypereides: The Forensic Speeches*. Oxford.
Worthington, I. 1992. *A Historical Commentary on Dinarchus: Rhetoric and Conspiracy in Later Fourth-Century Athens*. Ann Arbor.

Athenians in Sicily in the Fourth Century BC

DAVID WHITEHEAD

During the last quarter of the fifth century BC, Athenian military expeditions to Sicily twice ended in failure: first in (427–)424, and then in (415–) 413. The second of these episodes, which fills the sixth and seventh books of Thucydides and led to the calamity he describes there, had a shocking impact at the time (Thuc. 8.1–2) and for some years afterwards – eclipsed only, indeed, by the defeat and humiliation (in 404) of the great imperial city that had mounted the campaign. Large numbers of Athenians had died in and around Syracuse, but 'at least seven thousand' was Thucydides' estimate of those taken alive (Thuc. 7.87.4).[1] In 405/4, when thanking and rewarding a foreigner who had shown himself a friend, the Athenian *dēmos* recalled this earlier occasion when he had sought to ameliorate the condition of their suffering fellow citizens.

The euergetism (and its consequences) of this man, the (?)grain-shipper Epikerdes of Kyrene, is commemorated by a pleasing conjunction of literary and documentary evidence. Demosthenes 20.42 cites in court in 355 the honorific decree for Epikerdes, who 'gave a hundred *mnai* to the citizens at that time taken prisoner in Sicily, under such dire circumstances, and became the principal means of preventing them all from dying of hunger'; and *IG* i^3 125 (ii^2 174) is that very decree, enacted in recognition of Epikerdes' efforts 'for (their) preservation' (ἐς σω[τηρίαν, lines 11–12). Contrary to the orthodox understanding of this as an example of ransoming, Kendrick Pritchett has insisted that what Epikerdes did in 413 was exactly what Demosthenes says he did: provide money for food.[2] The case is well and convincingly made, in my opinion. Tucked away at the end of it, however, is an argument of a different kind – to the effect that there was a *third* expedition to Sicily,[3] half a century later, which this time (in the aftermath of another Athenian military failure) did involve some ransoming. My purpose here is to put this notion to the test.

Isaios 6.1

Pritchett's suggestion of an Athenian expedition to Sicily in the second quarter of the fourth century is not new; it was first made by the great (and still unsurpassed) commentator on Isaios, William Wyse.[4]

The passage that allows Isaios 6 (*On the Estate of Philoktemon*) to be dated to the year 364[5] is section 14: 'fifty-two years have passed since the expedition to Sicily, (reckoning) from its departure when Arimnestos was archon [early summer 416/415], yet the elder of these two alleged sons of Kallippe and Euktemon has not yet passed his twentieth year; if these years are deducted, more than thirty still remain since the events in Sicily.' No problem there. Rather, the problem has already arisen in the very opening chapter. This is how the unknown speaker, Isaios' client, explains to the jury why he has come forward in support of his friend Chairestratos, the claimant to Euktemon's estate:

ὅτι μέν, ὦ ἄνδρες, πάντων οἰκειότατα χρῶμαι Φανοστράτῳ τε καὶ Χαιρεστράτῳ τουτῳί, τοὺς πολλοὺς οἶμαι ὑμῶν εἰδέναι, τοῖς δὲ μὴ εἰδόσιν ἱκανὸν ἐρῶ τεκμήριον· ὅτε γὰρ εἰς Σικελίαν ἐξέπλει τριηραρχῶν Χαιρέστρατος, διὰ τὸ πρότερον αὐτὸς ἐκπεπλευκέναι προῄδειν πάντας τοὺς ἐσομένους κινδύνους, ὅμως δὲ δεομένων τούτων καὶ συνεξέπλευσα καὶ συνεδυστύχησα καὶ ἑάλωμεν εἰς τοὺς πολεμίους

That I am on very close terms, gentlemen, with both Phanostratos and Chairestratos here, I think most of you know, but for those who do not I will state a cogent proof: Chairestratos sailed off to Sicily in command of a trireme, and although, having gone on such a journey myself, I knew in advance all the dangers there would be, at the request of these men I sailed out with him and shared his misfortune when we encountered the enemy and were captured.

At first sight one might naturally suppose that this is the ill-starred expedition of 415–413, a supposition then strengthened, of course, by section 14 when it arrives. However, in section 60 Chairestratos is referred to as a youngish man (to be exact: τηλικοῦτος for one with his record of liturgies, etc.), and John Davies has calculated his date of birth as ca. 390.[6]

Possible textual solutions to this 'notorious crux' (Davies) had been passed in review by Wyse. Given that the manuscripts themselves offer no useful variants,[7] emendation provides the only escape route(s). They are of two types:

(i) The phrase εἰς Σικελίαν of section 1 can be either deleted, as an intrusive gloss

> generated by section 14 (Schoemann), or changed – either to produce another destination (Macedonia, Thessaly: Weissenborn) or another kind of phrase altogether (ἐν ἡλικίᾳ ὤν 'being of military age': Buermann).
> (ii) Alternatively, the toponym in section 1 is right but the personal name wrong: not Chairestratos but his father Phanostratos (Reiske, followed by Dobree, Scheibe, and Jebb).

To Wyse, type (i) solutions were all 'rude remedies.' Emendation to Φανόστρατος he evidently exempted from this stricture, but he noted that

> a difficulty still exists. The natural inference from the words δεομένων τούτων ['at the request of these men'] is that Chaerestratus was alive when his father, Phanostratus, was preparing for a voyage to Sicily. If the allusion is to the disaster of 415 B.C., Chaerestratus was now well over 50, and the contradiction with §60 [C's age in 364: see above] is not removed. On the other hand the language is very misleading, if the speaker meant by 'Phanostratus and his family,' Chaerestratus being excluded ... Thus all the corrections are unsatisfactory. My own conclusion is in favour of the text of the MS. Xenophon and Diodorus do not afford an exhaustive account of the foreign relations of Athens between 369 B.C. and 365/4 B.C., and with our imperfect knowledge it is presumptuous to pronounce that a mission to Sicily in this period involved no peril.[8]

(Before reaching this conclusion, Wyse briefly sets out the evidence for Athenian *diplomatic* involvement in Sicily from the 390s onwards, culminating in the treaty with Dionysios I of Syracuse in 368/7,[9] and observes that 'so far as the chronology of the speech is concerned, Chairestratus might perfectly well have been ordered to Sicily between 369 B.C. and 367 B.C.' And Wyse also raises the possibility that the 'enemy' who captured the young trierarch and his friend (ἑάλωμεν εἰς τοὺς πολεμίους) may have been Carthaginians, with whom Dionysios was at war in 368 [Diod. 15.73].)

The Teubner edition of Isaios by Thalheim, published the year before Wyse's edition, also retained Χαιρέστρατος (and εἰς Σικελίαν), summarily dismissing emendation to Φανόστρατος as erroneous;[10] and Forster's Loeb edition likewise adhered to the paradosis, supporting it with a Wyse-inspired footnote.[11] For some the question was not closed: the Budé editor Roussel joined the long line of those favouring Reiske's Φανόστρατος,[12] and a generation later Raubitschek expressly followed him.[13] But in our own time there has been no challenge, as far as I am aware, to the magisterial pronouncement by Davies:

> The notorious crux in Isaios vi. 1 does not admit of the solution adopted by

Raubitschek ... The logic of this crux is complex. If the words εἰς Σικελίαν are emended or deleted, there is no reason to emend the word Χαιρέστρατος. If they are retained, either they refer to the expedition of 415–413 or they do not. If they do so refer, then (*a*) either (i) Chairestratos was trierarch in 415–413, aged at least 18, or (ii) Χαιρέστρατος is the wrong reading. Since Chairestratos was born c. 390, (i) is excluded, and Reiske's emendation is called for: but then (*b*) either (i) Chairestratos was at least adolescent in 415, or (ii) Chairestratos was not one of δεομένων τούτων. Again (i) is excluded, but so is (ii), the logic of Isaios vi. 1–2 being conclusive against it (see Wyse ad loc.). *There is no means by which Isaios vi. 1 can be made to refer to 415–413* [...].[14]

As regards what it does, in that event, refer to, Davies said no more here (under PA 14093) but made his (Wysian) position clear under a later entry, PA 15164:[15]

A birth-year c. 390 suits [Chairestratos] well enough. The trierarchy of his mentioned in §60 [οὑτοσὶ δὲ Χαιρέστρατος τηλικοῦτος ὢν τετρηράρχηκε] should be identical with his trierarchy to Sicily (§1, where Χαιρέστρατος is not to be altered: see 14093), and should belong in (?)366/5 if Sundwall's restoration [Χαιρέστρ]ατος Κηφι(σιεύς) for the name of the syntrierarch on *Krete* in that year ([IG] ii² 1609, lines 81–2) is correct. If so, Chairestratos' colleague on the ship, Aristomenes, should be the speaker of Isaios vi.[16]

For all the loose ends to be tied up in this way would be gratifying indeed. That Chairestratos and the speaker of Isaios 6 were actually syntrierarchs, while less than fully explicit in section 1, is most certainly a reasonable understanding of the passage (συνεξέπλευσα καὶ συνεδυστύχησα) and one recently shared by Vincent Gabrielsen.[17] And section 60, likewise, reads as though Chairestratos has been trierarch only once (as opposed to his father's seven times).[18] Pivotal to everything, therefore, is Sundwall's restoration in *IG* ii² 1609.[19] Other than Chairestratos' own father, there are no other known trierarchs – indeed, it seems, no other known liturgists of any kind – from the (sizeable) deme Kephisia whose names end in -ατος. On the other hand there are, of course, numerous other -ατος names that would fit this irregularly *stoichedon* line: long ones like Agesistratos, Kallistratos, Mnesistratos, and Pheidestratos if one retains τριήρ] immediately before the name; shorter ones like Epistratos, Leostratos, Nikeratos, and Sostratos if one were to lengthen the abbreviation to τριήρ[αρχ.[20] The link thus falls short of proof positive. Without it, we fall back on Isaios 6.1 itself, which nonetheless does (if left unemended) appear to attest to Athenian military activity – of an official character – in Sicily in the first half of the 360s.

IG ii² 283

This partially preserved Athenian honorific decree thanks and rewards Ph[- -] of Salamis (namely, Cypriot)[21] for a series of acts which include the following (lines 8–10): [πολλοὺς τῶν πολιτῶν] λυτρωσάμενος ἐξ[22] Σικ[ελίας ἀπέστειλε Ἀθ]ήναζε τοῖς αὐτοῦ ἀναλ[ώμασιν ('having ransomed many of the citizens he sent them away from Sicily to Athens at his own expense').

Insofar as the episode in question has been contextualized at all, a date of 413 used to be regarded as self-evidently correct. 'On est tenté,' remarked Ducrey, 'de rattacher aux mêmes événements le décret rendu par les Athéniens en honneur de Ph... de Salamine.'[23] And Panagopoulos commented that 'there are still in the Attic orators of the Fourth century, and in inscriptions, echoes of ... beneficial activities towards citizens (sc. from 413)'; a footnote backs this up with the case of Epikerdes (discussed earlier) and with citations of *IG* ii^2 283 ('believed to have been issued for the same reason'), Andokides 3.30, and Isaios 6.1 and '13' (= 14).[24] However, we have now seen that Isaios 6.1 has nothing to do with 415–413; and Pritchett has pointed out that the same goes for the inscription, dated by Kirchner on the basis of its letter forms to the mid-fourth century (before 336/5). After mentioning the debate about the Isaios passage, Pritchett declares: '*IG* ii^2 283, which has not been brought into the discussion, and Isaios 6.1 complement each other ... There was a second Athenian expedition to Sikily that is not treated in modern histories. The Athenians apparently suffered a defeat.'[25]

Unfortunately, while the second and third of these assertions are (as we have seen) tenable, on other counts, the first is almost certainly not. True, by detaching *IG* ii^2 283 from the calamity of 415–413 Pritchett frees it up to become what it always should have been, a *fourth*-century datum; however, the general thrust of opinion actually puts it *too* late in the fourth century for Pritchett's purposes. If one sets aside McKechnie's location of it, without discussion, in the period 338–22,[26] Kirchner's *terminus ante quem* of 336/5 (see above) has held firm, and there has been an increasing tendency to favour an absolute date not far short of that. Anne Bielman categorizes the document as 'milieu ou seconde moitié du IVe siècle av. J.-C.,'[27] but others have opted definitely for the latter. Adolphe Kuenzi connected it with the immediate aftermath of Chaironeia, ca. 337.[28] Peter Garnsey settled, more cautiously, for the late 340s or early 330s.[29] And now two bona fide epigraphists have argued specifically for the latter. Michael Walbank opines that a date 'just before Chaironeia' would allow for the Sicilian context to be the activities of Timoleon and his mercenaries between 344 and 338, and the honorand's provision of a talent εἰς τὴν φυλακήν (lines 12–13) to be linked with the anticipated Macedonian invasion.[30] And in a full re-examination of the stone and all issues arising, Stephen Lambert finds that its lettering 'is tending markedly towards Tracy's more narrowly defined "Common Style, c. 345–320"'; and for a precise context within these limits he endorses Kuenzi's thesis of an immediately *post*-Chaironeia one, amidst anxieties about food supply and military security.[31]

Overview

There is no way, then, to bring Isaios 6.1 and *IG* ii² 283 together in the same chronological context. Had there been such a way, one could have proceeded to test the assumption – taken for granted by Pritchett – that the latter as well as the former reveals an otherwise unnoticed 'Athenian expedition' to Sicily in the fourth century. With a gap of thirty years between them, the issue obviously does not arise in that form. But must we, instead, postulate *two* such expeditions?

In a word: no. *IG* ii² 283 as it stands would require additional, external evidence before one was entitled to construe lines 8–10 (quoted above) as something Ph[--] had done in the aftermath of an actual, official Athenian military operation. We are merely told that he had spent his own money ransoming Athenians from Sicily.

Who then were the Athenians? Garnsey summarizes the possibilities – and the problems of adjudicating between them – admirably: 'it is unclear whether these Athenians were mercenaries (which might point to a date in the late 340s) or captives of pirates.'[32] The first of these alternatives has now been taken up by Walbank, whose case is persuasive enough but couched in wholly general, circumstantial terms.[33] On balance, therefore, the 'pirates' (*leistai*) option has marginally the more to recommend it. Piratical activity in the region at this time, especially after the death of Dionysios I of Syracuse in 367, is well documented,[34] and though McKechnie's description of the beneficiaries of Ph[--]'s action in *IG* ii² 283 as 'captives taken by *leistai*'[35] presents as fact what can only be supposition, the circumstantial probability of its being correct[36] is strong on two counts.[37] One is the parallel afforded by *IG* ii² 284 (*Syll*³ no. 263). In this decree, and at much the same time ('vers 350–340 av. J.-C.'),[38] the Athenians thank and reward Kleomis of Methymna who had 'freed those captured by the (*sc.* Aegean) *leistai*' (το]ὺς ἁλόντα[ς ὑπ]ὸ τῶν λῃιστῶν ἐλ[ύσατο]: lines 10–11). And the other is the fact, self-evident from the phraseology of the opening (extant) lines,[39] that Ph[--] was an importer and trader. As such, and as someone just as eager to please the Athenians as they are to thank him, he is more likely (I would argue) to have seen an opportunity to do so in the plight of innocent folk – including other *emporoi*? – undeservedly kidnapped than soldiers of fortune who had known the risks they were running.

Pritchett's fourth-century 'Athenian expedition' to Sicily can derive no cogent support, then, from the decree for Ph[--]. What does support it – as an event in the first half of the 360s – is the unemended text of Isaios 6.1, itself possibly supported by lines 81–2 of *IG* ii^2 1609. One must say 'possibly' not only because of the less-than-certain restoration of these lines themselves but also because of the larger problem of the stone's date. Two years before Pritchett made his suggestion, Davies had argued, in virtuoso fashion, in favour of 366/5 in *Athenian Propertied Families*; this remains to my mind the most persuasive option,[40] though other alternatives between 372/1 and 365/4 have continued to find advocates.[41]

If Davies is right, at any rate, the timing is suggestive. The great watershed in this era of Sicilian affairs, with wider repercussions, is of course 367: the death of Dionysios I of Syracuse, dominant figure of the region and, latterly,[42] friend and ally of Athens. His son and successor Dionysios II, though now an honorary Athenian citizen (Tod no. 133, now Rhodes-Osborne no. 33), did not let that fact inhibit him from reverting to the dynasty's longer-term pro-Spartan stance. In his sole appearance in the pages of Xenophon's *Hellenica*, Dionysios II's first act is to send a dozen triremes east, to the southern Peloponnese, to help the Spartans (re-)capture the perioikic town of Sellasia[43] (Xen. *Hell.* 7.4.12). It would be no great surprise if the Athenians' angry response, upon learning that Syracusan-sponsored forces were operating in northern Lakonia, had been to send a corresponding flotilla in the other direction – with the unhappy results that Chairestratos and (?)Aristomenes were to experience.[44]

Notes

1 For general discussion see Freeman 1891–4: 3.407–11, 716–19; Ducrey 1968: 80; Kelly 1970; Panagopoulos 1978 (1999): 132–44; Pritchett 1985: 201.

2 Pritchett 1991: 272 with n. 386. For the ransoming interpretation see Meritt 1970, and still in Bielman 1994: 1–7, no. 1 (where Pritchett is cited but his views are not discussed).

3 Pritchett (1991: 272 n. 386) says 'second'; in this he obviously discounts the expedition of 427–424 to treat that of 415–413 as the first. While the latter is in every respect the more important of the two, the former does deserve its place in the sequence; cf. Thuc. 6.1.1.

4 Wyse 1904: 488–9.

5 'If the year of Arimnestus be counted in, we get Ol. 103. 4, 365/4 B.C. for the date of the speech, with the modern way of reckoning Ol. 104. 1, 364/3 B.C.' (Wyse 1904: 500).

6 Davies 1971: 531.

7 Manuscript M and Aldine *editio princeps* (Venice 1513), based on manuscript L, have Μενέστρατος for Χαιρέστρατος, but there is no one of that name in the case. For the emendations of Schoenmann and others see, in summary, Wyse 1904: 82, *apparatus*.

8 Wyse 1904: 489.

9 Tod no. 136, *SV* no. 280, now Rhodes-Osborne no. 34; translation, Harding no. 52. The orthodox date is spring 367, but Harding points out that the prescript restorations that produce it were queried by Lewis 1954: 37–8; and for a more radical challenge – questioning even whether this is necessarily Dionysios I, rather than his son – see Buckler 1980: 234–42 (summarized in *SEG* 32.58). I adhere to orthodoxy in what follows here.

10 Thalheim 1903: 86.

11 Forster 1927: 202*c*: 'If the reading here is correct, Chaerestratus, who is still a young man at the date of this speech (§60) and therefore cannot have taken part in the famous Sicilian expedition of 415–413 B.C., must have sailed to Sicily on some occasion of which we have no historical record. The emendation Φανόστρατος, adopted by most editors, is precluded by the words δεομένων τούτων, which can only refer to Phanostratus and Chaerestratus; although Phanostratus might have taken part in the Sicilian expedition, Chaerestratus could not have been then alive and therefore would not have requested the speaker to accompany his father to Sicily.'

12 Roussel 1922: 107.

13 Raubitschek 1954: 69 n. 10.

14 Davies 1971: 531 (with my emphasis).

15 Thus because it had been the larger purpose of Raubitschek (1954) to equate the families, each with a Phanostratos, in Isaeus 6 and in Antiphon 6. Rejecting this, Davies was obliged to pass comment under both entries.

16 Davies 1971: 562–6 (with full documentation on the Kephisia connection), at 564. For more on Davies' '(?)366/5' dating of *IG* ii^2 1609, see below at nn. 40–1.

17 Gabrielsen 1994: 176: 'Isaeus 6.1 may represent a rare instance of two syntrierarchs in charge of their ship simultaneously ... Clearly, if a syntrierarchy was really in question, this form of cooperation was exceptional, arising from a special request to an experienced trierarch to help his inexperienced colleague during a long and difficult voyage (cf. also Dem. 24. 11–13).'

18 After the trial – at some time between 356 and 340 – he was the eponym of a naval symmory (*IG* ii^2 1618.99).

19 Sundwall 1910: 46 with 54 (discussion, citing Isaios 6. 1 and Wyse).

20 The full word τριήρ[αρχος seems excluded by the space available.

21 On the Salamis in question see Bielman 1994: 14 with n. 5; Lambert 2002: 75–6.

22 The *xi* is clear; the ἐς printed by Bielman 1994: 13, without comment, is therefore a slip (as Lambert 2002: 74 now tacitly confirms).

23 Ducrey 1968: 80 n. 5.

24 Panagopoulos 1978 (1999): 141 with n. 4.

25 Pritchett 1991: 274, with 272 n. 386 (end); for 'second' here see above, n. 3.

26 McKechnie 1989: 126.

27 Bielman 1994: 13. She elaborates at 14 ('Les traits caractéristiques qui s'en [palaeographic and formulaic criteria] dégagent incitent à placer ce document vers le milieu du IVe siècle av. J.-C.') and n. 1 there ('Parmi les caractéristiques paléographiques, relever la regularité et l'aspect géométrique de l'écriture (N, M, H notamment). Cependant, certains O ou Ω tendent déjà à s'amenuiser [l.5, TON̈'). But Stephen Lambert informs me that he finds these criteria unsubstantiable; for his own dating see below, at n. 31.

28 Kuenzi 1923 (1979): 41, 52.

29 Garnsey 1988: 150–4, at 151, 153.

30 Walbank 2002: 63.

31 Lambert 2002, esp. 78–9 (for 'Tracy,' see Tracy 1995: 76–81: '*Litterae Volgares Saec. IV*').

32 Garnsey 1988: 151 n. 6; cf. now Lambert 2002: 77. (Subsequently, though, both incline to the latter: see below, n. 36.)

33 Walbank 2002: 63.

34 Ormerod 1924 (1978): 159–60; Ientile 1983: 77–80; McKechnie 1989: 126–7; Bielman 1994: 15; de Souza 1999: 51–3.

35 McKechnie 1989: 126.

36 Besides McKechnie, see also Garnsey 1988: 153; Bielman 1994: 15; Ferone 1997: 144; Lambert 2002: 79.

37 McKechnie 1989: 122–6 (and cf. already, in brief, Ziebarth 1929: 18 would add a third: the information, later on in *IG* ii^2 283, that Ph[--] had also provided a generous donation "for security" (εἰς τὴν φυλακὴν [ἐπέδωκε τάλαντον] ἀργυρίου: lines 12–13). McKechnie argues for a link, if not always then often, between this phrase and *leistai*. For doubts in this particular instance, however, see Bielman 1994: 15 with n. 6; and, as Stephen Lambert points out to me, one would like to see a parallel for an anti-piracy *epidosis*. The project, rather, was surely concerned with domestic defence; cf. Lambert 2002: 78.

38 Bielman 1994: 15–18 (no. 5), at 15.

39 On which see now Lambert 2002: 76–7.

40 Davies 1969.

41 For a convenient summary of the possibilities and arguments see Gabrielsen 1989: 99 with n. 20, who insists himself that the question is still open.
42 See above, at n. 9.
43 Xen. *Hell.* 7.4.12; dated to spring 365 by Cartledge 1987: 389. (Cartledge's 'several boatloads of mercenaries,' it should be noted, does scant justice to a force which must have numbered well over two thousand men, even if not all the rowers transformed themselves into combat troops.)
44 I am greatly indebted to Dr Stephen Lambert, for alerting me to the recent work (culminating in his own) on *IG* ii[2] 283 and for other observations which materially improved an intermediate draft of this paper.

References

Bielman, A. 1994. *Retour à la liberté: libération et sauvetage des prisonniers en Grèce ancienne*. Athens and Paris.
Buckler, J. 1980. *The Theban Hegemony 371–362 BC*. Cambridge, MA.
Cartledge, P.A. 1987. *Agesilaos and the Crisis of Sparta*. London.
Davies, J.K. 1969. 'The Date of *IG* ii[2] 1609.' *Historia* 18: 309–33.
– 1971. *Athenian Propertied Families 600–300 BC*. Oxford.
de Souza, P. 1999. *Piracy in the Graeco-Roman World*. Cambridge.
Ducrey, P. 1968. *Le traitement des prisonniers de guerre dans la Grèce antique*. Paris.
Ferone, C. 1997. *Lesteia*. Naples.
Forster, E.S. 1927. *Isaeus with an English Translation by Edward Seymour Forster*. London/Cambridge, MA (Loeb Classical Library).
Freeman, E.A. 1891–4. *The History of Sicily from the Earliest Times*. Oxford.
Gabrielsen, V. 1989. '*IG* ii[2] 1609 and Eeisphora Payments in Kind?' *ZPE* 79: 93–9.
– 1994. *Financing the Athenian Fleet*. Baltimore and London.
Garnsey, P. 1988. *Famine and Food Supply in the Graeco-Roman World*. Cambridge.
Harding, P. 1985. *From the End of the Peloponnesian War to the Battle of Ipsus*. Cambridge.
Ientile, M. Guiffrida. 1983. *La pirateria tirrenica*. Rome.
Kelly, D.H. 1970. 'What Happened to the Athenians Captured in Sicily?' *CR* 84: 127–31.
Kuenzi, A. 1923 (1979). *Epidosis*. Bern, repr. New York.
Lambert, S.D. 2002. 'Fish, Low Fares and *IG* ii[2] 283.' *ZPE* 140: 73–9.
Lewis, D.M. 1954. 'Notes on Attic Inscriptions.' *ABSA* 49: 17–50.
McKechnie, P.R. 1989. *Outsiders in the Greek Cities in the Fourth Century BC*. London/New York.
Meritt, B.D. 1970. 'Ransoming of the Athenians by Epikerdes.' *Hesperia* 39: 111–14.

Ormerod, H.A. 1924 (1978). *Piracy in the Ancient World.* Liverpool.

Panagopoulos, A. 1978 (1999). *Captives and Hostages in the Peloponnesian War.* Athens.

Pritchett, W.K. 1985. *The Greek State at War,* vol. 4. Berkeley and Los Angeles.

– 1991. *The Greek State at War,* vol. 5. Berkeley and Los Angeles.

Raubitschek, A.E. 1954. 'Philinos.' *Hesperia* 23: 68–71.

Roussel, P. 1922. *Isée, Discours: texte établi et traduit par Pierre Roussel.* Paris (Budé).

Sundwall, J. 1910. 'Eine neue Seeurkunde.' *AM* 35: 37–60.

Thalheim, Th. 1903 (1963). *Isaei orationes cum deperditarum fragmentis edidit Th. Thalheim.* Stuttgart (Teubner).

Tracy, S.V. 1995. *Athenian Democracy in Transition: Attic Letter-Cutters of 340 to 290 BC.* Berkeley.

Walbank, M.B. 2002. 'Notes on Attic Decrees.' *ZPE* 139: 61–5.

Wyse, W. 1904 (1967). *The Speeches of Isaeus.* Cambridge, repr. Hildesheim.

Ziebarth, E. 1929. *Beiträge zur Geschichte des Seeraubs und Seehandels im alten Griechenland.* Hamburg.

IG ii^2 1622 and the Collection of Naval Debts in the 340s

KATHRYN SIMONSEN

IG ii^2 1622 (EM 10386) is one of a series of inscriptions (*IG* ii^2 1604–32) that preserve the accounts of the fourth-century Athenian navy. The inventories span a fifty-five-year period, from approximately 378 to 323 BC. *IG* ii^2 1622 comes from the middle of the series, dated on internal evidence from archon dates (especially lines 379–85), to about 342/41. Tracy assigns 1622 to the cutter of *IG* ii^2 334, whom he dates to the period 345–320.[1] 1622 preserves an unusual entry category, a report on the collection of debts from naval officials between the years 345 and 342. This period of Athenian history, just after the Peace of Philokrates, is well served by contemporary sources, notably Aischines and Demosthenes, but no reference to this collection is to be found (although references to the misbehaviour of naval officials are).[2] Nevertheless, this paper will argue that the report recorded on 1622 is an important clue. If this report is added to other events, it provides insight into how the Athenians tried to deal with their loss of military prestige and their disenchantment with the Peace of Philokrates in the years just after the treaty was signed.

IG ii^2 1622 was found in the Peiraieus, but currently resides and is on display in the Epigraphical Museum in Athens. The stele is complete at the bottom and on the right-hand side. The top portion and the left-hand side are incomplete. It is 1.37 m high, 0.52 m wide, and 0.12 m thick. It was reconstructed from four adjoining fragments.[3] On the inscribed side of the stele, the surface of the marble has weathered to an orange-tan colour, so it is easy to identify recent damage (of which there is some). The reverse, however, was carved out for use as a gutter in Antiquity, and its surface is now a whitish-grey.[4] It seems probable that this inscription was one of those found by Ludwig Ross in the Peiraieus in 1834. Ross found a number of naval archive stelai reused as gutters while excavating the remains of a Late Antique portico near the Kantharos harbour.[5]

Five columns (**a–e**) remain on the main surface, with a short sixth column (**f**) on the right-hand side. Only the letters farthest to the right of column **a** survive, although it is almost certain that it dealt with the same subject as columns **b** and **c**. Columns **a–e** vary slightly in length. Columns **c** and **e** are about four lines longer than **a** and **b**. Column **d** is ten to fifteen lines shorter than the others, presumably because the subject recorded in column **d** was complete (the final entries deal with naval officials from tribe X), and a new group of entries was begun at the top of column **e**.

It is difficult to estimate how much is missing from the top of the inscription. Based on the contents of columns **c** and **d**, which deal with the debts of naval officials by tribe, a rough estimate may be made. A new section begins at line 379 in column **c**. The officials of tribes I and II appear in column **c**, those of tribes V–X in column **d**. The accounts of tribe II may be incomplete; those of tribe V are, as the tribe name (if nothing else) is missing at the top of the entry. The complete entries are of different lengths, from as short as thirteen lines (Hippothontis, col. **d**, lines 531–543; Aiantis, col. **d**, lines 544–56) to at least forty-six (Akamantis, col. **d**, lines 432–77). The others range between eighteen and thirty lines. If the entry for tribe II is complete, and if the missing entries were approximately twenty-five lines long (including blank spaces between entries), there would have been at least fifty more lines at the top of column **d**. As the height of the letters in the inscription is 4 mm, a minimum of 0.2 to 0.25 m of the inscription has been lost at the top.[6]

It is also possible to estimate the number of columns missing on the left-hand side of the inscription. The first two and one-half existing columns appear to deal with the payment of naval debts by trierarchs from tribes VIII–X. The entry for tribe VIII begins at line 76 in column **a** ([Ἱπποθωντίδ]ος is restored, but no other tribal name would be long enough for the space). The heading that started the entry for tribe IX is lost; tribe X's entry begins at line 248 in column **b** and ends at line 378 in column **c**. Thus, the accounts of the last three tribes required the equivalent of two full columns. Provided that as many trierarchs of the other tribes were as much in debt as those from these three tribes, four columns would have covered the payments for tribes I–VI with another partial column for tribe VII. With an allowance for headings and other material, at least five columns have been lost.

Where were these columns? Was the inscription another 0.5–0.6 m wider or was it originally opisthographic?[7] D.R. Laing, while studying the naval inscriptions in the late 1960s, was able to find traces of headings on the reverse sides of *IG* ii^2 1628 and 1631.[8] Some of the inventories were, therefore, opisthographic, although even 1628, the earliest of this pair, is fifteen years later than 1622. The gutter carved on the reverse of 1622 is well centred, which might suggest that it marks the middle of the inscription, or perhaps, the middle of one half. The gutters carved into 1631 were also well centred, and 1631 was intentionally and neatly broken in half before it was reused.[9] In light of the current evidence, it is not possible to be certain, although it is worth noting that while parts of both halves of 1631 survive, nothing can be attributed to a lost left side of 1622. It is tempting, therefore, to suggest that 1622 was inscribed on both sides, with five columns on each face. As there are no traces of summaries of any sort, such as appear, for example, at the start of *IG* ii^2 1611.3ff., the surviving inscription on 1622 may represent the back side of the original inscription.

As mentioned above, the inscription has suffered some damage relatively recently. The top fifteen lines of column **c** and twenty-four lines of column **d** were lost between the earliest publication of the inscription and Kirchner's second edition of *Inscriptiones Graecae* ii. A few more chips have been knocked from the surface of the inscription since Kirchner. Certain letters that were clear to Kirchner are now either partially or completely missing. Column **c** seems to have suffered the most, especially between lines 335 and 353, 365 and 368, and 380 and 388. The damage to this last section is most unfortunate, as these lines introduced and provided dates for a new section of the inscription dealing with the debts of former naval officials. The surviving letters conform to the readings in *IG*, but confirmation is no longer possible.

The surviving portions of *IG* ii^2 1622 deal with the payments of debts. Columns **a** to **c** report on debts repaid by trierarchs and are organized by tribe. Columns **c** and **d**, the focus of this paper, list payments made by certain types of naval officials. The last two columns again list the debts of or payments from trierarchs, but this time these are listed under the ship the trierarch had commanded and not by tribe. Because the initial entry headings, which would have explained the two different sets of trierarch entries, are lost, there is no immediate explanation for the change in accounting style. The tribal entries list one or two men only per ship (see lines 128ff.). The ship entries, on the other hand, usually name several men (five men, lines 657–62; six men, lines 599–606, 645–51). The surviving tribal entries seem to be payments in full, whereas some of those listed as debtors in the ship list have not repaid anything (e.g. 604–6). It may be that the first set of entries was made earlier in time and represents debts incurred before the introduction of the symmory system, which increased the number of men responsible for each ship.[10] The ship entries, with their larger number of debts, would then represent the effects of the post-357 symmory system.

The series of naval inventories attest to the problem of indebtedness. Large sections of the surviving inscriptions deal with the outstanding or repaid debts of trierarchs. It was common for trierarchs to sign out equipment when they fitted their ships out. They were supposed to surrender the equipment when they returned. While some equipment was lost at sea or broken, some seems to have been kept by trierarchs, perhaps with the idea of using it for their next tour of duty or for some other, less honourable reason. At times this habit caused a shortage of equipment and forced other trierarchs to resort to litigation or other more desperate measures.[11] The inventories down to *IG* ii² 1622 usually describe these debts in terms of equipment. A certain trierarch owed ropes or ladders or oar-port covers, and so on. The emphasis seems to have been on the return of the material itself (or a replacement). This is only sensible as the navy needed the equipment itself, and a monetary equivalent would not have been useful if shortages meant that there was nothing to be bought in the marketplace. After 1622, however, monetary values for debts and payments, while not nonexistent earlier, become more and more common.

The most interesting aspect of these naval debts, beyond the surprise that anyone would go into debt rather than surrender an anchor or some other piece of equipment, is the length of time that the debts were allowed to accrue. Some trierarchs owed several debts from several different ships, which must represent many years, if not decades, of service. Some debts were quite small, such as an anchor or a ladder, and may represent the surviving evidence of arguments between trierarchs and naval officials about culpability in the loss of the equipment. Other trierarchs, however, had substantial debts, which could represent several hundred drachmae or more. In theory, these defaulting trierarchs were public debtors, whom the Athenians traditionally treated harshly.[12] In practice, however, trierarchs do not seem to have suffered penalites very often, and even when their debts became outrageous, some effort seems to have been made to help them pay off their debts.[13] The possession of naval debts did not prevent a man from acting as a trierarch on a new ship (indeed, if it had, there would have been even more problems). One explanation for this unusual privilege is that at most times the need for trierarchs outweighed concerns about their debts.

It is less clear to what extent and for what reasons naval officials became indebted to the state, although the evidence suggests that they were frequently in debt and that these debts were often the result of the misappropriation of equipment.[14] In inscriptions earlier than *IG* ii² 1622, these debts do not normally appear, although this may be an accident of preservation. There are fragmentary references in *IG* ii² 1617, which may date to 356,[15] to debts owed by naval officials for wooden equipment. The debts were already a decade old when they were recorded (369/8, line 71; 368/7, line 92; 367/6, line 110). No titles are provided in the individual entries to indicate what positions these men held, so it is possible that the list was begun with a heading indicating the men's office. That they were νεωρίων ἐπιμεληταί is made clear by reference to *IG* ii² 1622. At least two of the men did not pay their debts (or finish paying their debts) until the 340s and are listed as ἐπιμεληταί there (Lysiphilos of Rhamnous, 1617.98 and 1622.553; Euthedemos Athmoneus, 1617.116 and 1622.498). One further reference to an official, a ταμίας τριηροποικῶν, comes at 1617.121–2. In addition, the heading at *IG* ii² 1611.17 includes a reference to debts owed by officials (ταῖς ἀρχαῖς), but it is not clear (because of the date of the inscription) what sort of officials these are – all naval officials or just symmory leaders.

The list of debts repaid by naval officials at *IG* ii² 1622.379–579 is at present unique. The men listed in these entries had been either ταμίαι or νεωρίων ἐπιμεληταί. Some of these debts were extremely old, going back into the early 370s, and some had to be paid by the official's heirs.[16] The reasons for their debts are not always provided, especially for the older cases. In other instances, however, an explanation is given; these explanations, though brief, support the idea mentioned above that one of the main causes for the indebtedness of officials was the misappropriation of equipment. For instance, one official had taken a large number of oars, of which 1,800 were found to be unusable when he returned them (lines 392–7); another had taken equipment from the trierarchs but had not returned the equipment to the storehouse (lines 444–77).[17]

The collection of these debts took four years (lines 379–85). Although there is no indication in the entry that this was a special effort, the fact that there is no evidence for anything similar during this period suggests that this collection was unusual. The surviving entries span the entire period between 378 and 346, again perhaps indicating that nothing had been done about these debts since the early 370s.[18] The question then arises, why at this point? What was happening in the mid-340s that someone would have thought that it was worthwhile to start this process?

The ten to twelve years prior to the initiation of the collection process recorded on *IG* ii² 1622 had not been the most glorious period in Athenian history. In 357 various members of Athens' confederacy revolted against her authority. This war lasted until 355 and led to the disintegration of the alliance. Also in 355 the Third Sacred War broke out between the Delphic Amphiktyony and Phokis. Although this war did not involve Athens directly, she was vaguely allied with the Phokians. Athens suffered some embarrassment when, as a result of crises of leadership at Phokis in 347/6, she and Sparta were first offered and then refused control of Thermopylai. Athens had also suffered humiliation the year before on Euboia. Athens had enjoyed an important victory there in 357, when she drove the Thebans out of Euboia and regained control of that important island. Unfortunately,

Athens decided to support the unpopular tyrant of Eretria, Plutarch, in 348 when he faced an uprising. The revolt seems to have been broadly based, and Athens' defence of Plutarch turned the Euboians against her. Although the Athenian expedition was initially successful in gaining a base on the island, it was defeated within a few months and the Athenians were compelled to recognize the independence of the Euboian *poleis*.

While these events were taking place, some Athenian politicians began to worry about the ever-increasing power of Philip of Macedon. Both the Athenians and Philip were interested in controlling the coastal regions of Thrace. Athenian involvement in this region was ancient. According to tradition she had sent colonies out to Sigeion and Elaious in the late seventh century.[19] One of Athens' great disappointments during the fourth century was her inability to regain control of her fifth-century colony at Amphipolis.[20] Philip, starting in the early 350s, took control of large regions of Thrace and provided his kingdom with access to the northern Aegean. Many of the cities he captured had ties to Athens. The most grievous losses for the Athenians were probably Amphipolis in 357 (since Philip's possession of this city prevented their recovery of it) and Olynthos in 348. Although the Athenians had put some effort into the defence of Olynthos, sending three separate expeditions, Philip's actions against the city coincided with the revolt of Euboia, and the divided Athenian forces lost on both fronts.

The events leading up to the end of the Sacred War gave Philip great influence in Greece and led the Athenians to seek peace with him. Negotiations began early in 346 and by the summer of that year, after two embassies from Athens to Philip led by Philokrates, the treaty was signed. Although some Athenians, notably Demosthenes, soon came to repudiate the Peace of Philokrates, it did provide a brief window of peace.

In addition to these broader historical issues, the structure of the Athenian navy itself requires some attention. Between 358 and 356 the organization of the navy was altered in an attempt to make trierarchic service less of a burden. Men subject to that liturgy were divided into symmories, following the pattern employed for the collection of the *eisphora*. This development coincided in 357 with the outbreak of the Social War and the successful expulsion of the Thebans from Euboia. The naval requirements for these two battlefronts led to a massive crisis in naval equipment in 357.[21] The Athenian navy had had equipment problems on a regular basis. It is clear from the inventories that the navy normally had many more hulls than sets of equipment. By and large, oars and steering oars, the most basic items for outfitting a warship, were in the greatest supply but were still not enough to provide for more than 70 to 80 per cent of the hulls.[22] Other items, such as the various types of hanging gear (which was more prone to decay), were in much shorter supply and must have affected the readiness of the fleet profoundly. These problems were due to several factors, including the acquisitiveness of trierarchs and officials and the lack of a common storage area, which meant that items could be lost (or caused to be lost) fairly easily.

Certain measures were taken to correct these problems. At least once, in 357/6, a motion was passed compelling everyone who possessed naval equipment to sell it to the authorities ([Dem.] 47.20, 44). There are many entries in the early inventories that refer to equipment that has been donated or surrendered in some manner (e.g. *IG* ii^2 1609.77–81; 83–7). The law of Periander, which established the naval symmories, may have made it compulsory for incoming trierarchs and ἐπιμεληταί of the dockyards to collect equipment owed by earlier trierarchs ([Dem.] 47.21–3). The lists of debts, which are a common feature of these inscriptions, would have served as a public reminder of the equipment owed by trierarchs and, in some instances, by officials. In 347/6 funding for the construction of a naval arsenal was approved.[23] Although the building was not completed until approximately 330/29, the existence of a central warehouse will have eased some of the confusion that must have surrounded the location of equipment. In addition, 100 sets of hanging gear were stored on the Acropolis, presumably in case of emergency, by 330/29.[24]

In 346/5 a *diapsephismos*, or general revision of the citizenship lists, was proposed by Demophilos (Aisch. 1.86). According to Athenian tradition this was the third such review in polis history.[25] Although the contents of Demophilos' decree are not entirely certain,[26] it seems likely that the results were an extraordinary scrutiny of citizenship.[27] Each deme seems to have been required to go through its lists (the *lexiarchikon grammateion* kept by the demarch and referred to by Demosthenes [57.60] and possibly the *pinax ekklesiastikos* [Dem. 44.35]). Each member of the deme appears to have had his status voted on by his fellow demesmen (Dem. 57), who would have been in the best position to know each other's status. Although it seems unlikely that there is any direct connection between the scrutiny of the citizenship lists and a concerted effort to collect outstanding naval debts, the two together may in fact shed some light on the concerns of Athenians in the mid-340s.

The *diapsephismos* was a major effort to prevent non-Athenians from posing as citizens and deriving profit from that status. This attitude might be argued to be the response of people who had suffered recently and perceived themselves to be under threat: too many foreigners had been sneaking in and stealing benefits, while real Athenians had lost out; this had caused a 'watering down' of the native martial spirit, leading to the recent defeats and embarrassments. If it is impossible to attack external enemies because of one's own military weakness or a peace treaty, some other target must be discovered. Solidarity and scapegoats can be found by attacking the enemy within – the pseudo-citizen.

The attempt to clear up debts owed by the naval officials makes sense in this context. Some of the debts repaid in *IG* ii^2 1622 were enormous and were certainly the result of criminal, or almost criminal, behaviour on the part of officials. In aggregate the debts represent a substantial amount of equipment and money; enough, perhaps, to have made the difference between success and failure in the recent emergencies. While the beginning of the construction of the arsenal, which was intended to house most of the equipment together, may have been one incentive for the collection of debts, the need to appear to be 'cleaning up the system' may also be adduced. Insufficient equipment and the theft of funds hindered the navy. It is almost possible to imagine someone standing in the assembly pointing out the evils caused by these dishonest officials: Would Olynthos and Euboia have been lost if these evil men had been forced to return what they had stolen? Everyone knows who owes how much! Why has no one bothered to do anything about this disgraceful mess for thirty years?

Although *IG* ii^2 1622 lists debts owed by trierarchs, it is not entirely clear if a similar effort was being made to tidy up old trierarchic debts as well. I have observed above that one explanation for the two different types of accounts of trierarchic debts is that the first list, which is organized by tribe and parallels the organization found in the officials' list, refers to debts incurred prior to 357 and represents the manner by which the older records were arranged. The use of repayment in cash, as opposed to kind, may be as much an indication of the age of the debts as a change in overall practice (and may have been the origin of the change): thirty-year-old sails, ropes, and ladders were no longer useful. Without the section headings, which would have explained the contents of the accounts, no firm conclusion is possible about the nature and scope of the debt repayments contained in columns **a**–**c**. Trierarchs, though not untouchable, probably had better excuses for possessing naval equipment and were, perhaps, less likely to incur general displeasure. Trierarchs did their duty in defence of the state and were the first ones who suffered, along with their crews, if equipment was missing or not enough ships could be outfitted for an expedition.

Officials, on the other hand, were much easier targets. Although officials were presumably respectable individuals, they were not necessarily of the liturgical class. They were certainly unlikely to suffer direct physical harm because of their misuse of equipment or funds. The ταμίας of 347/6 (*IG* ii^2 1622.420–31) would have found it difficult to explain why he needed eighteen sets of hanging gear. Some may have seen their time in office as an opportunity for creative speculation. The same line of reasoning, which blamed recent misfortunes on 'infiltrators,' may have seen a connection between the mismanagement of the navy and its poor performance. Naval officials, being fewer in number and less important to the running of the navy (more easily replaced) than trierarchs, may have found themselves the object of their fellow citizens' anger.

The debt collection of 345–342 is not referred to in our surviving sources. Without *IG* ii^2 1622, nothing would be known about it at all. The laconic nature of the entry's heading does not indicate who proposed the process or why, and the incomplete nature of the inscription does not permit us to learn how extensive the debts were or whether the collection process included trierarchs as well. Nevertheless, this unique record may provide us with insight into important political and social issues in Athens just after the Peace of Philokrates.

Notes

1 Tracy 1995: 82–7.
2 See for example Dem. 22.17.
3 When I went to see the inscription in the summer of 2002, I could trace the joins between three fragments. As the topmost portion of the inscription has been lost since it was first published, it may be that this missing portion represents the fourth fragment.
4 It says something about the continuity of tradition in Greece that identical gutters, cut into marble slabs, may be seen just around the corner from the Epigraphical Museum, lining the sides of the steps that lead up to the National Museum.
5 Laing 1968: 244 and n. 1.
6 The missing portion is now somewhat larger as the topmost parts of columns **c** and **d** have been lost; see below.
7 I was unable to observe any traces of letters on the reverse, but it was not possible to make a prolonged, close investigation.
8 Laing 1968: 245.
9 Laing 1968: 249.
10 Dem. 18.102–8; also Gabrielsen 1994: 182–99.
11 Especially in 357, see below. [Dem] 47 and 50; Gabrielsen 1994: 146–9.
12 Gilbert 1895: 355; Hansen 1991: 262.
13 See for example the case of Pausanias at *IG* ii^2 1623.144–59. Some trierarchs were allowed to make donations to the grain fund as partial payments on their debts (e.g. *IG* ii^{2}1628. 353–68). See also Gabrielsen 1994: 162–9.

14 Dem. 22.17; *1G* ii² 1622.387ff.; Gabrielsen 1994: 149–57.

15 Gabrielsen 1994: 149.

16 E.g., Lykon of Kephisia was ἐπιμελητής in the archonship of Nausinikos (378/7); Mantias of Thorikos was ταμίας in the archonship of Kalleas (377/6).

17 Further evidence for the misappropriation of fund or equipment is provided by Demosthenes (22.17), who refers to a ταμίας τριηροποιῶν who ran off two and one-half talents.

18 It should be noted that none of the surviving inventories can be shown to predate 378 (*IG* ii² 1604 is the earliest, dating to ca. 377). It may be that in the preparations and negotiations leading up to the establishment of the Second Athenian League, old debts were collected or forgiven. Likewise, it may be that the changes in the running of the navy in 357 (manifested in the inscriptions by a change in their format; compare 1604–10 with 1611 and 1612) and the crisis over the lack of naval equipment led to an attempt to record the debts of officials (such as that in 1617); see Gabrielsen 1994: 157–8.

19 Osborne 1996: 123.

20 Harris 1995: 42–3.

21 [Dem.] 47.20.

22 See Gabrielsen 1994: 146–9. However, it should be observed that the navy probably had many more hulls than it could reasonably expect to man. As hulls were presumably the most difficult and most time-consuming to build, it made sense to build new hulls even if they were not needed immediately. It was not necessary to have equipment for all of them, as not all ships would see action at any one time and the equipment from two or three damaged ships could be cannibalized to outfit a new ship.

23 *IG* ii² 505 and 1668.

24 Gabrielsen 1994: 149.

25 The earlier reviews were in 510 (*Ath. Pol.* 13.5) and 445/4 (Philoch. F 119; Plut. *Per*. 37.2.4). See also Hansen 1991: 53, 95.

26 See, for instance, the dispute between Diller 1932 and Gomme 1934; also Hansen 1982: 183.

27 Hansen (1991: 95) suggests that it was in response to the return of *klerouchoi* from Thrace, and the fear that some of these might not have been true Athenians.

References

Diller, A. 1932. 'The Decree of Demophilos, 346–345 BC.' *TAPA* 63: 193–205.

Gabrielsen, V. 1994. *Financing the Athenian Fleet*. Baltimore.

Gilbert, G. 1895. *Greek Constitutional Antiquities.* New York.

Gomme, A.W. 1934. 'Two Problems of Athenian Citizenship Law.' *CP* 29: 123–40.
Hansen, M.H. 1982. 'Demographic Reflections on the Number of Athenian Citizens 451–309.' *AJAH* 7: 172–89.
– 1991. *The Athenian Democracy in the Age of Demosthenes.* Oxford.
Harris, E.M. 1995. *Aeschines and Athenian Politics.* Oxford.
Laing, Jr., D.R. 1968. 'A Reconstruction of I.G. II^2, 1628.' *Hesperia* 37: 244–54.
Osborne, R. 1996. *Greece in the Making, 1200–479 BC*. London.
Tracy, S.V. 1995. *Athenian Democracy in Transition: Attic Letter-Cutters of 340–290 BC*. Berkeley.
Tritle, L.A. 1988. *Phocion the Good.* London.

The Slave-Names of *IG* i^3 1032 and the Ideology of Slavery at Athens*

BRUCE ROBERTSON

In Classical Athens, personal names mattered. Like most ancient Greeks, Athenians believed that the lexical connotations of a name expressed its bearer's personality or role. For example, Odysseios' name is associated with the verb *odussthai*, 'to will pain to,' six times in the *Odyssey* (1.62; 5.340, 423; 16.145–7; 19.275; 19.406–9); Hesiod feels compelled to explain away the munificent connotation of Pandora's name in the *Works and Days* (80–2); and Herodotos records that King Leotychides of Sparta takes the Samian Hegesistratos' name as quite suited to one about to lead an army (> *hêgeomai*, 'lead,' and *stratos*, 'army'; 9.91). The tragedies of Classical Athens approach names similarly. The punning on Pentheus' name (> *penthos*, 'grief'; Eur. *Bacch.* 367–8) or Helen's (*hel-* > *haireô*, 'to take or kill'; Aes. *Ag.* 681–2), to take only two examples, verge on the bathetic to a modern Western audience; to the Athenians, they were apparently profound moments.[1] Attuned to the same sort of lexical analysis, Aristophanes creates comic names whose elements express a personality appropriate to the character and his situation, such as the Kleon-lover and -hater, Philo-kleon and Bdely-kleon (*Vesp.* 133–4). Elsewhere he makes comic an unexceptional name, such as Pheidippides in *Clouds*. Strepsiades' controversy with his wife about their social position translates into a debate about the constituent elements of their son's name. She wishes her son to have a name that reflects her aristocratic heritage; thus she insists upon the suffix *hippos*. Strepsiades, however, insists on the root *pheid-* to honour his father, he claims, although the audience might suspect that he hopes for a son more frugal than his wife.

This lexical approach to names was not a mere literary habit. The late-fifth-century Athenian epitaph of Myrrine expends one-third of its text on the 'truthfulness' of her name, meaning 'myrtle' or sometimes 'wreath of myrtle' (*IG* i^3 1330). Given the sacred uses of that plant, it seemed to the author that the girl's position as first priestess of Athena *Nike* was fated from birth. Names as a token of identity could even become a hot topic in the Athenian courts, as Demosthenes' *Against Boiotos* records. Finally, in *Kratylos,* agreement on the ideal appropriateness of personal names launches a discussion of nouns in general. Socrates and his interlocutor Hermogenes agree that names should reflect character. An impious son, for instance, should bear a name reflecting his vice, not such names as Theophilos (> *theos,* 'god;' *philos,* 'friend') or Mnesitheos (> *mnêsi-* 'mindful'; *theos,* 'god': 394e).

Socrates cannot provide examples of a suitable pejorative name because the lexical elements of citizens' names nearly always carried positive connotations. When a father named his child in the first two weeks after birth,[2] he had a small opportunity to select lexical elements that would define him or her. To be sure, custom constrained the father: first-born males were often named after the paternal grandfather (Pl. *Lach.* 179a; Dem. 43.74) and other relatives were similarly honoured (e.g. Is. 3.30; Pl. *Prm.* 126c; *APF* 8792 VIII). Yet the father could also make his homage through selected name elements, such as the *dēmos* echoing down the family of Demosthenes and the *glaukos* which recurs in Aischines' mother's line,[3] combining these with elements from outside the family line. Alford describes such naming practices as a 'variable system,'[4] one that encourages the selection of family names and common name-elements but does not enforce it. This, in the words of Morpurgo Davies, tells us something about 'a set of deliberate choices in name-giving and name-preserving that, in their turn, reflect specific attitudes to language but also to community life, kinship, continuity, etc.'[5]

Citizens were not the only ones whose names were thought to reflect their status. While denigrating his subject's father, Theophrastos' model slanderer observes that he began life as a slave with the name Sosias, but that when he was in the army he became Sosistratos and changed to Sosidemos when he was enrolled in a deme (*Char.* 28.2).[6] The author seems to suggest that name elements such as *stratos* and *dēmos* did not suit those of lowest status and that slaves' names ought to reflect their position.

This paper follows Theophrastos' lead by comparing and contrasting the connotations of some name elements borne by slaves and citizens in Athens roughly around the fourth century BC.[7] The names of the enslaved and the free offer an interesting problem because this status distinction was one of the bases of Classical Athenian thought: through legal texts, penal practices, and literature, the slave and free became polar opposites.[8] There were, of course, other free persons at Athens besides the citizens and other foreigners than the slaves, but the Athenians were the only full participants in the polis, and their literature expresses this opposition between slave and citizen (e.g. Dem. 21.49) or concerns itself with a lack of opposition ([Xen.] *Ath. Pol.* 1.10). Similarly, their laws placed slave and free at opposite ends of the scale of juridical personhood: a citizen was inviolate in body, whereas a slave not only *might* be punished for wrongdoing with bodily suffering but, with some minor exceptions,[9] *had* to be tortured if offering evidence to court.[10] As Vidal-Naquet puts it, in Athenian ideology the slave was the 'anticitoyen, étranger absolu.'[11]

Even in fields seemingly unrelated to political status, such as work, leisure, sex, and gender, this dichotomy shaped Athenian thinking.[12] Citizens who worked in trades associated with slave labour were disparaged (Xen. *Mem.* 2.8), and a young Athenian *eromenos* who prostituted himself was considered to have left the habits of free persons and so was to be stripped of the future right to participate in the political activities that were his privilege as a citizen (Aisch. 1.3, 19–20, 159).

This analysis of names will show that taken as a whole, slave-names represent their bearers as mere foreigners through ethnic adjectives and stereotypical ethnic names, whereas the relatively higher frequency in citizen-names of name-elements with military and political connotations reflects their status as the important participants in these institutions. The analysis will also demonstrate how these trends in naming and the naming itself, as a social act with lasting effects, contributed to the perception that differences between slave and free were 'natural.' The act of naming thus formed one of the ways in which this ideology was formed within Athenian society. The analysis will also compare the connotations of those animals used as slaves' and citizens' name-elements and of the theophoric names borne by these two groups. The paper concludes with an examination of the elements used in slave-names that express the character or circumstances of the named, suggesting that these reflect a morality prescribed by masters for slaves revolving around behaviour that is dutiful and pleasing to the master.

Who Named the Slaves at Athens?

While the Athenian citizens were usually named by older members of their own status group, there are at least three circumstances in which the slave could be named: within his own society and according to its practices, by those seizing or selling him, and by his master.[13] The only direct evidence from Athens is the statement of Hermogenes in Plato's *Kratylos*:

ἐμοὶ γὰρ δοκεῖ ὅτι ἄν τίς τῳ θῆται ὄνομα, τοῦτο εἶναι τὸ ὀρθόν. καὶ ἂν αὖθίς γε ἕτερον μεταθῆται, ἐκεῖνο δὲ μηκέτι καλῇ, οὐδὲν ἧττον τὸ ὕστερον ὀρθῶς ἔχειν τοῦ προτέρου, ὥσπερ τοῖς οἰκέταις ἡμεῖς μετατιθέμεθα (Pl. *Krat.* 384d).

While arguing for the arbitrariness of all words, Hermogenes uses the renaming of slaves as an example of inconsequential renaming. From this, we should conclude that the renaming of slaves to whom he refers was a reasonably familiar event. Furthermore, Hermogenes specifies the people who do the renaming with the first-person plural pronoun. In doing so, he must be referring to fellow slave owners at Athens but not to the slave dealers, for the latter were a reviled lot (Ar. *Eq.* 1030; Pl. *Resp.* 344b), and it would be a poor rhetorical tactic to link oneself and one's audience with them in debate.

Corroborating evidence can be extracted from the Attic stelai (*IG* i^3 421–30), where there are listed among the confiscated possessions forty-five slaves, forty-four of whom have legible names. Nineteen of these are non-Greek ethnic adjectives used as names; ten are Greek names borne by slaves of foreign origin;[14] and one is a name whose meaning makes it likely to be applied only to a slave.[15] Thus thirty out of forty-four slaves on this list, or 68 per cent, had names that were different from the sort given to the free within their original culture. The remaining fourteen are merely inconclusive; we cannot be certain if some of their names were changed as well (though the names of Philomenes the Cretan and Olas seem likely to be birth names). It might be thought that Greek names are more likely to be birth names, but the Attic stelai show that many foreigners were given Greek names. Of the eighteen Greek names that survive, thirteen, or 72 per cent, are classified above as likely cases of renaming.[16] This is important because some of the analysis that follows will specifically consider the elements in Greek slave-names.

Furthermore, the kinds of names given to the slaves on the Attic stelai vary from owner to owner, showing that this renaming was indeed in the hands of the owners. The slaves of the metic Kephisodoros are identified as his slaves with ethnic adjectives alone, and the same name is used for different slaves: Thraitta, for instance, appears three times (*IG* i^3 421.34, 35, 40). Perhaps this was Kephisodoros' practice, or perhaps he had not given these slaves their names before his arrest. In contrast, the listed slaves of Axiochos, son of Alkibiades, are all given well-formed Greek names even though they are of foreign origin.[17]

To conclude, a master had the power of renaming his slaves, as Plato's Hermogenes states, and as the Attic stelai make clear, the majority of slaves were indeed renamed. In fact, a master had more freedom in naming than did the father of a citizen, since, in some circumstances, tradition urged the latter to use family name-elements, whereas there is no such constraint on a master. In these circumstances, if a master chose not to rename his slave, this choice too can be treated as an expression of his or her idea of slaves, and hence as evidence for the idea of slavery at Athens. Thus even though we cannot be sure that every master chose to rename his slave, we will proceed on the basis that major trends found in a large sample of slave-names reflect the onomastic choices of their masters, whether citizen or metic.

Samples of Slave-Names

Though the Greek slave-names are well studied, their potential as evidence for the idea of slavery has not yet been exploited. Lambertz (1907) offers a catalogue of names similar in approach to that of Bechtel (1902); Collins (1978) takes a prosopographical approach to the slaves manumitted from Delphi; and Masson (1972) provides an overview with improvements on Lambertz. From the historian's point of view, however, these works share certain failings: they do not quantify the differences they perceive in naming patterns, and when providing relative quantitative statements they do not specify to what comparandum those statements apply. The following discussion will apply its findings to the larger questions of the ideology of slave and citizen at Athens; as well, all comparisons between slaves' and citizens' names will be quantified from within their samples.

Our knowledge of Athenian slave-names in the Classical period derives in large part from only two sources: roughly 40 per cent come from *IG* i^3 1032 (= *IG* ii^2 1952), a naval list, and another 30 per cent from manumission documents dating to ca. 330 BC (*IG* ii^2 1553–78). Of the remaining 30 per cent, a large proportion is found on inscriptions and surmised to be slaves, sometimes on the evidence of their names; other names found in literary texts have been subject to textual corruption. Our source for slave-names, therefore, is already limited, and random sampling does little to improve our understanding until the two key documents are understood. A collection of slaves who are about to be manumitted and are able to raise the 100 drachmai required for this manumission rite, represents, I suspect, unusual cases. For this reason, though the manumission documents make interesting comparative material, this paper will focus on the slave-names from *IG* i^3 1032.

The most thorough analysis of *IG* i^3 1032 is Laing's. She concludes that it lists the crews of eight triremes, including the slaves on board, who were the possessions of Athenian citizens or metics.[18] In total, the surviving text includes 146 names that are either complete or can be restored with confidence, and these names and their analysis are presented in the appended table 5.2, labelled S1 to S146.[19] According to Laing's estimates, slaves provided from 20 per cent to over 40 per cent of each ship's complement, suggesting that this fleet was staffed in a time of depleted manpower or emergency.[20] Xenophon records just such a circumstance, when the rescue fleet to Arginousai in 406 BC was filled with all available men, including slaves (*Hell.* 1.6.24). It has therefore been suggested that the document lists the casualties from that engagement. Laing points out, though, that this list differs in form from other late-fifth-century casualty lists: the names are not listed by tribal membership, and the inscription is written in Ionic lettering; furthermore, the name of one of the trierarchs on the document also appears on a fourth-century base.[21] For these reasons, it is more likely that the document was an honorific list recording some remarkable accomplishment of these crews. Laing suggests it honours the eight triremes that got away from Aigospotamoi with Konon upon their return to the city in 393.[22]

For our purposes, whether Laing is correct or whether the document relates to an expedition against Eretria in 411 – a theory Laing refutes[23] – this inscription provides a sample of slave-names in Athens in the very late fifth or very early fourth century. From the document we can conclude that the vast majority of these slaves had served in Athens before joining the fleet (like those who sailed in the battle of Arginousai) and were not purchased abroad to fill the fleet's complement. Rowing a trireme was a considerable skill and required training (Thuc. 1.142.6–9). On the one occasion that we do hear of slaves acquired abroad working in Athenian ships, it is one of the indications Nikias gives of the poor state of his fleet at Syracuse (7.13). A fleet that deserved the honour of public recognition should not have made this dishonourable use of slaves, nor, if it did, would it have advertised the fact on its return. Neither can it be the case that the officers on board bought any great number of slaves to make up for casualties or desertions among the complement of slaves, for we do not find large numbers of slaves owned by a small group of citizen-sailors.

A comparable set of Athenian citizens' names is required in order to determine which aspects of slave-names are unusual. Ideally, this set would be randomly selected from the same short time frame from which we conclude the slaves' names appeared, perhaps the last decade of the fifth century and the first decade of the fourth. However, this approach would restrict the sample to names that are very securely dated, and since accurate dates are far more likely to be associated with more prominent citizens, this method would unwittingly under-represent lower strata of Athenian society. Fortunately, Greek naming is a social phenomenon that changes slowly,[24] and it is therefore reasonable to compare our slaves' names with a sample spanning an adjacent century. Since Osborne and Byrne's 1994 *A Lexicon of Greek Personal Names* (*LGPN II*), like all similar works, assigns centuries BC to persons whose dates are uncertain, we must choose between the fifth and fourth centuries. In fact, my experience with samples from each of these centuries and with a sample spanning suggests that the difference between slave-names and citizen-names is so marked that either would suffice. However, because the nature of the evidence in the early fifth century is quite different from later times, on balance it seems best to provide a fourth-century sample. This was produced by random selection from *LGPN II*,[25] and the appended table 5.1 lists these names using labels from P1 to P110.

Similarities between the Names of Slaves and Citizens

Although the purpose of this paper is to explore the differences between slave- and citizen-names, we should outline the general similarities between them. The names given to the slaves of *IG* i^3 1032 do not constitute a set of words wholly separate from citizens' names or based on different underlying principles, as, for instance, are the names of Greek dogs.[26] With the exception of foreign ones, these slave-names were composed in the common manner, and though there are many slave-names with less-than-pleasant connotations (even excluding the ethnic ones),[27] names with positive connotations are by no means rare.

Furthermore, the very names are sometime the same: 56 per cent of the slaves' names on *IG* i^3 1032 are attested with certainty for an Athenian citizen in the fifth or fourth centuries.[28] If we add persons in the same period whom *LGPN II* considers likely to be citizens, the proportion is 66 per cent. Furthermore, of those that are unattested, some contain elements that are common to Greek onomastics in general; and for that matter, any sample of citizens' names of this size will contain a certain proportion of unique names. Among our sample of fourth-century Athenian men, for instance, there are five unique names, or 5 per cent of the total sample. In this respect we might agree with Robert's pronouncement, echoed in Matthews: 'Une fois de plus, on constate que la notion de "nom d'esclave," presque autant que celle de "nom de courtisane," ne correspond pas à une réalité stable; c'est plus ou moins tôt, suivant les régions, que noms d'esclaves et noms de citoyens puisent dans un même fonds.'[29] Slaves were named, then, with what were commonly used by Greeks as anthroponyms; further evidence that the Athenians never lost sight of the fact that slaves and free shared, at the very least, their humanity.

Ethnicity

Nevertheless, there are some clear differences between the collected names of Athenian slaves and citizens. The most obvious is the predominance of slave-names that make reference to cultures outside of Greece: non-Greek ethnic adjectives such as Thraix and patently non-Greek names like Manes account for a large proportion of slave-names.[30] Although the interpretation can at times be difficult, in most contexts names like Thraix should be understood as well-formed anthroponyms and not simply as plain ethnic labels (i.e. 'the Thracian slave of so-and-so'). As Fraser's study points out, Greek custom freely admits ethnic adjectives as proper names (e.g. Thettalos or Lakedaimonios);[31] and there is ample evidence from comic plays for such words being used in addressing slaves (Karion: Ar. *Plut. passim*; Daos: Men. *Georg*. 32). Twenty-four, or 16 per cent, of the slave-names recorded in *IG* i^3 1032 are barbarian ethnic adjectives or names of barbarian peoples.[32]

Equally interesting are names such as Manes and Tibeios, foreign names used as the names of slaves. Masson suggests that in these cases 'un esclave venu d'un pays non grec a conservé son nom indigene' and offers the example of Manes.[33] It is true that this name is common in Phrygia and other barbarian nations of Asia Minor.[34] However, it is so common among Athenian slaves as to provide fully 5 per cent of our sample. Given that many slaves came from areas such as Thrace, which did not have this name, Manes would have to have been extremely common in Phrygia and other parts of Asia Minor for all of these slaves to have been called by that name before captivity. It is more likely that Manes and similar names are like those modern ethnic nicknames that employ a name commonly used, or thought to be commonly used, by the bearer's ethnic group. This, in any case, was Strabo's impression of Athenian practices: τοὺς οἰκέτας ... τοῖς ἐπιπολάζουσιν ἐκεῖ ὀνόμασι προσηγόρευον, ὡς Μάνην ἢ Μίδαν τὸν Φρύγα, Τίβιον δὲ τὸν Παφλαγόνα (7.3.12). Furthermore, Demosthenes uses Manes as a typical slave's name alongside Ludos, a name that was clearly not borne by the slave before captivity (45.86). In total, eighteen names from our sample derive from foreign names, or 12 per cent. Rarer, but similar in effect, are the slave-names like Aisopos (table 5.2, S3) that refer to a famous non-Greek, presumably a compatriot of the slave.[35]

Against the forty-three slave-names that in these ways mark the bearer as an ethnic barbarian, only three identify a foreign Greek: Arkadion (S11), Lakon (S87), and Chionides (S144). Similarly, from the forty-four legible slave-names recorded on the Attic stelai, only one bears a Greek ethnic name (Messenios: *IG* i^3 430.9). This emphasis on the barbaric origin of slaves accords with the fundamental identification of slaves with non-Greek foreigners in Greek and especially Athenian writing on the subject. Quoting Euripides (*IA* 1400), Aristotle writes,

τὸ φύσει ἄρχον οὐκ ἔχουσιν, ἀλλὰ γίνεται ἡ κοινωνία αὐτῶν δούλης καὶ δούλου. διό φασιν οἱ ποιηταὶ "βαρβάρων δ' Ἕλληνας ἄρχειν εἰκός," ὡς ταὐτὸ φύσει βάρβαρον καὶ δοῦλον ὄν. (Arist. *Pol.* 1252b7–9)

He claims that barbarians do not have the innate ability to dominate and are by nature (*phusei*) equivalent to slaves. The prevalence of slave-names making reference to a foreign tribe or language shows that like Aristotle and like Euripides' *Iphigeneia*, many who named the foreign slaves in our sample considered a slave's ethnicity to be an important characteristic of him as a slave. Moreover, the wide use of ethnic adjectives and only a few common foreign personal names shows that the polis reduced the variety and complexity of barbarian life to a handful of common labels. Research into modern racial epithets has shown how such names not only express prejudice but are intrinsic to systems of racial discrimination.[36]

Individuation

Another obvious difference between Athenian citizens' and slaves' names is that the latter are less individuated. Of the 146 slaves named on *IG* i^3 1032, seventy-two, or 49 per cent are repetitions,[37] whereas the sample of fourth-century Athenian men contains eighteen repetitions, only 16 per cent of the names.[38]

Among other evidence for weak individuation among slave-names is Demosthenes' use of the phrase Σύρος ἢ Μάνης ἢ τίς ἕκαστος ἐκείνων (45.86) to refer to any given domestic slave. The expression is well chosen: these two names account for fourteen of the slaves in our sample, or 10 per cent. Finally, in *IG* i^3 1032 we find two slaves within the same household having the same name, a practice that was avoided in the naming of Athenian children. Lines 228–30 read:

Ἡρακλείδης
Ἱερομνήμονος
Ἡρακλείδης δεύτε(ρος)

The inscription records that the Herakleides in line 230 is the second slave thus named in the household of Hieromnemon.[39]

A simple functionalist explanation for the difference is at hand: onomastic individuation was critical to the smooth operation of the polis, but since slaves rarely performed official roles, repetition among slave-names was largely inconsequential. But this explanation is not sufficient. The organizational methods of the polis proved able to accommodate homonymous brothers or cousins. Conversely, *IG* i^3 1032 is evidence to the fact that slaves were, at least at times, officially identified by name. Rather, the difference in onomastic individuation between the names of these status groups represents an ideological distinction between slave and citizen. The Athenian males believed that their sons, while identified with the group by general onomastic traits, should be recognized within the polis as distinct individuals whose personal traits and abilities might uniquely contribute to his society. Slaves, on the other hand, are perceived as more interchangeable and less distinguished one from another.

It might be objected that although it is safe to assume that many slaves were 'general dogsbodies,'[40] some households show a remarkable degree of differentiation in the roles of slaves. The Attic stelai record the skills of the slaves to be sold (e.g. *IG* i^3 422.70–8), and Xenophon's *Oikonomikos* lists the extensive criteria applied in choosing a housekeeper (9.11–13). Division of labour, however, is not the same thing as individuation. Indeed, division of labour demonstrates the point: a slave housekeeper *can* be selected and bought according to such criteria, and one with a proper set of skills is worth as much as (that is, interchangeable with) another who has the same skills (Arist. *Pol.* 1255b22–7). This is all in keeping with Aristotle's pronouncement that the slave is a tool of the *oikos* (1253b23–1254a16). As such, his or her role is to produce according to the will of the master; he or she is not capable of excelling or making a unique contribution in the manner of a citizen.

Name-Elements Relating to Activities of the Polis in War and at Peace

As he further defines the natural roles of slaves and free, Aristotle writes:

Βούλεται μὲν οὖν ἡ φύσις καὶ τὰ σώματα διαφέροντα ποιεῖν τὰ τῶν ἐλευθέρων καὶ τῶν δούλων, τὰ μὲν ἰσχυρὰ πρὸς τὴν ἀναγκαίαν χρῆσιν, τὰ δ' ὀρθὰ καὶ ἄχρηστα πρὸς τὰς τοιαύτας ἐργασίας, ἀλλὰ χρήσιμα πρὸς πολιτικὸν βίον· οὗτος δὲ καὶ γίνεται διῃρημένος εἴς τε τὴν πολεμικὴν χρείαν καὶ τὴν εἰρηνικήν. (Arist. *Pol.* 1254b27–32)

According to Aristotle, nature forms the citizen to be suitable for the activities of life within a polis; that is, for the duties of war and of peace. The slave, he states, is not suited for these activities but rather for work under compulsion. That this opinion was widely shared is illustrated in Herodotos' tale of the Scythian slaves' children, who violently resisted their fathers' masters when the latter returned to their land after many years of absence. The rebellion succeeded until the masters put down their arms and took up instead the instrument used to control slaves: a whip. At this point, says Herodotos, the slaves ἐκπλαγέντες τῷ γινομένῳ τῆς μάχης τε ἐπελάθοντο καὶ ἔφευγον (4.4).

In fact, as in legend, slaves, in particular slaves of the Athenian type, were non-combatants. They might, as the slaves from *IG* i³ 1032 did, occasionally row in the navy (land battle being more prestigious), and in desperation the polis could mobilize its servile manpower, but in doing so it usually made offers of franchise, suggesting that to an Athenian, a slave who fought was no longer a slave.[41] Nor did slaves have a role in conflicts within the polis.[42]

It is not surprising, then, that the names of slaves and free citizens use elements relating to the military differently. When choosing names for their sons and daughters, Athenians were fond of name-elements with martial meanings or connotations (such as Nikomachos or Archestrate). To compare the frequency of these elements among slave and free, I have selected as military those elements in tables 5.1 and 5.2 that denote combat: *machê* ('battle'), *ptolemos* ('battle'); the military forces and their subgroups or commanders: *lochos* ('an armed band'), *naus* ('ship'), *phrourarchos* ('commander of a watch'), *phularchos* ('commander of the cavalry furnished by each tribe'); *stratos* ('army'); force and strength: *alkê* ('prowess'), *damazô* ('overpower'), *kratos* ('power'), *menô* ('stand fast'), *nikê* ('victory'), *sthenos* ('strength'); violent temperament or aspect: *deinos* ('terrible'), *thrasus* ('bold'); and motivations for battle: *tinô* (mid.'avenge oneself'). The results are presented in tables 5.1 and 5.2, and in figure 5.1. Among the citizen-names, there appeared thirty-three military name-elements spread over twenty-nine names, or 26 per cent of all citizen-names. In contrast, our sample of slave-names provided only eight elements with military connotations, or five such names per 100, a frequency one-fifth of that of the citizen-names. This is not simply a function of the high concentration of ethnic names among the slaves. Even with these removed, the remaining 103 names provide a frequency of only eight military names for each 100. Thus when Theophrastos portrays his Slanderer alleging that a citizen *parvenu* added the element *stratos* to his name, he makes reference not only to the meaning of the element but also to its value as an onomastic token of status within the context of citizen ideology (*Char.* 28.2).

In his final transformation, the father of the Slanderer's victim becomes a citizen and adds another appropriate name-element, such as *dēmos*. As the tables show, the frequency of citizens' name-elements that refer to life in the community in peacetime is also higher than the percentage of similar slaves' name-elements. To make this comparison, I selected 'civic' elements, those that refer to the polis and its parts: *agora* ('assembly, market place'), *astu* ('the city'), *polis* ('the city'); the citizen population: *dēmos* ('the people'); the institutions of the *polis*: *euthunos* ('corrector, judge'), *nomos* ('custom, law'); and leadership and rule: *archē* ('rule, power'), *hēgeomai* ('to lead'). As shown in the tables, names containing these elements appear three times per 100 slave-names (four times per 100 with ethnics removed) and fifteen times per 100 citizen-names.[43]

Finally, 'aristocratic' name elements, ones that express traditional Greek values of personal excellence, are far more frequent among the citizens than the slaves. In this category I included *euainetos* ('much extolled'), *eudoxos* ('of good repute'), *hippos* ('horse'),[44] *kallos* ('beauty'), *kleos* ('fame'), and related words *kudos* ('glory'), *kōmos* ('revel'), *prophantos* ('far-famed'), *timē* ('honour'), *prōtos* ('first'), and *medō* ('rule'). A total of 24 per cent of the citizens' names comprise these words and only 8 per cent of the slaves' names.

In summary, name-elements referring to corporate activity for, by, or in the interest of the polis or referring to the traditional values of its elite are significantly more frequent among the citizen-names than the slave-names, and in this way citizens' names reflect their position as inheritors of the rights, duties, virtues, and privileges of the life of the polis. As for the slaves, their names particularly express their foreign origins, and the infrequency of political elements makes the point that, as the comic poet wrote, οὐκ ἔστι δούλων οὐδαμοῦ πόλις (Anaxandrides fr. 4 [Kassel-Austin] = Ath. 6.263b).

Names and Ideology

These different naming habits did not merely produce a population of slave- and citizen-names that were a reflection of the polis' ideology of slavery; they also contributed to the perpetuation of that ideology. In their classic account of idealist sociology, Berger and Luckmann offer a general account of how social acts influence ideology (though they interestingly do not mention naming). They describe this process, which they call 'social construction,' as a three-stage process. First, they say, people create some artefact or practice based upon their conception of the world.[45] This then enters into the social realm, becomes an object of consciousness for the society at large, and appears to be 'natural.'[46] Finally, future generations born into the social world that includes these social objects 'internalize' them as part of their understanding of the nature of the world. In this way, although the society is, at least in part, constructed through social practices, it is experienced as a pre-given.[47]

This theory explains how naming contributed to the ideology of slavery at Athens. Corresponding to the first stage of social construction, each citizen who named a child or each person who controled the name of a slave added to the society a linguistic artefact that formed a link between the principal characteristics of the named (in this case, status) and the connotations of the name. The Athenians, far from considering these links illusory, believed they expressed something real about the person: in Berger and Luckmann's terms, the names are perceived as social objects. Finally, the conceptions of slaves and citizens expressed in the name-elements became part of the 'natural' world into which an Athenian was born and silently moulded his understanding of the distinction between himself and slaves. When he grew to be head of his own household, the Athenian therefore considered, for example, ethnicity to be a fundamental quality of his non-Greek slaves and in turn addressed them in ways that emphasized it. In doing so, he continued the cycle and perpetuated the illusion of an objectively established difference between the slave and the free.[48]

Animal Name-Elements

Alongside name-elements that are patently political, the naming system transmitted ideas of citizenship and slavery through metaphors. Here, due to the relative infrequency of these elements, we descend into a region of impressions whose verity a larger sample could test. The frequency of references to animals in general is, in fact, higher among the citizens' names, but what concerns us here is the connotation of the animals associated with slaves and free citizens. With only one exception, these elements are not shared between slave and free in our samples.[49] Among the free, the horse is the most common name-element relating to animals. Its associations with wealth and social status were, as we noted, important to Strepsiades' wife in *Clouds*, and here we should take note that certain forms of equestrian activity were the privilege of citizens alone (Dem. 61.23).[50] Furthermore, due to the state of the ancient harness, horses were not suitable for servile activity such as dragging heavy loads.[51]

Such work was done in large part by oxen, and it is noteworthy that *tauros* is an element that appears in a slave's name. Naturally, bulls were not meagre creatures in Greek thought: they appear as a metaphor for social prominence in the *Iliad* (2.480–3) and for sexual potency in Aristophanes (*Lys.* 81). Nevertheless, the slave's full name, Taurosthenes, makes it clear that it is the animal's suitability for hard labour that inspired the comparison, and not virility, since when used as a beast of burden the ox was castrated and disciplined.[52] Similarly, the slave named Murmex ('ant') had as his namesake an animal whose attitude to work was admired (Arist. *Hist. an.* 622b19–28).[53]

Another, more sinister metaphorical image of the bull in Greek literature is as the victim of the overwhelming strength and violence of the lion (Hom. *Il.* 16.487–90; 18.579–84; 20.165; Arist. *Eth. Nic.* 1118a). Thus a brave warrior (Ar. *Eq.* 1036–7) and even a healthy male child (Ar. *Thesm.* 510) were called 'a lion.' (The only Athenian lion slave-name I have found is that of Leon, a public slave [*IG* ii^2 1492.111].) Interestingly, we see here that the wild animal is conceptually closer to the ideal of the citizen than is the domesticated one.[54] Once again, Aristotle provides a theoretical grounding for this popular conception: he states that the domestic animal is like the slave in providing assistance regarding bodily necessities (Arist. *Pol.* 1254b 23–6).[55]

Another animal that appears among the slave-names is the *pithêkos* ('ape' or 'monkey'). In Athenian literature this is a beast considered lacking in beauty (Pl. *Hp. mai.* 289a) and *andreia* (Pl. *Lach.* 196e).[56] Thus it is the opposite of the lion and associated with servility: Plato writes, κολακεία δὲ καὶ ἀνελευθερία οὐχ ... ἐθίζῃ ἐκ νέου ἀντὶ λέοντος πίθηκον γίγνεσθαι (*Resp.* 9.590b). Aristophanes also plays with the servile connotations of the ape when he imagines a sycophant being sold as an ape to a visiting foreigner (*Ach.* 904–908); indeed apes were considered excellent exotic pets (Theophr. *Ch.* 5.25).[57] No Athenian citizens are known to have borne names containing this element at any time.

The distinction between slave and free appears even in the names that refer to animals commonly considered pests. The slave-name Mus ('mouse': table 5.2, S100) connotes a shy animal found around the house (Ar. *Vesp.* 1179–85). The *kōnōps* ('mosquito'), after whom the citizen Konopion (table 5.1, P66) was named, was notorious, then as today, for its buzzing and more importantly, its bite.[58] Something of the aggressive nature of Athenian civic ideology is reflected in this, as it was in the chorus of Aristophanes' *Wasps*: the citizen, according to the laws and tales of the polis, is the one who performs acts of military violence or sexual penetration; similarly, the lion and the mosquito, unlike the mouse, attack their victims openly and boldly do them some harm (Ar. *Eq.* 1037–8). Though his stature is small, the mosquito's character is like the citizen's.

Name-Elements Referring to Social Relations

Elements that appear to refer to one's position in society are also interestingly distributed. For example, the word *kleos* ('fame') appears in 14 per cent of citizens' names and only once among the slaves, in the name Iatrokles (table 5.2, S75). A total of 3 per cent of the citizens' names contain *charis* or related words, but this element never appears among the slaves.[59] The word *aristos* also is more common among the citizens (table 5.1, P9–14;

table 5.2, S9, 10). However, the name-elements do not consign these slaves wholly to the shadows of their masters. For instance, two slaves are named Euainos ('much extolled': S46, 47) and the names of another two contain the element *timē* ('esteem, honour': S136, 137). The path to such distinction, though, is different for slaves and citizens. Slave-name elements delineate a set of positive servile character traits that do not appear in the citizens' names. Obvious examples are Ergophilos (> *ergon*, 'work,' *philos*, 'friend', 'dear': S39); *euarchos* ('easily or well governed'), appearing three times among the slave-names (S48–50); and Parmenon (> *paramenō*, 'to remain faithful'), appearing twice (S108, 109).[60] Particularly notable are those names that suggest the ability to please or amuse others: seven such names appear among the slaves of *IG* i^3 1032, but only one is used in the sampled citizens.[61] Perhaps it is in this context that we can explain the greater number of slave-names containing the element *kallos* ('beauty': S77–9).

Other slave-names express the quality of life enjoyed under the current master. Unambiguous examples of this are Eubios (S51) and Eutuchos (S54), but many other names hover between a sense that expresses both the slave's character and his circumstances. The compound *euarchos* (S48–50) could mean either *easily* or *well* governed; [62] Alypetos (S4), connoting 'not causing pain,' may also mean 'one not pained.' The ambiguity of these terms is probably intentional and expresses reciprocity between master and slave: a slave who is 'well governed' is also one who is 'easily governed,' and a slave that does not cause grief will not suffer punishment.[63] Similarly, the name Eukrines (S53) expresses both the ideal 'well-arranged' personality and labour of the good slave as well as an exceptional relationship with his master, in whose eyes he is 'easily discerned' from others. By so naming his slaves, a master, in part, promoted his own position. Bad relations with a slave were considered a vice (Dem. 21.49–50), and so names such as these ultimately reflect well on the master as a slave owner. Similarly, we might expect that these sorts of names acted as an advertisement of the slave's finer qualities and increased his value.

Furthermore, these names reflect – and express – the social 'horizon' of the two status groups. These domestic slaves had no formal association with the polis at large; their social presence was within the *oikos* and thus always on a personal level. For this reason, slaves had a larger proportion of names that referred to what we would call their 'relationships' with others. In comparison, male citizen-names do not so heavily emphasize the effects of the individual in personal relationships, even between son and father. Instead, from birth onwards a male citizen looked outside the *oikos* to the state at large, in which context he was to represent and glorify his *oikos* primarily through action, not necessarily with a pleasant disposition.

Theophoric and Heroic Names

The category of Greek personal names that were formed from the names of the gods was of interest to the ancient philosophers and today provides evidence for the popularity of cults.[64] As the tables and chart show, if anything, theophoric elements appear more frequently among slaves, 16 per cent of whose names are theophoric, compared to 8 per cent of the sampled citizens' names. It is not surprising that Athenian citizens should conceive of slaves as associated with the gods like themselves. Unlike at Rome, where slaves developed alternative cults, slaves at Athens worshipped alongside the free.[65] They participated in the family cult (Ar. *Ach.* 259–60); if Greek speaking, they might be initiated into the Eleusinian mysteries ([Dem.] 59.21); and they played a major role in the festival of the Choes.[66]

Nevertheless, there remain some salient differences between the theophorics borne by slaves and citizens. Slave-names referring to the gods Artemis or Apollo account for five of the names on *IG* i[3] 1032 (table 5.2, S6–8, 13, 14), but neither of those gods appears in the sample of citizens' names.[67] Similarly, Hekate appears once among the names of slaves (S36), and never among the Athenians of the fifth and fourth centuries listed in *LGPN II*. Conversely, four theophoric citizens' names contain the element *Dios*, the genitive form of Zeus (table 5.1, P31–3, 36),[68] though this element is absent from the slave-names. In his study of the religion of slaves in Greece, Bömer observes roughly the same distinction: 'Betrachtet man den Kreis der Götter, die mit den griechischen Sklaven in Verbindung treten, so fällt sofort ins Auge, dass die "alten Götter," Zeus, Poseidon, Hades, fehlen ...'[69] Furthermore, he provides abundant evidence for the religious association of Apollo and Artemis with slaves.[70]

The absence of Zeus from the lives of slaves can be interpreted in many ways. Bömer offers this explanation: 'Die alten Götter zwar, nicht von ungefähr mit den grossen Bereichen Himmel, Erd und Unterwelt nahezu identisch, liegen ausserhalb der Welt der Sklaven.'[71] A more immediate concern may have been Zeus' political role: 'All sovereignty among men proceeds from Zeus ... the city and its council enjoy the special protection of Zeus *Polieus* and Zeus *Boulaios*. The head of every household places his court and possessions under the protection of Zeus *Herkeios* and Zeus *Ktesios*.'[72] Furthermore, Zeus' sexual potency and rule over Olympus make him an archetype of the patriarch and thus a model for the head of the *oikos* and the antithesis of his slaves.[73]

A more complicated phenomenon is the strong association of slaves with the younger gods Apollo, Artemis, and Hermes. The slave markets or manumissions associated with the *temenē* of Apollo are not a sufficient reason, since other gods have similar association with slaves and do not appear among slaves' names. Apollo, it is true, undergoes a servile experience, but his sister and Hekate do not. Probably these names reflect the citizen's conception of the goddesses as important deities in such slave-exporting nations as Lydia and Lykia.[74]

The frequency of heroic names in the slave sample is also strikingly high. Altogether 4 per cent of the slave-names are the same as or make reference to a hero of Greek myth, whereas none of the citizen-names were formed from these sources. Heroes, like the gods, were the common possession of slave and free. For slaves captured from other Greek states, such tales were part of their common heritage. Indeed heroic legends, as expressed in public art, were available to all, and painted mythological scenes were found on the very domestic implements with which household slaves performed their daily duties.

Most frequently, it seems, heroic slave-names express the foreign origin of the bearer. Many of these are from the slave-exporting East: Marōn (table 5.2, S97) was the eponymous hero of Maroneia, a town on the Thracian coast; Sarpedon (S114) was associated with Karia and Crete, both regions whose inhabitants became slaves at Athens; and Hylas (S139) was a child of the king of Mysia, lost on the Asiatic coast by the Argonauts while still a youth. The fact that Hylas was never an adult is perhaps also important, since adult slaves were addressed as *pais*.[75]

It is possible to see a political comment in other mythical slave-names. The name Herakleides accounts for six of the names on *IG* i^3 1032, a high proportion of all the theophoric names in this sample. Dorian opponents of Athens in the Peloponnesian War were said to be descendants of the Herakleidai, the children of Herakles (Tyrtaios fr. 2.12–15 [West]; Thuc. 1.12). One imagines that during the war these slave-names became popular at Athens as a means of suggesting that slavery is the fate of the enemy.

Conclusion

This paper is a first attempt at quantifying the linguistic differences between the names of slaves and citizens in Classical Athens. Analysis of these differences shows that name-elements that reflected the privileged role of the citizen in the Athenian polis were more frequently applied to citizens than to the slaves of *IG* i^3 1032. Furthermore, it shows how these acts of naming helped to maintain the idea of the slave and how the Athenians' conception of animals was adopted into the scheme. At the same time, the evidence of names suggests that the slave owners projected upon their slaves an ethic of personal interaction different from the ethic of polis-based action that citizens projected upon their sons. Finally, it is clear that owners associated the sphere of myth and religion with slaves as much as citizens associated this with their sons, although some kinds of divinities and heroes were linked in names more with one status group than the other.

These preliminary results also suggest avenues for further research. A diachronic study of male citizens' names would be useful, as would a comparison of women citizen's names with those of their male counterparts and the slaves. The other major source of Classical Athenian slave-names, the manumission documents of *IG* ii^2 1553–78, should be analysed as well. It might be expected that like the persons that bore them, the elements of these names would be intermediary, reflecting a status somewhere between slave and citizen.

Notes

* This paper is a revision of material from my PhD thesis, begun after Professor Harding introduced me to Greek epigraphy in his highly engaging, coffee-fueled graduate seminar at the University of British Columbia.

1 Dodds 1960, *ad* 367.

2 Golden 1986: 252–6.

3 *LGPN II*, s.v. 54.

4 Alford 1988: 43.

5 Morpurgo Davies 2000: 24–5.

6 τούτου ὁ μὲν πατὴρ ἐξ ἀρχῆς Σωσίας ἐκαλεῖτο, ἐγένετο δὲ ἐν τοῖς στρατιώταις Σωσίστρατος, ἐπειδὴ δὲ εἰς τοὺς δημότας ἐνεγράφη, Σωσίδημος (Theophr. *Char.* 28.2).

7 The study of slave-names has proven to be useful to social historians of other periods. For the American South, see especially Inscoe 1983 and Cody 1987.

8 Just 1989: 166–7.

9 Garlan 1988: 42.

10 Hunter 1992: 278–9.

11 Vidal-Naquet 1981: 218.

12 Fisher 1993: 99–108.

13 For a brief discussion of the naming of the slaves listed in the Delphic manumission documents of the second and first centuries, see Reilly 1978.

14 [P]eisistratos, a Karian (*IG* i^3 421.9); Potainios, a Karian (*IG* i^3 422.77); [A]rete, a Thracian (*IG* i^3 422.195); [Gr]ylion, a Thracian (*IG* i^3 422.196); [Hab]rosyne, a Thracian (*IG* i^3 422.197); D[io]nysios, a Scythian (*IG* i^3 422.198); [An]tigenes, a Thracian (*IG* i^3 427.3); Stroggylion, a Karian (*IG* i^3 427.5); Simos, a Scythian (*IG* i^3 427.7); and Apollo[ni]des, a Thracian (*IG* i^3 427.12).

15 Pistos (*IG* i^{3} 421.28).

16 An additional three persons are said to be *oikogeneis*, slaves born in the house: Skonus (*IG* i^{3}422.71–2); Alexitimo[s] (*IG* i^{3} 422.74–5); and [.....]on *or* [.....]ōn (*IG* i^{3} 426.16). The *kurioi* probably chose these names as well.

17 Arete, Grylion, Habronsyne, and Dionysios (*IG* i^{3} 422.195–9).

18 Laing 1965: 91.

19 I exclude from the survey the names which have not been restored by *IG* i^{3} 1032, but I make note of the existing elements of those names where appropriate. Also excluded are the names the status of whose bearers cannot be determined.

20 Laing 1965: 93.

21 Laing 1965: 100–2.

22 Laing 1965: 107–19.

23 Laing 1965: 105.

24 Morpurgo Davies 2000: 38–9.

25 The sample was drawn from all names appearing in contexts dated from 400 to 301 BC or to some part of the fourth century, marked in *LGPN II* #32 as 'f. iv BC' or 'm. iv BC.' The following were omitted: dubious datings like '?iv BC'; those whose dates were estimated across another century, such as 'v/iv BC' or 'iv/iii BC'; and those dated 'hell(enistic).' I omitted foreigners and those whose political status is unsure, listed under ATHENS* and ATHENS?, respectively. Names that were too fragmentary for the purposes of this paper were also excluded. The names were sampled by producing 300 sets of three random numbers: the first, representing the page, from one to 481; the second, representing the column, from one to three; and the third, representing the number of names down from the top of the page, from one to forty. If the name corresponding to a set was not that of a fourth-century male, it was discarded. All random numbers were generated with Hypercard 2.0 for the MacOS operating system.

26 The number of citizen- and slave-names that also appear among the known Greek dog-names illustrates the difference between these naming systems. Only one citizen's name (Dorkeus: table 5.1 P38) and two slaves' names from the samples (Syros: table 5.2 S124–29; Charon: S143) are also attested among the dog-names in Baecker 1884: 1–7. The very different principles of dog-naming are listed at Xen. *De Ven.* 7.5 and Arrian *De Ven.* 31.2.

27 Though it is difficult to determine exactly which names should be considered of this class, Charon (table 5.2 S143), Pithekos ('monkey, ape': S111) and the five names derived from Simos ('snub-nosed,' S116–120) are probably good examples. The one citizen's name of this sort is Phoxias (>*phoxos*, 'pointed, especially of the head': table 5.1 P102). See below on Konopion (>*kōnōps*, 'gnat, mosquito': P66).

28 I exclude Manes as a citizen's name, since I can see no clear indication that the

person making the dedication on *IG* ii^2 4633 is a citizen. Similarly, the Aisopos at schol. Ar. *Vesp.* 566 is most likely a scholiast's error.

29 Firatli and Robert 1964: 179–80; see also Matthews in *OCD*, s.v. 'names, personal, Greek.'

30 Masson 1972: 13.

31 Fraser 2000.

32 The names that contain these elements are: Assyrios, Daos, Getas, Kar, Phoinix, Skythes, Syros, Thraix, and Triballos.

33 Masson 1972: 15.

34 Robert 1970: 369.

35 *IGPN II*, following a scholium, records Aisopos at Ar. *Vesp.* 566 as a contemporary poet and, therefore, Athenian citizen; but Koster (1978: 90) notes rightly, 'de fabularum auctore agit Ar.; quae in sch. traduntur, aliunde nota non sunt.'

36 Allen 1983; Palmore 1962.

37 In table 5.2: Agathon S1–2; Apollonios S7–8; Artimas S15–19; Euainos S46–7; Euarchos S49–50; Euphron S55–6; Gelon S23–4; Gerus S26–9; Hermaios S40–1; Hermon S43–5; Herakleides S60–5; Kallistratos S78–9; Karion S80–3; Manes S89–96; Nomenios S103–5; Parmenon S108–9; Phoinix S141–2; Simias S116–17; Simos S118–20; Syros S124–9; Thraix S68–73; Tibeios S134–5. If we omit the foreign or ethnic names, the remaining slave-names are 28 per cent repetitions.

38 In table 5.1: Demostratos P28–9; Diodoros P31–2; Dionysios P34–5; Euthydemos P46–7; Eukleides P50–1; Gnathios P22–3; Nikostratos P76–7; Stratios P93–4; Sosthenes P96–7.

39 It is just possible that the homonymity of the slaves is a coincidence and we should instead supply the genitive of the name Deuteres. But that name appears only once, on a late-sixth-century black-figure vase (Immerwahr 1990; 440).

40 Garlan 1988: 62.

41 Garlan 1988: 163–76.

42 Vidal-Naquet 1981: 216–17.

43 Note though that at *IG* i^3 1032.126 what appears to be a slave-name begins Eudem[--].

44 Dubois (2000) provides a recent study of some instances of this element.

45 Berger and Luckmann 1966: 33–9

46 Berger and Luckmann 1966: 55–9.

47 Berger and Luckmann 1966: 119–20

48 Of course, this account simplifies the chronological progression of events: all three stages were constantly taking place within the polis (Berger and Luckmann 1966: 119). For a similar study of the whip as a symbol of Greek slavery, see Hunter 1992: 276–7.

49 *Hippos* in Xanthippos (table 5.2 S106).

50 The impression that *hippos* appears more frequently among citizens' names should be tempered by the presence of the slave Hippodameia and freedman Ktesippos in the *Odyssey* (18.102; 19.288).

51 Isager and Skydsgaard 1992: 85–6

52 Isager and Skydsgaard 1992: 89.

53 It should be noted, though, that Aristotle also admires the social organization of ants: he considered them to be 'political' animals along with humans (*HA* 488a10).

54 Thus Alkibiades' reply when scolded by his wrestling opponent for having bitten, like a woman: 'οὐκ ἔγωγε,' εἶπεν, 'ἀλλ' ὡς οἱ λέοντες' (Plut. *Alc.* 2.3).

55 See also Garlan 1988: 139, 149.

56 With respect to *andreia,* it should be noted that the name-element *anēr* ('man') never appears among the sample of slaves and occurs four times among citizens.

57 Garlan (1988: 47) notes that distant Africa exported slaves and monkeys. It is possible, then, that the name also makes reference to ethnicity.

58 Davies and Kathirithamby 1986: 166–7.

59 On the social import of *charis,* see MacLachlan 1993. At *IG* i^{3} 1032.354 there is a name beginning Chair[--], which may or may not be a slave's.

60 Parmenon might make reference to the *paramōnē,* an obligation of the freed slave to remain with his former master for a period of time. The *paramōnē* is attested only in later documents, however.

61 Slaves (table 5.2): Alypetos ('not causing pain': S4), Gelon (<*gelōs,* 'laughter': S23–4), Euphron ('cheering': S55–6), Lysanias (< *luō* , 'loose,' and *ania,* 'sorrow': S88), Pausanias (< *pauō,* 'stop,' and *ania,* 'sorrow': S110). Citizen (table 5.1): Euphranor (<*euphrainō,* 'to cheer, delight': P55). The simple explanation for this difference – that slaves were named once their personalities were developed and citizens were named before evidence of such qualities – does not suffice, since, as we will see, Athenians applied such concepts to their female infants.

62 The passive intent of the name is ensured by the passive sense of this adjective as applied to slaves at Arist. *Oec.* 1344b.

63 There is a possibility that any number of these names is given in sarcasm, but that would not alter the fact that the presence or absence of these qualities is an onomastic concern.

64 Parker 2000.

65 Bömer 1961: 238.

66 Hamilton 1992: T29, 56, ?59, ?60 and p. 51.

67 They are not, of course, wholly absent from all extant citizens' name, but rather our sample strongly suggests they are less frequent among citizen's names than among the names of slaves.

68 For Dio- as a naming element referring to Zeus, and not to divinities in general (LSJ, s.v.), see *HPN* 132–4, and Sittig 1912: 11.

69 Bömer 1961: 235.
70 Bömer 1961: 7–59, 235.
71 Bömer 1961: 235.
72 Burkert 1985: 130.
73 Burkert, 1985: 128–9.
74 Burkert 1985: 149.
75 For a fictional slave with the name Hylas, see Ar. *Eq.* 67.

References

Alford, R.D. 1988. *Naming and Identity: A Cross-Cultural Study of Personal Naming Practices.* New Haven, CT.

Allen, I.L. 1983. 'Personal Names That Become Ethnic Epithets.' *Names* 31: 307–17.

Baecker, E. 1884. 'De Canum Nominibus Graecis.' PhD thesis. Vienna.

Bechtel, F. 1902. *Die attischen Frauennamen nach ihrem Systeme dargestellt.* Göttingen.

Berger, P., and T. Luckmann. 1966. *The Social Construction of Reality.* Garden City, NY.

Bömer, F. 1961. *Untersuchungen über die Religion der Sklaven in Griechenland und Rom,* vol. 3. Mainz.

Burkert, W. 1985. *Greek Religion.* Cambridge, MA.

Cody, C.A. 1987. 'There Was No "Absalom" on the Ball Plantations: Slave-naming Practices in the South Carolina Low Country, 1720–1865.' *American Historical Review* 92: 563–96.

Collins, L. 1978. *Slaves in Ancient Greece: Slaves from Greek Manumission Inscriptions.* Chicago.

Davies, M., and J. Kathirithamby. 1986. *Greek Insects.* London.

Dodds, E.R., ed. 1960. *Euripides' Bacchae,* 2nd ed. Oxford.

Dubois, L. 2000. 'Hippolytos and Lyippos: Remarks on Some Compounds in Ἱππο-, -ιππος,' in S. Hornblower (ed.), *Greek Personal Names,* 41–52. Oxford.

Firatli, N., and L. Robert. 1964. *Les stèles funéraires de Byzance gréco-romaine.* Paris.

Fisher, N.R.E. 1993. *Slavery in Classical Greece.* London.

Fraser, P. 2000. 'Ethnics as Personal Names,' in S. Hornblower (ed.), *Greek Personal Names,* 149–57. Oxford.

Garlan, Y. 1988. *Slavery in Ancient Greece,* trans. J. Lloyd. Ithaca.

Golden, M. 1986. 'Names and Naming at Athens: Three Studies.' *EMC/CV* 30:245–69.

Hamilton, R. 1992. *Choes and Anthesteria: Athenian Iconography and Ritual.* Ann Arbor.

Hunter, V. 1992. 'Corporal Punishment in Classical Athens.' *Phoenix* 36: 271–91.
Immerwahr, H.R. 1990. *Attic Script: A Survey*. Oxford.
Inscoe, J.C. 1983. 'Carolina Slave Names: An Index to Acculturation.' *Journal of Southern History* 49: 527–54.
Isager, S., and J. E. Skydsgaard. 1992. *Ancient Greek Agriculture: An Introduction*. London.
Just, R. 1989. *Women in Athenian Law and Life*. London.
Koster, W.J.W., ed. 1978. *Scholia in Vespas*. Groningen.
Laing, D. 1965. *A New Interpretation of the Athenian Naval Catalogue, IG II^2 1951*. Cincinnati.
Lambertz, M. 1907. *Die griechischen Sklavennamen*. Vienna.
MacLachlan, B. 1993. *The Age of Grace: Charis in Early Greek Poetry*. Princeton.
Masson, O. 1972. 'Les noms des esclaves dans la Grèce antique,' in *Actes du Colloque 1971 sur l'esclavage*. Paris.
Matthews, E., and S. Hornblower. 2000. 'Introduction,' in S. Hornblower (ed.), *Greek Personal Names*, 1–14. Oxford.
Morpurgo Davies, A. 2000. 'Personal Names and Linguistic Continuity,' in S. Hornblower (ed.), 15–39. *Greek Personal Names*. Oxford.
Palmore, E.B. 1962. 'Ethnophaulism and Ethnocentrism.' *American Journal of Sociology* 67: 442–5.
Parker, R. 2000. 'Theophoric Names and the History of Greek Religion,' in S. Hornblower (ed.), 53–79. *Greek Personal Names*. Oxford.
Reilly, L.C. 1978. 'The Naming of Slaves in Greece.' *Ancient World* 1: 111–13.
Robert, L. 1970. *Études anatoliennes: recherches sur les inscriptions grecques de l'Asie mineure*. Amsterdam.
Sittig, E. 1912. 'De Graecorum Nominibus Theophoris.' PhD thesis. Vienna.
Vidal-Naquet, P. 1981. 'Les esclaves grecs étaient-ils une classe?' in *Le Chasseur noir: formes de pensée et formes de société dans le monde grec*, 211–21. Paris.
West, M.L., ed. 1992. *Iambi et Elegi Graeci ante Alexandrum Cantati^2*, vol. 2. Oxford.

Figure 5.1 Frequencies of Names in Lexical Categories

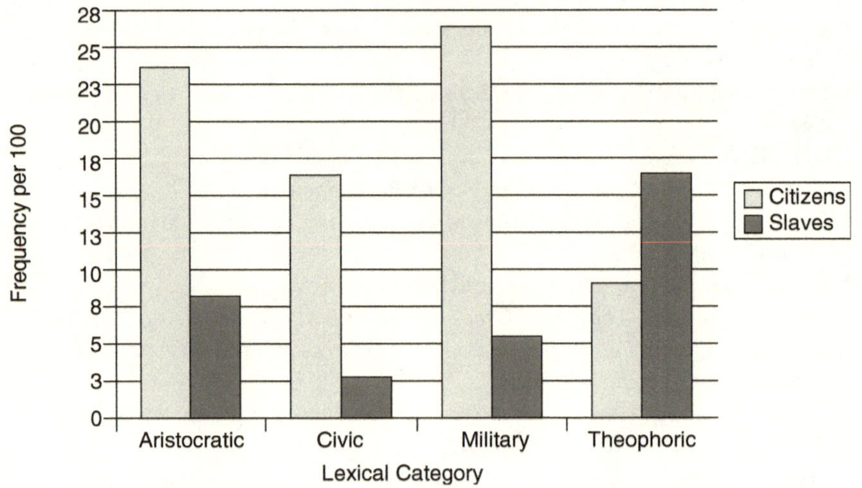

Table 5.1 Analysis of a Sample of Fourth-Century Athenian Citizens' Names

Label	Name	Number	1st Element	Definition	2nd Element	Definition	Aristocratic	Civic	Military	Theophoric
P1	Ἀγάθαρχος	18	ἀγαθός	good	ἀρχή	rule, power		y		
P2	Ἀγακλῆς	3	ἀγακλής	very glorious			y			
P3	Ἀλκιβιάδης	8	ἀλκή	prowess, courage, boldness	βίος	life			y	
P4	Ἀλκίμαχος	25	ἀλκή	prowess, courage, boldness	μάχη	battle			y	
P5	ἈΑμεινοκλῆς	6	ἀμείνων	better	κλέος	fame	y			
P6	Ἀμφινομίδης	1	ἀμφι-	around	νόμος	custom, law		y		
P7	Ἀντίλοχος	13	ἀντι-	opposite; against; instead; equal to	λόχος	armed band			y	
P8	Ἀντί[οχ]ος	47	Ἀντίοχος	(Antiochos: hero after whom the tribe Antiochis was named)				y		
P9	Ἀριστοκλείδης	14	ἄρσιτος	best	κλέος	fame	y			
P10	Ἀριστοκλῆς	62	ἄρσιτος	best	κλέος	fame	y			
P11	Ἀριστολέων	1	ἄρσιτος	best	λέων	lion	y			
P12	Ἀριστόπολις	1	ἄρσιτος	best	πόλις	city	y	y		
P13	Ἀριστοτέλης	29	ἄρσιτος	best	τέλος	fulfillment, completion; end	y			
P14	Ἀριστώνυμος	33	ἄρσιτος	best	ὄνομα	name	y			
P15	Ἀστῖνος	2	ἄστυ	city				y		
P16	Αὐτοκλῆς	25	αὐτός	self	κλέος	fame	y			
P17	Ἀφόβητος	1	ἀ-	alpha privatum (expresses absence)	φοβέω	frighten				
P18	Ἀχιλλεύς	2	Ἀχιλλεύς	Achilles						y

Table 5.1 (*Continued*)

Label	Name	Number	1st Element	Definition	2nd Element	Definition	Aristocratic	Civic	Military	Theophoric
P19	Βαβυρίας	1	Βαβύρας	rich, fat			y			
P20	Βλεπαῖος	2	βλέπω	see, look						
P21	Βόηθος	26	Βοηθός	assisting, auxiliary						
P22	Γνάθιος	6	γνάθος	cheek, jaw						
P23	Γνάθιος	13	γνάθος	cheek, jaw						
P24	Γνίφων	2	[unknown]	[unknown]						
P25	Δείνων	8	δεινός	fearful, terrible; mighty					y	
P26	Δημήτριος	324	Δημητήριος	of or pertaining to Demeter						y
P27	Δημοκράτης	30	δῆμος	the people	κράτος	strength, might		y	y	
P28	Δημόστρατος	19	δῆμος	the people	στρατός	army		y	y	
P29	Δημόστρατος	51	δῆμος	the people	στρατός	army		y	y	
P30	Δημοχάρης	33	δῆμος	the people	χαίρω	rejoice, be glad; welcome		y		
P31	Διόδωρος	12	Διός	Zeus	δῶρον	gift				y
P32	[Δι]όδωρος	115	Διός	Zeus	δῶρον	gift				y
P33	Διοκλῆς	87	Διός	Zeus	κλέος	fame	y			y
P34	[Δ]ιονύσιος	221	Διονύσιος	of or pertaining to Dionysos						y
P35	Διονύσιος	766	Διονύσιος	of or pertaining to Dionysos						y
P36	Δίων	9	Δίος	Zeus						y
P37	Δόκιμος	9	δόκιμος	trustworthy						
P38	Δρακοντίδης	3	δράκων	dragon, serpent						
P39	Ἔκφ[α]ν[τ]ος	6	ἔκφαντος	shown forth, revealed			y			
P40	Ἐλπίας	2	ἐλπίς	hope, expectation						

Table 5.1 (*Continued*)

Label	Name	Number	1st Element	Definition	2nd Element	Definition	Aristocratic	Civic	Military	Theophoric
P41	᾽Επαμείν[ων]	10	ἐπί	upon, over, towards, with	ἀμείνων	better				
P42	᾽Επιχαρίδης	7	ἐπιχαρής	gratifying, agreeable						
P43	῾Ερομογ[ένης]	24	῾Ερμῆς	Hermes	γίγνομαι	come into being; become				y
P44	Εὔδραστος	1	εὐ	well	δράω	do				
P45	Εὔθιππος	11	εὐθύς	straight	ἵππος	horse	y			
P47	Εὐθύδημος	35	εὐθύς	straight	δῆμος	the people		y		
P46	Εὐθύδημος	29	εὐθύς	straight	δῆμος	the people		y		
P48	Εὐθύκρατος	11	εὐθύς	straight	κράτος	strength, might			y	
P49	Εὔθυνος	6	εὔθυνος	corrector, judge				y		
P50	Εὐκλείδης	39	εὐκλής	of good report, famous			y			
P51	Εὐκλείδης	55	εὐκλής	of good report, famous			y			
P52	Εὐκλ[ῆς]	48	εὐκλής	of good report, famous			y			
P53	Εὐρυπτόλεμος	4	εὐρύ	far-reaching	πτόλεμος	battle (epic form)			y	
P54	Εὐσθένης	1	εὐ	well	σθένος	strength, might			y	
P55	Εὐφράνωρ	29	εὐφραίνω	cheer, delight, gladden						
P56	῾Ηγέλοχος	11	ἡγέομαι	go before, lead the way; lead	λόχος	armed band		y	y	
P57	῾Ηγησίας	32	ἡγέομαι	go before, lead the way; lead				y		
P58	Θεογένης	49	θεός	god	γίγνομαι	come into being; become				
P59	Θέογνις	12	θεός	god	γίγνομαι	come into being; become				

Table 5.1 (*Continued*)

Label	Name	Number	1st Element	Definition	2nd Element	Definition	Aristocratic	Civic	Military	Theophoric
P60	Θεόδωρ[ος]	82	θεός	god	δῶρον	gift				
P61	Θεόπομπος	67	Θεόπομπος	sent by the gods						
P62	Θουκλείδης	3	θεός	god	κλέος	fame	y			
P63	Κηφίσιος	2	Κηφισός	name of various rivers				y		
P64	Κηφισόστρατος	1	Κηφισός	name of various rivers	στρατός	army		y	y	
P65	Κιχήσιππος	2	κιχάνω	reach, arrive at	ἵππος	horse	y			
P66	Κωνωπίων	1	κώνωψ	gnat, mosquito						
P67	Λυσίας	71	λύω	loose						
P68	Λυσίστρατος	63	λύω	loose	στρατός	army			y	
P69	Μέλη[το]ς	11	μέλω	think of, care for						
P70	Μενεκλῆς	26	μένω	stand fast (esp. in battle)	κλέος	fame	y		y	
P71	Μνήσαρχος	12	μιμνήσκω	remind, recall to memory	ἀρχή	rule, power		y		
P72	Μυρτίλος	4	μύρτος	myrtle						
P73	Νίκανδρος	38	νίκη	victory	ἀνήρ	man			y	
P74	Νικέας	3	νίκη	victory					y	
P75	Νικόμαχος	10	νίκη	victory	μάχη	battle			y	
P76	Νικόστρατος	38	νίκη	victory	στρατός	army			y	
P77	Νικόστρατος	135	νίκη	victory	στρατός	army			y	
P78	Νίκων	30	νίκη	victory					y	
P79	Ξενοκλῆς	47	ξένος	stranger, friend	κλέος	fame	y			
P80	Ξενόκριτος	4	ξένος	stranger, friend	κριτός	picked out, chosen				
P81	Οἰνοκλῆς	3	οἶνος	wine	κλέος	fame	y			

Table 5.1 (*Continued*)

Label	Name	Number	1st Element	Definition	2nd Element	Definition	Aristocratic	Civic	Military	Theophoric
P82	Ὀνήσανδρος	5	ὀνίνημι	profit, benefit, help	ἀνήρ	man				
P83	Ὀψιάδης	4	ὄψιος	late						
P84	Παλαθίων	1	παλάθη	cake of fruit						
P85	Πανδαίτης	1	πᾶς	all, everything	δαίς	meal, banquet				
P86	Παντακλῆς	10	πᾶς	all, everything	κλέος	fame	y			
P87	Πεδίαρχος	2	πεδίον	plain	ἀρχή	rule, power		y		
P88	Πείσανδρος	4	πείθω	win over, persuade	ἀνήρ	man				
P89	Πολυκλῆς	31	πολύς	many	κλέος	fame	y			
P90	Πρόφαν[τος]	1	πρόφαντος	appearing at a distance, far seen, hence far-famed			y			
P91	Σάτυρος	38	Σάτυρος	Satyr						y
P92	Σπουδωνίδης	1	σπουδή	haste, speed						
P93	Στράτιος	11	στρατός	army					y	
P94	Στράτιος	16	στρατός	army					y	
P95	Στρο[μβ]υ[λίων]	1	στρόμβος	spun object; a top						
P96	Σωσθένης	1	σώζω	save	σθένος	strength, might			y	
P97	[Σ]ωσθένης	9	σώζω	save	σθένος	strength, might			y	
P98	Σωτιμίδης	1	σώζω	save	τιμή	worship, esteem, honour	y			
P99	Τείσανδρος	19	τίνω	(mid.) avenge oneself, punish	ἀνήρ	man			y	
P100	Τεισίας	16	τίνω	(mid.) avenge oneself, punish					y	
P101	Φανόμαχος	14	φαίνω	reveal	μάχη	battle			y	

Table 5.1 (*Concluded*)

Label	Name	Number	1st Element	Definition	2nd Element	Definition	Aristocratic	Civic	Military	Theophoric
P102	Φοξίας	2	φοξός, ή, όν	pointed, (esp. of head)						
P103	Φορμίων	6	φορμός	basket for carrying grain, etc						
P104	Φρούραρχος	3	φρούραρχος	commander of watch					y	
P105	Φύλαρχος	2	φύλαρχος	commander of the cavalry furnished by each tribe					y	
P106	[Φ]υλεύς	7	unknown	[unknown]						
P107	Χαιρήμων	6	χαίρω	rejoice, be glad; welcome						
P108	Χαρέας	1	χαίρω	rejoice, be glad; welcome						
P109	Χάριππος	5	χαίρω	rejoice, be glad; welcome	ἵππος	horse	y			
P110	Χρέμης	6	unknown	[unknown]						

Table 5.2 Analysis of Slaves' Names from *IG* I³ 1032s

Label	Name	Line No.	1st Element	Definition	2nd Element	Definition	Aristocratic	Civic	Military	Theophoric
S1	Ἀγάθων	374	ἀγαθός	good						
S2	Ἀγάθων	460	ἀγαθός	good						
S3	Αἴσωπος	397	Αἴσωπος	(Aesopos, slave and author)						
S4	Ἀλύπητος	243	ἀλύπητος	not pained or grieved; not causing pain						
S5	Ἀντιφάνης	258	ἀντι-	opposite; against; instead; equal to	φαίνω	reveal				
S6	Ἀπολλωνίδης	250	Ἀπόλλων	Apollo						y
S7	Ἀπολλώνιος	268	Ἀπολλώνιος	of or pertaining to Apollo						y
S8	Ἀπολλώνιος	396	Ἀπολλώνιος	of or pertaining to Apollo						y
S9	Ἀριστόβολος	247	ἄριστος	best	βουλή	counsel, advice; council	y			
S10	Ἀριστόδημος	364	ἄριστος	best	δῆμος	the people	y	y		
S11	Ἀρκαδίων	346	Ἀρκαδία	Arcadia						
S12	Ἀρκέσας	233	ἀρκέω	help, aid						
S13	Ἀρτεμίδωρος	480	Ἄρτεμις	Artemis	δῶρον	gift				y
S14	Ἀρτέμων	359	Ἄρτεμις	Artemis						y
S15	Ἀρτίμας	135	Ἀρτίμας	(Artimas, name from Lydia, etc.)						
S16	Ἀρτίμας	253	Ἀρτίμας	(Artimas, name from Lydia, etc.)						
S17	Ἀρτίμας	372	Ἀρτίμας	(Artimas, name from Lydia, etc.)						
S18	Ἀρτίμας	402	Ἀρτίμας	(Artimas, name from Lydia, etc.)						
S19	Ἀρτίμ<α>ς	337	Ἀρτίμας	(Artimas, name from Lydia, etc.)						

Table 5.2 (*Continued*)

Label	Name	Line No.	1st Element	Definition	2nd Element	Definition	Aristocratic	Civic	Military	Theophoric
S20	Ἀρχέφιλος	113	ἀρχή	rule, power	φίλος	friend, dear		y		
S21	Ἀσσύριος	109	Ἀσσύριος	Assyrian						
S22	Ἄττας	345	Ἄττας	(Phrygian name)						
S23	Γέλων	257	γέλως	laughter						
S24	Γέλων	462	γέλως	laughter						
S25	Γέτας	108	Γέτας	(reference to foreign tribe)						
S26	Γῆρυς	116	γῆρυς	voice, speech						
S27	Γῆρυς	261	γῆρυς	voice, speech						
S28	Γῆρυς	404	γῆρυς	voice, speech						
S29	Γῆρυς	459	γῆρυς	voice, speech						
S30	Γλαυκία[ς]	262	γλαυκός	bluish green, esp. of the eyes						
S31	Γρίσων	130	γρίσων	pig						
S32	Δάμων	111	δαμάζω	overpower; subdue; tame					y	
S33	Δᾶος	234	Δᾶος	the name of a non-Greek people.						
S34	Δεξίθε[ος]	377	δέχομαι	receive	θεός	god				
S35	Δημήτ[ριος]	379	Δημητήριος	of or pertaining to Demeter						y
S36	Ἑκατώνυμος	464	Ἑκάτη	Hekate	ὄνομα	name				y
S37	Ἔμπορος	457	ἔμπορος	traveller; merchant						
S38	Ἐπιμέλης	369	ἐπιμέλης	careful, attentive						
S39	Ἐργόφιλος	450	ἔργον	work	φίλος	friend, dear				
S40	Ἑρμαῖος	239	Ἑρμαῖος	of or pertaining to Hermes						y

Table 5.2 (*Continued*)

Label	Name	Line No.	1st Element	Definition	2nd Element	Definition	Aristocratic	Civic	Military	Theophoric
S41	Ἑρμαῖο[ς]	381	Ἑρμαῖος	of or pertaining to Hermes						y
S42	Ἑρμάφιλος	367	Ἑρμῆς	Hermes	φίλος	friend, dear				y
S43	Ἕρμων	378	Ἕρμος	Hermos River						
S44	Ἕρμων	400	Ἕρμος	Hermos River						
S45	Ἕρμων	455	Ἕρμος	Hermos River						
S46	Εὔαινος	242	εὐαίνετος	much-extolled			y			
S47	Εὔαινος	467	εὐαίνετος	much-extolled			y			
S48	Εὐαρχίδης	249	εὔαρχος	easily governed						
S49	Εὔαρχος	458	εὔαρχος	easily governed						
S50	Εὔαρχος	465	εὔαρχος	easily governed						
S51	Εὔβιος	348	εὐβίοτος	easily finding their food, of certain animals						
S52	Εὐβολίδης	240	εὔβουλος	well-advised; prudent						
S53	Ἐυκρίνης	342	εὐκρνής	well-arranged; in good order						
S54	Εὔτυχος	110	εὐτυχής	well off, successful, lucky						
S55	Εὔφρων	267	εὔφρων	cheerful, cheering						
S56	Εὔφρων	244	εὔφρων	cheerful, cheering						
S57	Ζώπυρος	338	ζώπυρον	spark, ember						
S58	Ἡγίας	252	ἡγέομαι	go before, lead the way; lead				y		
S59	Ἡραῖος	398	Ἡραῖος	of Hera						y
S60	Ἡρακλέδης	270	Ἡρακλείδης	descendant of Herakles						y
S61	Ἡρακλείδης	228	Ἡρακλείδης	descendant of Herakles						y

Table 5.2 (*Continued*)

Label	Name	Line No.	1st Element	Definition	2nd Element	Definition	Aristocratic	Civic	Military	Theophoric
S62	Ἡρακλείδης	230	Ηρακλείδης	descendant of Herakles						y
S63	Ἡρακλείδης	235	Ηρακλείδης	descendant of Herakles						y
S64	Ἡρακλείδης	401	Ἡρακλείδης	descendant of Herakles						y
S65	Ἡρακλείδ[ης]	360	Ἡρακλείδης	descendant of Herakles						y
S66	Ἡφαιστόδωρος	117	Ἥφαιστος	Hephaistos	δῶρον	gift				y
S67	Θραικυλίων	466	Θρᾶιξ	Thracian						
S68	Θρᾶιξ	248	Θρᾶιξ	Thracian						
S69	Θρᾶιξ	383	Θρᾶιξ	Thracian						
S70	Θρᾶιξ	390	Θρᾶιξ	Thracian						
S71	Θρᾶιξ	391	Θρᾶιξ	Thracian						
S72	Θρᾶιξ	395	Θρᾶιξ	Thracian						
S73	Θρᾶιξ	406	Θρᾶιξ	Thracian						
S74	Θρασῦλας	474	Θρασύς	bold, spirited, courageous					y	
S75	Ἰατροκλῆς	473	ἰατρός	one who heals, a physician	κλέος	fame	y			
S76	Ἱερόμβροτος	245	ἱερός	mighty, divine; holy	βροτός	mortal man				
S77	Καλλίας	137	κάλλος	beauty			y			
S78	Καλλίστρατος	392	κάλλος	beauty	στρατός	army	y		y	
S79	Καλλίστρατος	454	κάλλος	beauty	στρατός	army	y		y	
S80	Καρίων	119	Κάρ	Karian						
S81	Καρίων	140	Κάρ	Karian						
S82	Καρίων	366	Κάρ	Karian						
S83	Καρίων	403	Κάρ	Karian						

Table 5.2 (*Continued*)

Label	Name	Line No.	1st Element	Definition	2nd Element	Definition	Aristocratic	Civic	Military	Theophoric
S84	Κτίτας	266	κτίζω	found, build						
S85	Κυλίκων	470	κύλιξ	drinking-cup						
S86	Κύρσας	477	unknown	[unknown]						
S87	Λάκων	232	Λάκων	Laconian						
S88	Λυσανίας	471	λύω	loose	ἀνία	grief, sorrow, distress, trouble				
S89	Μάνης	323	Μάνης	(Manes, a Phrygian and Paphlagonian name)						
S90	Μάνης	332	Μάνης	(Manes, a Phrygian and Paphlagonian name)						
S91	Μάνης	405	Μάνης	(Manes, a Phrygian and Paphlagonian name)						
S92	Μάνης	451	Μάνης	(Manes, a Phrygian and Paphlagonian name)						
S93	Μάνης	452	Μάνης	(Manes, a Phrygian and Paphlagonian name)						
S94	Μάνης	472	Μάνης	(Manes, a Phrygian and Paphlagonian name)						
S95	Μάνης	479	Μάνης	(Manes, a Phrygian and Paphlagonian name)						
S96	Μάνη[ς]	328	Μάνης	(Manes, a Phrygian and						
S97	Μάρων	371	Μάρων	(Maron, eponymous hero of Maronia)						y

Table 5.2 (*Continued*)

Label	Name	Line No.	1st Element	Definition	2nd Element	Definition	Aristocratic	Civic	Military	Theophoric
S98	Μίκος	349	μικός	small						
S99	Μύρμηξ	241	μύρμηξ	ant						
S100	Μῦς	231	μῦς	mouse						
S101	Νάδος	453	Ναδυς	(Karian name)						
S102	Ναύσων	275	ναῦς	ship					y	
S103	Νομήνιος	254	νουμήνιος	of, or pertaining to, the new moon						
S104	Νομήνιος	350	νουμήνιος	of, or pertaining to, the new moon						
S105	[Ν]ομήνιος	389	νουμήνιος	of, or pertaining to, the new moon						
S106	Ξάνθιππος	478	ξανθός	yellow, golden	ἵππος	horse	y			
S107	Παντάρκης	237	πανταρκής	all-powerful			y			
S108	Παρμένων	468	παραμένω	remain faithful						
S109	Πα[ρμ]ένων	384	παραμένω	remain faithful						
S110	Παυσανίας	114	παύω	stop	ἀνία	grief, sorrow, distress, trouble				
S111	Πίθηκος	347	πίθηκος	ape; monkey						
S112	Πιστύρας	136	Πιστύρας	(Thracian name)						
S113	Πύρρος	358	πυρρός	with red hair						
S114	Σαρπη[δών]	362	Σαρπηδών	Sarpedon, a hero in the Iliad						y
S115	Σάτυρ[ο]ς	382	Σάτυρος	Satyr						y

Table 5.2 (*Continued*)

Label	Name	Line No.	1st Element	Definition	2nd Element	Definition	Aristocratic	Civic	Military	Theophoric
S116	Σιμία[ς]	259	σῖμος	snub-nosed						
S117	Σιμίας	340	σῖμος	snub-nosed						
S118	Σῖμος	129	σῖμος	snub-nosed						
S119	Σῖμος	463	σῖμος	snub-nosed						
S120	Σῖμος	322	σῖμος	snub-nosed						
S121	Σκύθης	128	Σκύθης	Scythian						
S122	Σπίνθαρος	132	σπινθήρ	spark						
S123	Στρομβιχίδης	272	στρόμβος	spun object; a top						
S125	Σύρος	120	Σύρος	Syrian						
S124	Σύρος	256	Σύρος	Syrian						
S126	Σύρος	399	Σύρος	Syrian						
S127	Σύρος	449	Σύρος	Syrian						
S128	Σύρος	469	Σύρος	Syrian						
S129	Σύρος	475	Σύρος	Syrian						
S130	Σωκράτης	112	σώζω	save	κράτος	strength, might			y	
S131	Σωσίας	334	σώζω	save						
S132	Ταυροσθένης	476	ταῦρος	bull	σθένος	strength, might			y	
S133	Τεῦκρος	121	Τεῦκρος	Teukros, son of Telamon and of Hesione of Salamis; step-brother of Aias						y
S134	Τίβειος	131	Τίβειος	(Paphlagonian name; ?name of a Paphl. people)						

Table 5.2 (*Concluded*)

Label	Name	Line No.	1st Element	Definition	2nd Element	Definition	Aristocratic	Civic	Military	Theophoric
S135	Τίβειος	255	Τίβειος	(Paphlagonian name; ?name of a Paphl. people)						
S136	Τιμαγόρας	134	τιμή	worship, esteem, honour	ἀγορά	assembly, market place	y	y		
S137	Τίμων	341	τιμή	worship, esteem, honour			y			
S138	Τρίβαλλος	115	Τριβαλλοί	the Triballi, a people on the borders of Thrace						
S139	Ὕλας	139	Ὕλας	Hylas, son of Teodamas, king of Mysia, stolen by Herakles and lost on Asian coast by Argonauts						y
S140	Φιλόστρατος	106	φίλος	friend, dear	στρατός	army			y	
S142	Φοῖνιξ	107	Φοῖνιξ	Phoenician						
S141	Φοῖνιξ	274	Φοῖνιξ	Phoenician						
S143	Χάρων	343	Χάρων	mythical ferryman of the Styx						y
S144	Χιωνίδης	461	Χῖος	Chian, from Chios						
S145	Χοιρίλος	138	χοῖρος	young pig, porker						
S146	Ὠφελίων	456	ὠφελέω	help, aid, assist; be of use or service						

PART TWO

Athens from the Outside: The Wider Greek World

Theopompos and the Public Documentation of Fifth-Century Athens*

FRANCES POWNALL

An important target of the fourth-century BC historian Theopompos' often vitriolic *Philippika* was fifth-century Athens, the subject of one of his notorious digressions (*FGrHist* 115 FF 153–6). I do not intend to examine here what can be discerned from it of Theopompos' political views, because Michael Flower has demonstrated convincingly that they are typical of the fourth-century intellectual elite, with a hostility to democracy, a preference for oligarchy, and a partiality for pre-fourth-century Sparta.[1] Instead, I shall argue that Theopompos takes the first critical look at inscriptions as imperialistic documents, for in two of the four preserved fragments from this digression in Book Twenty-Five (and by implication, a third), he buttresses his arguments against the Athenians' pride in their glorious fifth-century past with specific reference to Athenian public documentation. Thus, the exploitation of inscriptions for historical argument did not begin with Aristotle and his successors, as is often stated,[2] but with Theopompos.

Of course, historians prior to Theopompos also cite epigraphical documents but do so infrequently,[3] and, more importantly, without questioning their content. Herodotos makes many references to various monuments but rarely does he quote their inscriptions or give any indications that he has actually seen them for himself.[4] One notable exception is his statement (5.59) that he had seen the 'Kadmeian letters' inscribed on three tripods in the temple of Ismenian Apollo in Boiotian Thebes, commenting that they were 'very similar to letters in the Ionic alphabet' (τὰ πολλὰ ὅμοια ἐόντα τοῖσι 'Ιωνικοῖσι). As M.I. Finley observed, 'Thucydides notoriously failed to make any reference to documents in his statement of method (1.22),'[5] and certainly he makes little use of them in his history, except for his quotation of treaties, particularly in books five and eight – sections of his work considered by many to be largely unrevised.[6] Ironically, modern scholars often use inscriptions to supplement Thucydides' narrative, particularly his sketchy account in the Pentekontaetia of the growth of Athenian imperialism.[7] Xenophon follows in this tradition, with the important exception of his citation of the text of the King's Peace (*Hell.* 5.1.31),[8] later to be considered a shameful blot upon the Hellenic character (Isok. 4.120–1 and 175–80; 12.105–7). Ephoros, the question of whose priority to Theopompos is impossible to determine, cites several epigrams (*FGrHist* 70 F 122 and F 199), taking them at their face value. Androtion, another contemporary of Theopompos, includes summaries of various documents in his *Atthis*, as Phillip Harding himself has shown, but apparently only for the purpose of providing background information.[9]

It is only with Theopompos that a more skeptical attitude towards inscriptions appears. With the possible exception of the citation made purely in passing to an epigram at the temple of Aphrodite in Corinth (F 285), it is especially noteworthy that the extant references to inscriptions occur in the digression in Book Twenty-Five (FF 153–6), where Theopompos casts doubt upon the claims to achievement of fifth-century Athens (and inasmuch as the context for the fragment with the epigram is the participation in the Persian Wars of other, non-Athenian Greek states, it could well have come from this digression also).[10] Although it is unclear what exactly gave him the impetus to digress from his narrative, which at this point has reached the early 340s (F 152 and F 157),[11] it seems probable that Theopompos intended this excursus to be read in connection with an earlier one in Book Ten (FF 85–100), *On the Athenian Demagogues* (Ath. 4.166d = F 100), which was famous enough to have been given its own title in antiquity. In it, Theopompos singles out for attack the Athenian politicians who were most associated with the promotion of the fifth- and fourth-century empires and attributes to them demagoguery and corruption of the people, which led ultimately to their city's utter inability to fend off the threat posed by Philip.[12] From the tenor of the surviving fragments, the digression in Book Twenty-Five appears to be equally polemical in nature.

The largest fragment extant from it is a citation from Theon (*Progymnasmata* 2 = F 153):

παρὰ δὲ Θεοπόμπου ἐκ τῆς πέμπτης καὶ εἰκοστῆς τῶν Φιλιππικῶν, ὅτι ⟨ὁ⟩ Ἑλληνικὸς ὅρκος καταψεύδεται, ὃν Ἀθηναῖοί φασιν ὀμόσαι τοὺς Ἕλληνας πρὸ τῆς μάχης ἐν Πλαταιαῖς πρὸς τοὺς βαρβάρους, καὶ αἱ πρὸς Βασιλέα [Δαρεῖον] Ἀθηναίων [πρὸς Ἕλληνας] συνθῆκαι. ἔτι δὲ καὶ τὴν ἐν Μαραθῶνι μάχην οὐχ οἵαν ἅπαντες ὑμνοῦσι γεγενημένην, 'καὶ ὅσα ἄλλα' φησίν 'ἡ Ἀθηναίων πόλις ἀλαζονεύεται καὶ παρακρούεται τοὺς Ἕλληνας.'

From Theopompos in the twenty-fifth book of the *Philippika,* [there is the account] that the Hellenic oath which the Athenians say the Hellenes swore before the battle at Plataia against the barbarians is falsified, and the treaty of the Athenians with the King. And moreover he says that the battle at Marathon was not such as everyone hymns it to have been, 'and all the other things that the city of Athens brags about and uses to deceive the Hellenes.'

This is a complicated passage, containing what appears to be a paraphrase of Theopompos, followed by a verbatim quotation at the end. For our purposes, it is not necessary to discuss either the textual emendations to this passage,[13] or the question of the historicity of the Oath at Plataia and a fifth-century peace with Persia, notorious *cruces* in the study of Greek history.[14] We can, however, make two observations. First, it is likely that Theopompos actually saw the inscription on public display in the deme of Acharnai purporting to be a transcription of the Oath at Plataia, for the inscribed version claims that *the Athenians* took the oath,[15] while the other literary testimonies (Lyk. 1.80–1; Diod. 11.29.2–4) state that *the Greeks* swore before the battle. By attributing the oath to the Athenians alone, Theopompos reveals that the inscription, rather than the literary tradition, was his source. Likewise, it is worth noting that the fifth-century peace with Persia was publicly inscribed,[16] and it is a logical inference that Theopompos consulted it too. Second, his use of the verb καταψεύδεται, which has a wide range of meanings including falsification rather than outright fabrication, and the phrasing of his concluding sentence indicate that his point is not that these events did not occur,[17] but rather that the Athenian claim to glory in these events in particular is inflated and misleading. The reference to Marathon is especially telling for it, more than any other event of the Persian Wars, reflects the Athenians' systematic rewriting of history in their own favour and is rightly 'regarded as the epitome of the Persian Wars and Athenian imperial power.'[18] It is likely that Theopompos is directing his criticism at the popular version of the Persian Wars and their aftermath found in the Attic orators, who exaggerate the role of Athens in unifying the Greek resistance and punishing the barbarians and their sympathizers and downplay the contributions of other states.[19]

When we turn to the next two fragments extant from this digression, we find the only surviving argument of Theopompos against the details of the fifth-century peace with Persia as recorded in Athenian public documentation. F 154 is a citation from Harpokration (s.v. Ἀττικοῖς γράμμασιν)

... Θεόπομπος δ' ἐν τῇ κε τῶν Φιλππικῶν ἐσκευωρῆσθαι λέγει τὰς πρὸς τὸν βάρβαρον συνθήκας, ἃς οὐ τοῖς 'Αττικοῖς γράμμασιν ἐστηλιτεῦσθαι, ἀλλὰ τοῖς τῶν 'Ιώνων.[20]

... Theopompos says in the twenty-fifth book of his *Philippika* that the treaty with the barbarian has been falsified, as it is inscribed not in Attic letters, but in Ionic ones.

F 155 (Photios and the Souda, s.v. Σαμίων ὁ δῆμος) adds little new information:

... τοὺς δὲ 'Αθηναίους ἔπεισε χρῆσθαι τοῖς τῶν 'Ιώνων γράμμασιν 'Αρχῖνος [δ' 'Αθηναίοις] ἐπὶ ἄρχοντος Εὐκλείδου ... περὶ δὲ τοῦ πείσαντος ἱστρορεῖ Θεόπομπος.

... Archinos persuaded the Athenians to use the Ionic alphabet in the archonship of Eukleides [403/2] ... and Theopompos writes about the one who persuaded them.

Thus we learn that Theopompos objected to at least some of the details of a fifth-century peace with Persia recorded in the public documentation in Athens on the grounds that it was inscribed in the Ionic alphabet, officially introduced to Athens in 403/2, and not the older Attic script. It is possible, though of course this suggestion can remain only in the realm of speculation, that Theopompos was inspired in his judgment based on letter shapes by his knowledge of Herodotos (whose work he epitomized),[21] who commented, as we have seen, on the resemblance of the 'Kadmeian letters' at Thebes to the Ionic alphabet. While this particular argument (he may well have had others) based on the letter forms is not a conclusive one, in that occasional examples of the use of Ionic script in Attic documents prior to 403/2 have been found,[22] it does show that Theopompos examined the inscription with an unwillingness to accept its contents at face value. As was the case with καταψεύδεται in F 153, the verb ἐσκευωρῆσθαι contains a wide range of meanings varying from outright fabrication to falsification in some way,[23] and so once again it is likely that Theopompos is objecting to some of the details on the public inscription. Furthermore, he is our only source for the information that Archinos proposed the motion to adopt the Ionic alphabet in 403/2; this statement reveals not only that he examined both inscriptions, but also more importantly that he used one epigraphical document to call into question the details of another. Theopompos was evidently familiar enough with the archives at Athens to use public documentation comparatively as well as critically.[24]

While there are no references to epigraphical material in the final fragment extant from the digression on fifth-century Athens (F 156), the fragment does provide some clues as to the digression's contents. A scholiast to Aristophanes' *Birds* (556) records:

καλεῖται δὲ ἱερὸς (sc. ὁ πόλεμος), ὅτι περὶ τοῦ ἐν Δελφοῖς ἱεροῦ ἐγένετο. ἱστορεῖ περὶ αὐτοῦ καὶ Θουκυδίδης καὶ Ἐρατοσθένης ἐν τῷ θ̄ καὶ Θεόπομπος ἐν τῷ κε̄.

It is called 'sacred' because it took place over the sanctuary at Delphi. Thucydides writes about it, as do Eratosthenes in Book Nine, and Theopompos in Book Twenty-Five.

This passage makes it clear that Theopompos included in this digression a discussion of the fifth-century Sacred War,[25] a minor incident of sabre-rattling between Athens and Sparta that occurred just after Kimon's expedition to Cyprus and death (Thuc. 1.112.5). The inclusion of material on the Athenians' fifth-century aspirations for land empire reveals that Theopompos extended his criticism in the digression in Book Twenty-Five to their imperialism in general, thereby furthering his arguments in the digression on the demagogues in Book Ten.

We can perhaps infer more about Theopompos' criticism of the Athenians for their role in the fifth-century Sacred War if we examine the context for another digression, the *Wonders* (*Thaumasia*), in Book Eight (FF 64–76). From the relatively lengthy fragments extant from it, it is clear that the common element of the various wonders collected in this digression is the importance of pious behaviour, particularly with respect to portents and prophecies, and it seems likely, as Gordon Shrimpton suggests, that its connection to the rest of the *Philippika* is the Delphic oracle.[26] The point of departure for an excursus on Delphi and other oracular material at this point in Theopompos' narrative, which has apparently reached the mid 350s (the context for the comment on Byzantion in F 62 is likely to be the Social War), is Philip's entry into the so-called Third Sacred War, especially inasmuch as another fragment from Book Eight (F 63) discusses the composition of the Amphiktyonic League. Theopompos was clearly interested in this conflict, not only because it provided a means for Philip to become directly involved in the affairs of central and southern Greece, but also because of its moral implications. In a work entitled *On the Funds Plundered from Delphi* (FF 247–9) (it is unclear whether this was a different work altogether or a section from the *Philippika* that was circulated separately in antiquity), Theopompos gives a detailed list of the ironically fitting retributions suffered by the Phokian commanders and their supporters for their plundering of the sanctuary at Delphi (F 248). Because Philip's pretext for intervening in the Sacred War was explicitly to avenge these insults to Apollo,[27] the purpose of the *Thaumasia* is likely to have been to provide examples of those who are truly pious in order to demonstrate how Philip was using piety as an excuse to further his own political ends. If so, then Theopompos' inclusion of the fifth-century Sacred War in the digression in Book Twenty-Five undoubtedly had a similar purpose, to deflate any Athenian claims to piety in a conflict in which religious obligations served only as a convenient pretext for political and imperialistic aims.[28]

As the four fragments extant from this digression reveal, Theopompos criticizes the Athenians not only for inflating their claims to achievement against the Persians, but also for their imperialistic activities in the fifth century. In doing so, Theopompos is the first ancient historian to draw the connection between Athenian public documentation and imperialism (to my knowledge, this point has not been observed before). Moreover, he is obviously targeting the popular tradition of Athens' salvation of Greece in the Persian Wars and idealization of the fifth-century empire, the source of which, as we have seen above, is the oratorical tradition. It is clear from the digression *On the Demagogues* and his portrayal of Demosthenes, in which, as I have argued elsewhere, he presents him as a demagogue to Athens' ultimate detriment,[29] that Theopompos viewed the Athenian orators as corrupt and power-hungry agents of imperialism, who used the power of speech to manipulate the masses. As Lisa Kallet-Marx has argued convincingly, the necessity of empire for the democracy was an important ideological motif created and fostered by the Athenian *rhētores*.[30] Given Theopompos' attitude to the fifth-century empire, the Athenian orators, and democracy itself, it is likely that he is particularly reacting against the role of the *rhētōr* in this connection. It is surely no coincidence that by the third quarter of the fourth century, around the time that Theopompos was composing his *Philippika*,[31] Aischines systematically began to mine the public records in Athens to promote his demagogic rhetoric, as Rosalind Thomas has demonstrated.[32] Likewise, it is surely no coincidence either that by the mid-fourth century, most of the ten 'cardinal virtues' identified by David Whitehead as most significant to the Athenian democracy are present on honorific inscriptions,[33] indicating an increased awareness of the usefulness of public documentation to promote democratic ideology.[34] By his critical interpretation of Athenian inscriptions as imperialistic documents, Theopompos attempts to show that they are yet another method of propaganda of the democracy, exploited by the orators in particular.

Although the association between epigraphy and empire may seem self-evident, given the rapid increase in the production of inscriptions from the

450s onwards (the heyday of the Athenian empire) and the sheer monumentality of the inscriptions from the mid-fifth century in particular,[35] it seems to have gone unnoticed in the historiographical tradition before Theopompos. Of his predecessors and contemporaries, even those such as Thucydides, Xenophon, or Ephoros, whose attitude to democracy and imperialism was at best ambivalent, if not outright hostile, made little use of inscriptions. It was not until Theopompos, who left no stone unturned in his condemnation of Athens' imperial past – in antiquity he was characterized as a lover of the truth who spared no expense on the accurate investigation of his history[36] – that a critical examination of Athenian inscriptions as imperialistic documents was introduced into the realm of historiography.

Notes

* I am pleased to offer this contribution in honour of Phillip Harding, to whom I owe my interest in both epigraphy and fourth-century historiography as a neophyte graduate student at the University of British Columbia in the mid-1980s.

1 Flower 1994: 63–97; see also Pownall 2004: chap. 5.

2 E.g., Thomas 1989: 90–1; Higbie 1999.

3 As noted by, e.g., Finley 1985a and 1985b; Thomas 1989: 90. On the use of documentary evidence by ancient historians up to Philochorus, see Higbie 1999: 54–65 (with no discussion of fourth-century historians prior to Theopompos) and Sickinger 1999: 176–82.

4 *Pace* Fehling 1989 and West 1985, the lack of indication of autopsy does not indicate that Herodotos had any intention to deceive; see Pritchett 1993.

5 Finley 1985a: 15.

6 See, e.g., Gomme, Andrewes, and Dover 1981: Appendices 1 and 2; and Hornblower 1987: chap. 6; for an opposing view, Connor 1984: esp. 144–7 and Appendix 4.

7 See, e.g., Meiggs 1972: 18–22; Davies 1978: 76–98.

8 And failed even to cite that in full, if we are to infer with George Cawkwell (1979: 254) from Isokrates 4.120 that the terms were more detailed than Xenophon indicates.

9 Harding 1994: 36–8 and 43–4; Sickinger 1999: 179–82.

10 As suggested by Connor 1968: 97.

11 Jacoby (*FGrHist* IIC: 380), citing Schwartz, suggests that claims similar to those in this digression were made in the Athenian speeches about Olynthos.

12 Connor 1968 and Pownall 2004: chap. 5.

13 For discussion of the various proposed emendations, see Connor 1968: 78–81.

14 On the Oath of Plataia and other alleged fourth-century forgeries, see Habicht

1961 and Robertson 1976. On a fifth-century peace with Persia, see Badian 1993 (with earlier bibliography); Cawkwell 1997; and Samons 1998.

15 Rhodes-Osborne no. 88; Siewert 1972: 5–7.

16 This is the implication of Isokrates' comment at 4.20, as noted by Thomas 1989: 86 n. 234.

17 So Connor 1968: 81–9.

18 Thomas 1989: 224–6 (quotation from 225); cf. Walters 1981; Loraux, 1986: 155–71 (who reads political implications into the glorification of Marathon at the expense of Salamis).

19 The Athenian version of the Persian Wars can be seen already in Thucydides in the Athenian speech to the Peloponnesian League prior to the outbreak of the Peloponnesian War (1ines 73–8). On the Athenians' sanitation of the more unpleasant aspects of their fifth-century empire, see Chambers 1975 and Pownall 2004: chap. 2.

20 For a discussion of the proposed textual emendations to this passage, see Connor 1968: 89–91.

21 T 1 and FF 1–4; for the suggestion that the epitome was not a separate work but part of the *Philippika*, see Christ 1993.

22 Woodhead 1981: 18–19 and n. 11.

23 Connor 1968: 91–2.

24 The city archive in the Metroon was established at the end of the fifth century; see Thomas 1989: 38–45 and 68–83; Sickinger 1999: esp. chapters 4 and 5. For documents of the mid-fifth century, Theopompos could have visited the stelai on public display, or consulted the earlier archives in the Bouleuterion. As Sickinger notes (92): 'Had the preservation of archival texts of decrees throughout the fifth century been wholly haphazard and disorderly, Krateros could hardly have filled the nine books attested for his work.'

25 On the nomenclature, see Pownall 1998.

26 Shrimpton 1991: 19–20.

27 See esp. Justin 8.2.3 with Pownall 1998.

28 Cf. Connor (1968: 96 and n. 52), who does not, however, draw the connection to Theopompos' similar criticism of Philip's claim to piety in the Third Sacred War.

29 Pownall 2002.

30 Kallet-Marx 1994, esp. 246–51; *pace* Ober 1989, that the orators reflect the ideology of the people.

31 For a review of the very sketchy evidence for Theopompos' life, see Flower 1994: chap. 1.

32 Thomas 1989: 69–71.

33 Whitehead 1993.

34 On the complex relationship between the Athenian 'epigraphical habit' (for they

certainly erected more inscriptions by far than any other contemporary Greek state) and democratic ideology, see Hedrick, Jr. 1994; 1999; and 2000.

35 See, e.g., *ATL* esp. the physical dimensions of the stelai in the first volume, and Hedrick 1999: 399–400.

36 T 28 = Athenaios 3.85a: ἀνδρὸς φιλαλήθους καὶ πολλὰ χρήματα καταναλώσαντος εἰς τὴν περὶ τῆς ἱστορίας ἐξέτασιν ἀκριβῆ ...

References

Badian, E. 1993. 'The Peace of Callias,' in *From Plataea to Potidaea: Studies in the History and Historiography of the Pentecontaetia*, 1–72. Baltimore and London.

Cawkwell, G.L. 1979. 'Introduction' and 'Notes,' in R. Warner (trans.), *Xenophon: A History of My Times (Hellenica)*. Harmondsworth, England.

– 1997. 'The Peace Between Athens and Persia.' *Phoenix* 51: 115–30.

Chambers, J.T. 1975. 'The Fourth-Century Athenians' View of Their Fifth-Century Empire.' *PP* 30: 177–91.

Christ, M.R. 1993. 'Theopompus and Herodotus: A Reassessment.' *CQ* n.s. 43: 47–52.

Connor, W.R. 1968. *Theopompus and Fifth-Century Athens*. Washington, DC.

– 1984. *Thucydides*. Princeton.

Davies, J.K. 1978. *Democracy and Classical Greece*. Glasgow.

Fehling, D. 1989. *Herodotus and His 'Sources': Citation, Invention, and Narrative Art*, trans. J.G. Howie. Leeds.

Finley, M.I. 1985a. 'The Ancient Historian and His Sources,' in *Ancient History: Evidence and Models*, 7–26. London.

– 1985b. 'Documents,' in *Ancient History: Evidence and Models*, 27–47. London.

Flower, M.A. 1994. *Theopompus of Chios: History and Rhetoric in the Fourth Century BC*. Oxford.

Gomme, A.W., A. Andrewes, and K.J. Dover. 1981. *A Historical Commentary on Thucydides*, vol. 5. Oxford.

Habicht, C. 1961. 'False Urkunden zur Geschichte Athens im Zeitalter der Perserkrieg.' *Hermes* 89: 1–35.

Harding, P. 1994. *Androtion and the* Atthis. Oxford.

Hedrick, C.W. 1994. 'Writing, Reading, and Democracy,' in R. Osborne and S. Hornblower (eds), *Ritual, Finance, Politics: Athenian Democratic Accounts Presented to David Lewis*, 157–74. Oxford.

– 1999. 'Democracy and the Athenian Epigraphical Habit.' *Hesperia* 68: 387–439.

– 2000. 'Epigraphic Writing and the Democratic Restoration of 307,' in P. Flensted-Jensen, T.H. Nielsen and L. Rubinstein (eds), *Polis and Politics: Studies in Ancient Greek History*, 327–35. Copenhagen.

Higbie, C. 1999. 'Craterus and the Use of Inscriptions in Ancient Scholarship.' *TAPA* 129: 43–83.

Hornblower, S. 1987. *Thucydides*. London.

Kallet-Marx, L. 1994. 'Money Talks: Rhetor, Demos, and the Resources of the Athenian Empire,' in R. Osborne and S. Hornblower (eds), *Ritual, Finance, Politics: Athenian Democratic Accounts Presented to David Lewis*, 227–51. Oxford.

Loraux, N. 1986. *The Invention of Athens: The Funeral Oration in the Classical City*, trans. Alan Sheridan. Cambridge, MA and London.

Meiggs, R. 1972. *The Athenian Empire*. Oxford.

Ober, J. 1989. *Mass and Elite in Democratic Athens*. Princeton.

Pownall, F. 1998. 'What Makes a War a Sacred War?' *EMC/CV* 17: 35–55.

– 2002. 'Theopompus' View of Demosthenes,' in M. Joyal (ed.), *In Altum: Seventy-Five Years of Classical Studies in Newfoundland*, 63–71. S. John's, NL.

– 2004. *Lessons From the Past: The Moral Use of History in Fourth-Century Prose*. Ann Arbor.

Pritchett, W.K. 1993. *The Liar School of Herodotus*. Amsterdam.

Robertson, N. 1976. 'False Documents at Athens: Fifth-Century History and Fourth-Century Publicists.' *Historical Reflections* 3: 3–25.

Samons, L.J., II. 1998. 'Kimon, Kallias and Peace with Persia.' *Historia* 47: 129–40.

Shrimpton, G.S. 1991. *Theopompus the Historian*. Montreal and Kingston.

Sickinger, J.P. 1999. *Public Records and Archives in Classical Athens*. Chapel Hill and London.

Siewert, P. 1972. *Der Eid von Plataiai*. Munich.

Thomas, R. 1989. *Oral Tradition and Written Record in Classical Athens*. Cambridge.

Walters, K.R. 1981. '"We Fought Alone at Marathon": Historical Falsification in the Attic Funeral Oration.' *RhM* 124: 206–11

West, S. 1985. 'Herodotus' Epigraphical Interests.' *CQ* 35: 278–305.

Whitehead, D. 1993. 'Cardinal Virtues: The Language of Public Approbation in Democratic Athens.' *C&M* 44: 37–75.

Woodhead, A.G. 1981 (1992). *The Study of Greek Inscriptions*[2]. Cambridge (repr. Norman, OK).

Horton Hears an Ionian*

GORDON SHRIMPTON

And down on the dust speck, the scared little Mayor
Quick called a big meeting in Who-ville Town Square.
And his people cried loudly. They cried out in fear:
'We are here! We are here! We are here! We are here!'

Horton Hears a Who! Dr Seuss

Work on fourth-century BC documents has been greatly aided thanks to the edition and translation of many of them produced by this Festchrift's worthy honorand. Naturally, Phillip Harding's edition included the decree of Aristoteles, the 'charter' of the Second Athenian League (Harding no. 35). Recently, Sheila Ager concluded a study of this decree, with the following remark: 'Much of the instinctual rationale for ejecting the Theraian *dēmos* from *IG* ii 43 (and for seeking Athenocentric Cyrenaean motivations behind *SEG* ix 3) originates in an outmoded tendency to view history only in the context of the big players.'[1]

The subject of this essay is not the decree of Aristoteles itself, however, but the idea that Ager brings out in her remark that lesser-known – marginalized – people tend to disappear from the view of the historian in favour of subjects more central to the historical enterprise. In particular I wish to call attention to some of the people included in the League, particularly the Ionians, and to suggest that there is a sort of perspectival bias that tends to give them a low level of visibility, a bias that comes indeed from many of our ancient sources themselves. The point of view of writers like Thucydides and Xenophon was often Athenocentric, or at least (in Xenophon's case) oriented towards the mainland and away from Ionia and the Aegean islands.

Herodotos, too, despite his origin on the fringe of Ionia proper, addressed a war whose decisive battles were fought on the Greek mainland, against Persia on the face of things, but against Ionia too, in a way, because the Ionians were willy-nilly included in the invading forces of 480–479.[2] In later antiquity, Plutarch gave us many precious references to comments made by non-Athenians, but always in the context of a mainland subject, usually an Athenian. As a result, the information he provides is stripped of its context and difficult to interpret.

Who Were the Ionians?

A problem arises as soon as one tries to define 'Ionia.' The ancients themselves seem to have recognized more than one 'Ionia,' depending on whether one looked at the question from the point of view of (say) an Athenian or a Samian. My strategy will be to focus on the eastern Ionians and show who these people were to various onlookers, particularly in the sixth century (but in the fifth and fourth to some extent also), when people bearing, or given, the name of Ionians were a considerable force in the Eastern Mediterranean. In other words, while no satisfactory definition of 'Ionian' is likely to emerge from this study, I hope to bring out a picture of an energetic, cultured community on the Asiatic coast and the eastern and Cycladic islands that was the true 'education of Hellas' (to steal a phrase) long before Athens came to ascendancy.

Some time early in the archaic period a group of twelve cities (the Dodekapolis: Miletos, Myos, Priene, Ephesos, Kolophon, Lebedos, Teos, Klazomenai, Phokaia, Samos, Chios, and Erythrai) canonized themselves as 'the Ionians.' At first it was an ethnic and religious community with no apparent political organization or mission. It held regular meetings at a shrine to Poseidon called the Panionion on the promontory of Mykale, a place that is near the southern extremity of the region dominated by these member cities, where traces of an altar, presumably to Poseidon, have been found. The geographical centre of 'the Ionians' (i.e., the Dodekapolis) was actually Teos.[3] As need arose, with the advance of Persia particularly, meetings between the states were held to discuss matters of political and military urgency.

Herodotos (1.141–8, 170; 6.7–18) describes the Ionians as a group of cities or communities speaking diverse languages or dialects and somewhat lacking in cohesion, but in sufficient communication to hold meetings at the Panionion. In other words, these (eastern) Ionians attempted to define themselves by establishing a community of cult practice dedicated to Poseidon. There was another cult centre for the Ionians at large, however, on the island of Delos where they worshipped, among other divinities, Apollo and Artemis. I shall give the greater part of my attention to Delos because that island was destined to become the meeting place of the Athenian-led Delian League in the fifth century. Before the fifth century it may have had geographical significance for defining the territory of what might be called 'Greater Ionia.' If the Panionion was the religious focus of the eastern community, was Delos seen by them as a *limes*?

I shall return to Delos in a moment, but first a few remarks about the eastern Ionians. Attempts to give them an ethnic identity go back at least to the fifth century. Herodotos understood well the criteria by which an ancient community could establish its identity: 'common blood, common language, shared religious practice, and common customs' (8.144). For the Ionians he implicitly or explicitly supplies two, more narrow sets of criteria: the Ionians were, properly speaking, the peoples who met and worshipped Poseidon at the Panionion; otherwise, they were colonists from Athens and all celebrated the Apatouria.[4] He sets out these criteria more with a view to scrutinizing than endorsing them. He criticizes his contemporaries, who wanted to exclude this or that state from the Panionion on the grounds of ethnic purity, by showing the extent of racial mixing that had taken place in all the states that occupied the eastern Aegean. The concept of Ionic racial purity was entirely fictive in his eyes. Even the Apatouria becomes a problematical benchmark considering the fact that the Ephesians and Kolophonians no longer celebrated that festival.

On the face of things, Herodotos does not include Delos in his discussion of Ionian identity. This is remarkable because he cannot have been unaware of the significance of the island to the Ionian past. Philip Stadter points out, however, that he seems to use Delos to demarcate the boundary between the eastern and western parts of the Aegean.[5] It may be that in the eyes of the eastern Ionians, at least, Greece was divided into two sacred regions from archaic times, one around a shrine to Apollo in the west, the other around a shrine to Poseidon in the east, with another sacred precinct of Apollo dividing the two worlds. The western group had Delphi as its focus, around which the famous Delphic Amphiktiony was formed. Though this Amphiktiony had seats for 'Ionians,' the claimants came from Athens or from one or another of various Euboian cities. Apart from a puzzling reference to Priene in Aischines (2.116), there is no evidence that the Cyclades or Asia sent delegates to the Amphiktionic council at Delphi.[6]

Despite the manifest importance of Delphi, Delos was the birthplace of Apollo. The Homeric Hymn to Delian Apollo describes the Ionian festival held on the island (lines 147–64). It seems that this festival had lapsed during the empire, for Thucydides notes that the Athenians purified Delos in the winter of 426/5 and celebrated 'the quadrennial Delia for the first time after the purification' (3.104.2). Gallet de Santerre thought it possible that the earlier festival, going back into archaic times, was annual rather than quadrennial and celebrated in the spring.[7]

The Hymn describes Delos as having a hard, rocky soil (line 72) and few inhabitants (line 78). Everything of importance, right down to the pottery found on the island, had to be imported.[8] Athenian interest in Delos was evident throughout the archaic period,[9] but Delos seems to have had eastern sources of wealth from the earliest times. As far back as the thirteenth century BC, ivories had come to the island from such places as Megiddo and Ras Shamra, probably via Cyprus.[10] Importation of bronzes began after the middle of the eighth century after a long hiatus of significant contact with the outside world. Some imports of quality derived from the orient; nothing came from the Peloponnese.[11] From a detailed study of Ionic column capitals found on the island, Roland Martin found evidence for close contact with Naxos in the first half of the sixth century but later, increased influence from Samos and the Milesian coast.[12] The Samian preoccupation with Delos is probably to be associated with the activities of Polykrates (below), but in a larger context, one might think of the Ionians of the east cultivating their sacred foci more attentively in the face of aggression from Lydia and, more significantly, Persia as the century wore on.[13]

As a sacred focus of Ionia, Delos attracted the attention of Athens, which claimed to be the mother city of the Ionians. Solon called Athens 'the greatest city of Ionia.'[14] Both Herodotos (1.64) and Thucydides (3.104.1) tell us that Peisistratos purified the island. Not many years after Peisistratos, however, Polykrates took the island of Rhenea (the larger island to the west of Delos) and attached it to Delos with a chain to make it part of the sacred precinct, in effect. There is reason to believe that he extensively reorganized the festival at this time, a step that the Peisistratids must have seen as an affront. Polykrates expected an attack from a Spartan-Corinthian alliance. His purpose in meddling with Delos, therefore, was probably to organize and secure his western frontier.[15]

The likely date for Polykrates' intervention was 525/4, scarcely a year or two before his death. He was not around for long, therefore, to enforce his new arrangements, but they may have lasted nevertheless, because the Peisistratids, now under Hippias, do not seem to have been as aggressive as their father, and the regime was soon to become preoccupied with the reign of terror after the assassination of Hipparchos. Some circumstantial evidence suggests that the easterners did maintain Delos as a boundary between east and west rather than as the heart of Ionia, as the Athenians, no doubt, would have preferred. I have already pointed out Stadter's demonstration that Herodotos saw the island this way. Further, if Galette de Santerre is right about the archaic festival – that it was celebrated each spring rather than quadrennially – then the eastern Ionians were using Delos as a 'non-urban' sanctuary, which, if we believe Francois de Polignac's theory, places it at or near their border.[16]

The Greeks called the Persians 'Medes,' just as the Persians and other oriental nations called the Greeks 'Ionians.'[17] Of course, oriental sources, consisting of inscriptions and tomb reliefs, were never too particular in their views of foreign ethnicity. Sancisi-Weerdenburg points out how Persian reliefs blended Greeks, Karians, and Lydians in their pictorial references to the 'Hellenic world.'[18] Nevertheless, when the 'Greeks' first encountered people from the heart of Iran, those people were apparently calling themselves Medes, which must have been before ca. 560 and the rise of Kyros. Those 'Greeks,' for their part, were apparently calling themselves Ionians, a name by which Greeks were known throughout the Near East from as early as the seventh century.

Herodotos describes the first confrontations of Asiatic Greek city-states with non-Greek powers in his book one. Kroisos, he says, was the first of the barbarians to reduce some Greeks to tributary status and make alliances with others (1.6), though in fact, his predecessors had been attacking parts of Ionia before him. Mellink comments: 'It was very evident to every Lydian king from Gyges on that the Ionians and Karians had to be made into constructive allies as seafaring merchants and soldiers.'[19] But as useful as they may have been for their seafaring and soldiering skills, the Lydians at times coveted Ionian land more than their skills, for Roebuck pointed out long ago that territorial pressure from the inland peoples was a major cause of Ionian colonizing activity in the archaic period.[20]

To the Persians they were known as Yauna, and I have already noted their appearance on Persian inscriptions and reliefs. 'Greeks,' (i.e., Yauna) as Sancisi-Weerdenberg remarks, 'are mentioned together with the Carians as the peoples who brought the cedar timber from Babylon to Susa'(to build Darius' palace). The stonecutters for the palace were Greeks and Lydians and ornamentation was brought from Ionia.[21] The Assyrians called the Greeks Yaman. As early as 694, Sennacherib had 'Ionian' and Phoenician sailors under his command at Nineveh.[22] In the case of the Persians, their term Yauna corresponds generally to the Greeks who were incorporated into their empire. In other words, it does refer roughly to the Asiatic Greeks and nearby islanders.[23] The Assyrians, however, did not have quite the same relationship to the Greeks. So it seems wise to avoid hasty assumptions about the precise origin of the 'Yaman' with whom they dealt.

Towards the end of the seventh century, Greek involvement in the disputes of the Near East seems to have become fairly significant. In many cases, particularly where Egypt was involved, it can be stated with confidence that the Greeks in question came from Ionia or 'Greater Ionia' if places like Rhodes, for example, can reasonably be included in such a coinage. The brother of the poet Alkaios served as a mercenary for the Babylonians. The occasion was probably the battle between Nebuchadrezzar and Pharaoh Necho at Carchemish in 605.[24] A Greek shield was found on the site of the battle, and Boardman suggests that the Greek who lost it could have been fighting on the Egyptian side. He points to evidence of a possible Greek settlement near Ashdod, perhaps a frontier garrison left there by Necho after the battle.[25]

When we come to Egypt, we have more and better information. That Naukratis was primarily an eastern Greek settlement is affirmed by Herodotos (2.135, 178 [where the only non-eastern city is Aigina]) and is generally supported by the sixth-century pottery found there. From about 600, Boardman notes the likely presence of Chians as well as Samians and Milesians on the evidence of pottery finds, and, as we might expect, Egyptian contacts with Cyprus and Rhodes are clearly evident.[26] Pottery alone, however, cannot tell the whole story. Corinthian vases are also represented, as are Athenian and Spartan, but literary evidence does not testify to a strong Corinthian or Athenian, much less a Spartan, presence in the Delta during the sixth century. Again, Herodotos mentions Egyptian use of Greek mercenaries (2.153–4). In particular, in 1.163 he reports 30,000 Ionian and Karian mercenaries in service to Apries (ca. 570). He tells of fortresses at the frontier town of Tell Defenneh (Daphnai) as well as other sites (2.30). Daphnai, Memphis, and Thebes yield pottery evidence of a Greek presence. The pottery finds throughout Egypt seem to suggest a preponderance of eastern Greek styles and interests, but other wares such as Athenian are also found. In 591 Greeks and Karians joined the Egyptians as mercenaries in an invasion of Nubia. Many scratched their names on Egyptian monuments at Abu Simbel.[27] The Greeks who identify their places of origin were from Teos, Kolophon, and Ialysos (on Rhodes).[28]

The Education of Hellas

Places like Corinth, Chalkis, Rhodes, and the Cyclades were sending out colonies before the Ionians, but this does not necessarily mean that the eastern Greeks lagged seriously behind their western relatives in cultural development.[29] Whatever the reasons for Greek colonization, there is little doubt that the scattering of Greek establishments from Egypt to the Black Sea and from Ras Shamra to Marseilles gave the Greeks access to the vast and varied resources of the Mediterranean littoral. The Greek communities on the Asiatic shore, however, had rich resources closer to hand. They were usually situated on fertile coastal plains and had direct access to the peoples of the Asiatic hinterland. This was especially true of Lydia, which was fabulous for its wealth.

There was general agreement in the ancient world that Homer, the poet heard, read, and memorized by all educated Greeks, hailed from somewhere in or near Ionia. Chios and Smyrna are the places most frequently mentioned. The compilation of the Homeric epics was a great achievement, but it would have been all for naught without the alphabet to give it permanence. In a puzzling passage (5.58), Herodotos claims Ionian agency for this momentous contribution to the development of Greek civilization. Recently, Giuseppe Nenci has explained the passage and defended Herodotos' claim.[30]

Whether or not we believe that the Ionians introduced the alphabet to Greece, they led the way in exploring its full potential. The tradition of Milesian philosophers from Thales to Anaximenes is well known. But it is well to remember that other intellectuals from the sixth century were also Ionian. Xenophanes was from Kolophon, and Herakleitos was an Ephesian. Even Pythagoras, who has strong associations with Kroton in the west, was believed by some to have been born on Samos during the reign of Polykrates.[31] These intellectuals showed a keen interest in the phenomenal world and a passion for finding theoretical explanations for their observations.

Hekataios the mythographer and geographer, the first we can name in a tradition of *logopoioi*, hailed from Miletos also. After noting an absence of politically oriented traditions from Ionia, Oswyn Murray comments: 'This absence must be related as symptom or cause to the fact that it was from Ionia that the *logopoios*, the maker of tales, emerged, as the demotic counterpart in prose to the aristocratic epic poetry.'[32] 'Making tales' was an Ionic trademark. I have pointed out elsewhere that historical writing in all its major sub-genres emanated from the eastern side of the Aegean. Even the Athenians had to learn how to write their own history from Hellanikos, who hailed from Lesbos.[33] In the lyric age, nearly all parts of the Greek world were well represented. From the eastern side of the Aegean we have three great names: Sappho and Alkaios of Lesbos, and Anakreon of Teos. This brings me to a curious fact, the implications of which seem provocative. A full century or more after the Ionians had begun to explore and develop the potential of the alphabet for poetry – both epic and lyric – and prose, the Athenians, late in the fifth century, were putting the alphabet on the comic stage as if they regarded it as a bizarre new technology – not unlike the presence of the automobile in the silent films of the last century.[34]

I mentioned the Milesian philosophers. Philosophical wisdom was not the only kind in which the easterners made a worthy contribution to Greek culture. Plato gives an apparently canonical list of seven 'sages' (*Prt.* 343a). These people all lived in the early sixth century. Three are from the mainland (with one each from Athens and Sparta) and four are easterners.[35] It might be tempting to grant the Ionians the palm for literature and ideas, but still dismiss them as impractical theoreticians. When it comes to real progress in the pragmatic world of politics, we might say, the Athenians and their democracy were the unquestioned leaders. We should like to know more about early Ionian political sophistication, but Herodotos did not believe that democracy was an Athenian invention.

In fact, the most exemplary would-be democratic reformer in Herodotos' eyes was not Kleisthenes of Athens but Maiandrios of Samos (3.142–3). He called the whole citizen body together in assembly, deplored the tyranny of Polykrates, who had just been lured to his death on the mainland by Oroites, and offered to give the Samians *isonomia*. The attempt proved abortive, but clearly Herodotos believed that a government that gave all citizens equality before the law and differed from both tyranny and oligarchy was a concept known to the Samians about twenty years before Kleisthenes. There is a sadly fragmentary inscription from Chios, which dates from the second quarter of the sixth century. It is a law that confers the right of a citizen to 'appeal to the Council of the people (the *dēmosiē boulē*).'[36] These words along with other more fragmentary parts of the inscription testify to a strong democratic element in the Chian constitution in the early sixth century.[37]

With respect to the plastic arts, the development of a sophisticated order of architecture is impossible without the basic skills of surveying and engineering. When the eastern Greeks created theirs (the Ionic), they drew on oriental motifs to refine an order that combined elegance with practicality.[38] Corinth and Athens led the way in vase decoration, but in sculpture some of the earliest and best examples, though found on Delos, evidently derive from Naxos.[39]

It is tempting to think that the Athenian Empire changed all this, that it impoverished and demoralized the Ionians by its demands for tribute and its interference in local politics.[40] A recent article by Robin Osborne, however, puts these notions in considerable doubt.[41] The enquiring mind of the eastern Greek did not fall dormant. The fifth century saw the development and flourishing of *historiē*, first in the work of Herodotos and then with the emergence of the Hippocratic corpus.[42] In fact, the eastern city-states showed a resilience and energy that lasted well into Hellenistic times.[43] There is no denying, however, that when it came time for Greece to respond to the challenge of Persian expansion, the Ionians were Greece's first line of defence, and that line did not hold. The result was a lost opportunity for freedom, the exchange of one master, Persia, for another, Athens.

The Aftermath of Lade

Simon Hornblower recently declared that the Persian War 'gave the Greeks their identity,' and I suppose that is true in a geopolitical sense.[44] From a cultural perspective, however, I think it is not true. The Ionians had already done that. Geopolitically, the war simply realigned power structures in such a way as to remove any possibility that Ionia would ever enjoy its old prestige. The chain of events was relatively simple. In response to the Persian threat the Athenians equipped themselves with a large fleet, which gave backbone to Greek resistance in two major sea battles: Artemision and Salamis, both fought in 480 under Spartan command. After 479 and the Greek victory at Plataia, the allied mainland forces pursued the Persians into the Aegean, but tentatively at first. Soon the Aegean states were in revolt from Persia and turned to Athens for support. The Spartans, only nominal commanders of the alliance by now, soon withdrew, leaving maritime operations to the Athenians and their new Aegean allies. The Athenians, with their newfound sea-fighting experience, claimed the hegemony, and the allies established Delos as the meeting place of their new league. So Delos now became the heart of this newly 'unified' Ionian community.

Later in the fifth century, of course, the Delian League became the Athenian Empire and it was during that time that Herodotos of Halikarnassos was researching and writing his history. But none of this would have happened quite this way if the Ionians had won the battle of Lade in 494. The Ionian defeat at Lade, the disastrous culmination of the Ionian revolt from Persia, meant that Persian encroachment on Greek territory would not be stopped on the Asiatic side of the Aegean. It also meant that no direct and full history of this period would be recorded beyond the sparse and rather incriminating account found in Herodotos. Until Thucydides, who had other interests, history was written by eastern Greeks, the losers at Lade, and losers do not normally write their own history.

Thucydides shows us how the Athenians used their contribution to the victories over the Persians to justify their hegemony over their empire (1.73–4). He also depicted the Aegean Greeks as lazy, all too willing to give up their ships, pay tribute to Athens, and excuse themselves from military action, and by so doing give the Athenians a free hand in controlling the Empire (1.99; also 6.76.4). Herodotos seems to apply this characterization specifically to the Ionians when he explains their failure at Lade (6.12; also

4.142). The implication would seem to be that if the Ionians did not like being in the Athenian Empire, they had themselves to blame.[45] Better discipline and resolute opposition to the Persians at the critical moment could have produced a different and nobler result for them. This, or something like it, has been a fairly standard way of reading Herodotos since the beginning of the last century.[46] Fortunately, it has come under severe scrutiny in recent years.

Oswyn Murray saw Herodotos' remarks as a record of the Ionians' own admission: 'The emphasis on their lack of military spirit and on Ionian luxury is a self-created myth resulting from defeat.'[47] The empire obliged Ionians to turn against their neighbours at times. At Samos, in 440, the Athenians suppressed a revolt with help from Chios and Lesbos. Philip Stadter imagines the revulsion Herodotos probably felt at the sight of Ionians aiding their own subjugators: 'It was not bias that led Herodotus to characterize the Ionians as weak, fawning, and spineless, but anger and frustration at seeing their behavior in his own day.'[48] Sara Forsdyke has recently published a study of Herodotos' language in characterizing what she calls Athenian democratic ideology. The effect of tyranny in his view is to 'hold down' (*katechein*) the subject people and deprive them of chances for success.[49] But if we can believe Thucydides, some Athenians were not attempting to conceal the fact that their empire was (like) a tyranny in the late fifth century (Thuc. 2.63; 3.37.2). Herodotos called the fateful decision of the Athenians to give aid to the Ionian revolt 'the beginning of evils for Greek and barbarian alike' (5.97.3). The evils for the barbarian were a series of humiliating defeats, and for the Greeks – well, it began a chain reaction that led to the establishment of the Athenian Empire.[50] The most direct and thorough debunking of the idea that Herodotos endorsed the ideology of Athenian imperialism, however, comes from John Moles.[51]

The arguments of Forsdyke and Moles seem contradictory at first. On the one hand, if Herodotos was prepared to celebrate the delivery of Athens from tyranny and the success that democracy makes possible, then he must have approved of the reforms of Kleisthenes and the regime of democratic Athens that he created. Moles, on the other hand, shows how difficult it is to cling to the view that Herodotos had unreserved admiration for Keisthenes and his specific reforms or even for Athens itself. Kleisthenes was no Maiandrios. Worsted in oligarchic infighting, he took the demos into his faction. He acted in imitation of his maternal grandfather, Kleisthenes tyrant of Sikyon, who disbanded the old tribes out of contempt for them and replaced them with new and artificial ones. His grandfather changed the tribes in order to shore up his tyranny by depriving the people of a traditional hero. Kleisthenes of Athens abolished the original four Ionian tribes and manufactured ten new ones, naming them after local heroes (5.67–9). Herodotos seems to regard his actions as a deliberate affront to the Ionians.[52] Even worse, if we look at the famous debate allegedly held by three Persian grandees after the overthrow of the Magos and before Dareios came to power, we see that Kleisthenes was emerging from oligarchic feuding in a way characteristic of tyrants (3.82.3). How can Herodotos admire the institution but vilify its founder as a tyrant? But perhaps we are looking for consistency in the wrong place, or for the wrong kind of consistency. 'Herodotus admires Athens *qua* saviour of Greece but condemns the empire: a position consistent with two other aspects of his thinking: hatred of war (for which Athens bore most responsibility in fifth-century Greece) and genuine Panhellenism.'[53] To this we should add a deep commitment to the cause of freedom in all its manifestations. It seems likely that the ultimate problem that he saw in Athenian democracy lay in the inconsistency of the Athenians' gaining political freedom for themselves, then using their new power and confidence to deprive their fellow Greeks of autonomy.

I have shown so far that generally speaking, Ionia and the eastern Greeks were the cultural, intellectual, and, in terms of city-state organization, the political leaders of Greece right down to the end of the sixth century. They were 'the education of Hellas.' Ultimately, however, they were not up to the challenge posed by the Persian advance. We have little information regarding the reaction of eastern Greek intellectuals to the disastrous Ionian revolt – apart from Herodotos, that is. He responded to it in two ways: a direct and an indirect one.

To begin with the indirect response, Herodotos set the whole story of the Persian attack on Greece in the context of a wide-ranging, vast account of the history and geographical extent of the Persian Empire. Readers may draw what conclusions they like from perusing such a work, but the impression that seems unavoidable to me is both the remarkable nature of the success of the old city-states and a profound understanding of the resources that the Persians could bring to bear on a dwarfed Ionia. Pushing back the invaders was a miracle that Ionia could not quite pull off, but old Greece did, and the challenge was to explain both the understandable failure as well as the brilliant success. Herodotos accomplished both by emphasizing one simple concept: submission to hegemony. The Ionian states would not accept the leadership of a single one of their members in the interest of the common good (6.12); the Athenians saved Greece by setting aside their dispute with Aigina (7.145) and putting their fleet under Spartan command (7.161).

For Herodotos, to understand was not necessarily to forgive. Part of his direct approach to the disaster was, of course, his analysis of the failure of the Ionians to develop an effective command structure. Otherwise, by reporting the Ionian traditions regarding the revolt, he was able to bring out its shaky beginnings: 'There was ... some common ground in these traditions,' says Sara Forsdyke. 'All Ionians, it seems, could agree that Aristagoras, Histiaios, and the other Ionian tyrants had acted in their own self-interest, and were not truly interested [in] the cause of Greek freedom.'[54]

When the revolt was brewing, Aristagoras' fellow Milesian, Kadmos, published a 'Foundation of Miletos and all of Ionia,' which reiterated in a new form a claim at least one-half a century old that Athens had colonized Ionia. It was a good story on the basis of which to persuade the Athenians that they had a moral obligation to come to the aid of their 'offspring.'[55] Of course, there need not be anything threatening in the relationship of colony to mother city. In Greek practice, the parent state did not exact tribute from its colonies. Ionians who embraced the story at this time perhaps naively believed that they were giving life to an innocuous tradition on which to model a future relationship with Athens.

In fact, the Ionians were spinning a web in which they would soon find themselves ensnared. I do not intend to contribute to the debate over how insidious or benign that web (the Athenian Empire) might have been. In what follows, I simply wish to bring out the voices of the eastern Greeks and islanders during this time, and let them be heard.[56] Ion of Chios was born shortly before 480 and lived until some time in the 420s. His lifespan paralleled that of Herodotos just about exactly. His literary production is all lost, but fragments survive in sufficient quantity to get some idea of his work.[57] To him we can attribute certain reworkings of the Theseus myth that tied Chios more closely to Athens.[58] He wrote poetry and prose, which latter appeared in the Ionian dialect. He was an admirer of the Athenian general, Kimon, who led Athenian and allied forces during the first decade of the Delian Confederacy's existence.

Kimon's most brilliant victory was won at the mouth of the Eurymedon River in Anatolia. He ran into political trouble at home through the late 460s and into the 450s. He died in a sea fight off Cyprus in 450. His idea of enriching Athens and Ionia by attacking and plundering Persia probably sat well with many Ionians. When he was at the height of his influence, he actively encouraged an association of himself with the legendary Attic hero Theseus. He repatriated 'the bones of Theseus' to Athens from Skyros, probably around 476, and seems to have promoted the belief that he was a reincarnation of the old hero. Meanwhile, to return to Chios, it appears that the Chians had not signed on to the Milesian agenda of encouraging the belief that all of Ionia was a colony from Athens. They chose to promote themselves rather as producers of coveted wine, named their founder Oinopion ('Winedrinker'), and gave him a Cretan lineage. Not to be deterred, Ion exploited Theseus' heroic visit to Crete and made Oinopion a son of Theseus and thus brought Chios back to the Athenian fold.

It was about this time that the legend of Theseus began to attract fairly wide attention and not just among Athenian playwrights. Bacchylides, the dithyrambist from Keos, produced versions of the Theseus story that connected the hero to the Aegean.[59] It is not clear just what these poets hoped to achieve by addressing the story, unless it was mere servile flattery directed towards the newly powerful Athenians, but there is one possibility that deserves a moment's reflection. Part of the legend included Theseus' puzzlingly shameful abandonment of Ariadne, the woman who helped him elude Minos and defeat the Minotaur, on the island of Naxos. A rather speculative possibility comes to mind that perhaps the idea behind the reworking of the Theseus myth was to suggest the paradigm of a marriage to influence the relationship between Athens and the Aegean. If an absent-minded Theseus had left his prospective bride behind in the Aegean many years ago, perhaps Theseus *redevivus* in the form of Kimon would reclaim her. As a bride she would retain her personal freedom, at least, and her authority over the house and home – local autonomy. Perhaps, too, it would promote the idea that Ionians and islanders could continue to marry into the Athenian family and share the fruits of empire.

Perikles put an end to the marrying of Athenians with non-Athenians by his citizenship law of 451/0. From this time on, the 'bride' would be at best a concubine. Athenian citizens needed freeborn Athenian parents. Only a few years later, he passed the coinage decree. Now the Ionians and islanders were forbidden from minting their own silver coinage and were even obliged to adopt Athenian weights and measures. This second decree had nominal impact on some states, but Chios suffered significantly. The Chians had been minting silver coins. Perhaps worse, they were now forced to market their famous wines in jars that conformed to the Attic standard rather than preserving the one that had served them well, it seems, for decades, if not centuries previous. The humiliation probably weighed more heavily than the inconvenience.[60]

Not all the voices from the Aegean followed the form of Ion and his ilk. There is a story about a man from the poor and insignificant island of Seriphos (Plut. *Them.* 18.3) who railed at Themistokles, alleging that his greatness and fame was only possible because he was Athenian. Themistokles responded that being from Seriphos was a guarantee of obscurity, but the Seriphian would not have achieved greatness even if he were born in Athens. The story, even if apocryphal, captures a plausible resentment directed towards Athens from the island communities. More noteworthy was the literary output of Stesimbrotos of Thasos, a younger contemporary of Ion, who produced a biographical work called 'On Themistokles, Thoukydides, and Perikles.'[61] The Thoukydides mentioned here was the son of Melesias, apparently, and not the historian (Thucydides). Stesimbrotos is quoted from time to time by Plutarch, and it appears that he attacked Themistokles and Perikles ferociously. We do not know what he said about Thoukydides. Stesimbrotos foreshadows attitudes that anticipate Theopompos in the fourth century. He chooses the more aggressive advocates of Athenian imperialism to attack but still preserves fond memories of Kimon. Even Kimon, however, would soon be sacrificed under the savage knife of Theopompos.

A few loose ends remain before I turn to a brief look at the fourth century. When the Delian League began and the allies located the *Synedrion* on Delos, I suggested that they had changed the old configuration of the Aegean in more than a political sense. Two religious solitudes came together, the eastern centred on Poseidon and the western centred on Delphic Apollo. In 454, the treasury of the League was moved from Delos to Athens, and Delos returned to its old status, presumably, a kind of boundary marker between east and west.[62] As I noted above, it looks as if Polykrates of Samos wanted Delos and its surrounding islands to mark his western frontier in the sixth century. Is it pure irony, or is there some meaning to the fact that it was the Samians who made the proposal to remove the treasury and return Delos to something like its old position?[63]

During the sixth and fifth centuries the Ionians prospered, but at the same time they were falling under the control of various external powers. Their cultural leadership as I call it, self-indulgent luxury as some of the ancients saw it, combined with their political vulnerability made them the objects of much criticism. Fornara and Samons show the extent to which their alleged softness attracted vicious comment from such figures as Archilochos of Paros, Theognis, and one of their very own, Xenophanes of Kolophon, who left Ionia rather than live under tyranny.[64] Fornara and Samons see Herodotos' Dorian origin as a platform from which to criticize the effete Ionians, but I find that idea unconvincing. It is true that Herodotos rarely missed a chance to remind his audience that his native Halikarnassos was Dorian (1.144; 2.178.2; 7.99.2), but he probably disassociated himself from Halikarnassos, since in the earliest quotation of his proem that we have (from Arist. *Rhet.* 3.9; see also Plut. *Mor.* 604), he called himself a Thourian. It is also worth remembering that he wrote in the Ionic dialect, and by so doing associated himself openly with the Ionians and particularly with a long line of Ionian intellectuals.

The life of luxury, however, need not be a cause of reproach. When Perikles allegedly claimed that Athens was the 'education of Hellas' (in the Funeral Oration: Thuc. 2.41.1), he did so after rehearsing all the pleasurable things the Athenians obtain from all parts of the world (2.38). The critical claim, however, comes at 2.40.1: 'We love beauty without extravagance and intellectual pursuits without becoming soft.' 'Softness' or 'toughness,' of course, is measured by military success.

When we enter the fourth century, the choices that lay before an Ionian with literary pretensions were even more restricted than before. Epigraphical evidence shows that local Ionian dialects were dying out, although an Atticized version of Ionic would survive to become the *koinē* of Alexander's empire.[65] Owing to the increasing prestige and influence of people like Plato, Isokrates, and even Xenophon, it became necessary to master the Attic dialect, preferably in the style of Isokrates, if one wanted a serious hearing. Two of the most important figures from Ionia, Ephoros of Kyme and Theopompos of Chios, sojourned in Athens and emerged writing fluent Attic in the Isokratean style.

Ephoros and Theopompos each chose a different path through the minefield that lay before their feet. From the fragments of Ephoros and those places in which Diodoros of Sicily seems to be closely epitomizing his work, it appears that he found a way to approve of just about everything and praise everybody even when on opposite sides of a conflict. There was a joke about him in circulation in antiquity that captures the extent of the mischief of which he was capable in seeking to detract from the pretensions of the Greek mainland powers by drawing attention to his own relatively small hometown. It is said that Ephoros would interrupt his narrative from time to time to assure his readers that, in the meanwhile, the people of Kyme were having a peaceful time (F 236).

Theopompos was a Chian born in 379 or 378/7 and died in or around 323. There was nothing coy about his preparedness to thrust his native Ionia before the attention of his readers. Ephoros had dared to include the occasional gratuitous visit to Kyme. Theopompos devoted eight continuous books to a digression in his *Philippika* on the subject of the history of eastern Greece and the western Persian satrapies, easily the longest in a digression-filled work.[66] One fragment reveals that he too, like his earlier countryman Ion, related the foundation story of Chios (F 276). The Chians were the first to produce red wine, learning the art from their founder, Oinopion son of Dionysos. With this brief genealogy, Theopompos almost certainly 'corrected' the version of Ion, and disengaged the Chian foundation myth from the Theseus legend. In a substantial digression in book ten, he also attacked Athenian political leaders like Perikles and Themistokles as had Stesimbrotos before him. Unlike his forebears, however, he included the old hero Kimon and just about everyone else in his list of grasping villains.

The word Theopompos used for these Athenian villains was 'demagogue,' a word also used by his contemporary Aristotle to describe all popular leaders of Athens, but especially for those who corrupted the people and the democracy after the death of Perikles. Kleon was the paradigm (*Ath. Pol.* 28.1–3). It is doubtful to me, however, that Aristotle and Theopompos shared the same point of view regarding these demagogues. Aristotle was concerned about the deterioration of politics within Athens after the loss of the firm but enlightened hand of Perikles. His view, in other words, was Athenocentric. But the demagogues also shared a harsh and aggressive attitude towards the empire. It was this that made Athenian leaders, from Kimon to Perikles and beyond, demagogues in the eyes of the Chian historian, who was by no means committed to an Athenian perspective. For Theopompos, whenever the Athenians sought to remind anyone of their past heroism in the cause of Greece, they were simply 'crowing' and duping the Hellenes.[67] Later antiquity branded Theopompos as malicious (T 25). Perhaps this was right, but there always remains the possibility that 'malice' is just another word for independence of mind.

I began with the decree of Aristoteles and the Second Athenian League. It looks as if the League grew out of a sequence of bilateral alliances with various places like Thebes (Harding no. 33) and Byzantion (Harding no. 34), but the first in the sequence was one made between Athens and Chios in 384/3 (Harding no. 31). By the time we come to line 25 (Harding) of the decree of Aristoteles, the Chians are now found alongside the Thebans as examples of the sort of alliance now open to all. No matter how scrupulous the Athenians may have been to avoid the abuses of the old empire, the establishment of a pecking order in the process of extending the League just seems inevitable. It started as the Athenians and Chians, but progressed quickly to Athenians and the others who wished to join. For the most part, history records the founding of the Second Athenian League. As ever, the contributions of smaller states or those just beyond the main focus of the attention of our ancient sources must be worked out by Jack Cargill, Sheila Ager, and so many others, work that will draw on the foundation of the documents made available by epigraphists like Phillip Harding.

Notes

* I am grateful to the Social Sciences and Humanities Research Council of Canada for a generous grant that made research for this paper possible. Thanks go also to an anonymous reader for some helpful suggestions.

1 Ager 2001: 119. For an extensive discussion and bibliography regarding this decree, see Cargill 1981 and Cargill 1996.

2 Roebuck 1953 = Roebuck 1979: 21–8. Attempts had been made to assess the

importance of Ionia before Roebuck's article, as he shows, but scholars were far from reaching a consensus. Roebuck argued that the fleet numbers given by Herodotos for the Ionian contingents at Lade are both credible and testify to considerable wealth in the Ionian states at the beginning of the fifth century. In general, see Huxley 1966.

3 Roebuck 1955 = Roebuck 1979: 26–68. On the Panionion, see Stillwell, MacDonald, and McAllister 1976: 670.

4 Herodotos 1.143–7; McInerney 2001: 57–9; van Wees 2002: 327; Thomas 2001.

5 Stadter 1992.

6 Sanchez 2001: 39–40.

7 de Santerre 1958: 247.

8 Coldstream 1977: 213–16.

9 de Santerre 1958: 282–308.

10 Poursat 1973.

11 Rolley 1973: 491–525. Contrast this with Samos: Shipley 1987: 42–3.

12 Martin 1973.

13 Malkin (2001: 8) situates the Ionian debate over their ethnic identity in the context of the Persian conquest.

14 *Ath. Pol.* 5.2.

15 de Santerre 1958: 307–9; Shipley 1987: 92–4.

16 de Polignac 1995: 21–31.

17 Braun 1988: 1–3; Burkert 1992: 12–13; Boardman 1999: 20, 285 n. 52.

18 Sancisi-Weerdenburg 2001: 324–5.

19 Mellink 1988: 211.

20 Roebuck 1959.

21 Sancisi-Weerdenburg 2001: 329–30.

22 Boardman 1999: 285, n. 36.

23 Except for certain mainland Yauna, who Sancisi-Weerdenburg (2001: 329) suggests were probably Macedonians.

24 Burn 1960: 243–4. He may have been involved in the battle of Carchemish or other immediately subsequent campaigns. See also Boardman 1999: 52.

25 Boardman 1999: 51, 285 n. 52.

26 Boardman 1999: 119–28.

27 Boardman 1999: 128–36.

28 Fornara no. 24.

29 Roebuck 1979: 159–60.

30 Nenci 1998.

31 Kirk, Raven, and Schofield 1983: Milesians, 75–162; Xenophanes and Herakleitos, 163–212; for the traditions regarding Pythagoras' origins, 222–4.

32 Murray 1988: 471.

33 Shrimpton 2001; Pearson 1939.

34 Shrimpton 2001: 59; Wise 1998: 15–18; Svenbro 1988: 182–6.

35 Burn 1960: 207–9.
36 Meiggs-Lewis no. 8; Fornara (no. 19) translates a small (the most legible) part of the surviving text. Roebuck 1986.
37 Roebuck (1979: 160–1) argues for a high degree of political sophistication at old Smyrna on the basis of the (reconstructed) town's grid plan and the evident distribution of wealth throughout a large and prosperous community.
38 Boardman, Dorig, Fuchs, and Hirmer 1967: 16–17.
39 Stewart 1990: 108–19.
40 Fornara and Samons 1991: 76–150. Fornara and Samons (113) do not argue that the tribute was crippling financially, but that the Athenians turned the Delian League into an empire deliberately and much sooner than most scholars think. Some Athenian practices (parading the tribute through the theatre of Dionysos before all the people of Athens, to mention but one) were galling to the allies.
41 Osborne 1999.
42 Thomas 2000.
43 Shipley 2000: 59–107.
44 Hornblower 1991: 11.
45 Fornara and Samons 1991: 106–9.
46 How and Wells 1912: 1.120, 2.36.
47 Murray 1988: 471–2.
48 Stadter 1992: 807.
49 Forsdyke 2001.
50 Shrimpton 1997: 218–19.
51 Moles 2002.
52 Woodhead (1981: 179–90) showed a fascinating way whereby this apparent contradiction could find some resolution. For a stimulating and even more adventuresome study, see Fornara and Samons 1991: 1–75.
53 Moles 2002: 51.
54 Forsdyke 2001: 529.
55 Barron 1986: 91.
56 The debate over the popularity of the Athenian Empire has been a long one and still continues. The classic argument for its popularity is still de Ste Croix 1955. More recent studies are by Osborne 1999 and Fornara and Samons 1991.
57 Dover 1986.
58 Barron 1986: 92.
59 Campbell 1992 no. 17, no. 18, fr. eleg. 29. Shapiro 1992; Tyrrell and Brown 1991: 159–88.
60 Barron 1986: 96–100. Barron (103) points out that despite the coinage decree, in general the Chians 'did well out of the empire.'
61 *FGrHist* 107.

62 For background see Meiggs 1972: 48. Plutarch provides us with the information that the proposal to move the treasury came from Samos: *Aristid.* 25.3.
63 Shipley (1987: 111) reminds us that the Athenians and allies had just lost a large fleet owing to a disaster in Egypt. Perhaps this left the treasury of the League vulnerable.
64 Fornara and Samons 1991: 106–7.
65 Buck 1955: 175–6.
66 Shrimpton 1991: 72–8; on his attitude to his native Chios, see 35–6.
67 FF 154, 153; Shrimpton 1991: 80.

References

Ager, S.L. 2001. 'Fourth-Century Thera and the Second Athenian League.' *Ancient World* 32: 119.

Barron, J.P. 1986. 'Chios in the Athenian Empire,' in J. Boardman and C.E. Vaphopoulou-Richardson (eds.), *Chios: A Conference at the Homereion in Chios, 1984,* 89–103. Oxford.

Boardman, J. 1999. *The Greeks Overseas: Their Early Colonies and Trade*[4]. London.

Boardman, J., J. Dorig, W. Fuchs, and M. Hirmer. 1967 (1966). *The Art and Architecture of Ancient Greece.* London.

Braun, T.F.R.G. 1988. *Cambridge Ancient History* 3[2], part 3. Cambridge.

Buck, C.D. 1955. *The Greek Dialects*[2]. Chicago and London.

Burkert, W. 1992. *The Orientalizing Revolution: Near Eastern Influence on Greek Culture in the Early Archaic Age,* trans. M.E. Pinder and W. Burkert. Cambridge.

Burn, A.R. 1960. *The Lyric Age of Greece.* London.

Campbell, D.A. 1992. *Greek Lyric.* Vol. 4, *Bacchylides, Corinna, and Others.* Cambridge, MA.

Cargill, J. 1981. *The Second Athenian League: Empire or Free Alliance?* Berkeley and Los Angeles.

– 1996. 'The Decree of Aristoteles: Some Epigraphical Details.' *Ancient World* 27: 39–51.

Coldstream, J.N. 1977. *Geometric Greece.* London.

de Polignac, F. 1995. *Cults, Territory, and the Origins of the Greek City-State,* trans. Janet Lloyd. Chicago.

de Santerre, H.G. 1958. *Délos primitive et archaïque.* Paris.

de Ste Croix, G.E.M. 1955. 'The Character of the Athenian Empire.' *Historia* 3: 1–41.

Dover, K. 1986. 'Ion of Chios,' in J. Boardman and C.E. Vaphopoulou-Richardson (eds.), *Chios: A Conference at the Homereion in Chios, 1984,* 27–37. Oxford.

Fornara, C.W. and L.J. Samons II. 1991. *Athens from Cleisthenes to Pericles*. Berkeley and Los Angeles.

Forsdyke, S. 2001. 'Athenian Democratic Ideology and Herodotus' *Histories*.' *AJP* 122: 329–58.

Hornblower, S. 1991. *The Greek World*. London and New York^2.

How W.W., and J. Wells. 1912. *A Commentary on Herodotus in Two Volumes*. Oxford.

Huxley, G.L. 1966. *The Early Ionians*. London.

Kirk, G.S., J.E. Raven, and M. Schofield. 1983. *The Presocratic Philosophers*^{2}. Cambridge.

Malkin, I., ed. 2001. *Ancient Perceptions of Greek Ethnicity*. Cambridge, MA.

Martin, R. 1973. 'Complements à l'étude des chapitaux Ioniques de Délos,' in *Études déliennes publiées à l'occasion du centième anniversaire du début des fouilles de l'École française d'Athènes à Délos*, 371–98. *BCH* Supplement I. Paris.

McInerney, J. 2001. 'Ethnos and Ethnicity in Early Greece,' in I. Malkin (ed.), *Ancient Perceptions of Greek Ethnicity*, 51–73, Cambridge, MA.

Meiggs, R. 1972. *The Athenian Empire*. Oxford.

Mellink, M. 1988. *Cambridge Ancient History* 2^2. Cambridge.

Moles, J. 2002. 'Herodotus and Athens,' in E.J. Bakker, I.J.F. de Jong, and H. van Wees (eds.), *Brill's Companion to Herodotus*, 33–52. Leiden.

Murray, O. 1988. *Cambridge Ancient History* 2^2. Cambridge.

Nenci, G. 1998. 'L'Introduction de l'alphabet en Grèce selon Hérodote (v 58).' *REA* 100: 579–89.

Osborne, R. 1999. 'The Archaeology of the Athenian Empire.' *TAPA* 129: 319–32.

Pearson, L. 1939. *Early Ionian Historians*. Oxford.

Poursat, J.-Cl. 1973. 'Ivoires de l'Artemision,' in *Études déliennes publiées à l'occasion du centième anniversaire du début des fouilles de l'École française d'Athènes à Délos*, 415–25. *BCH* Supplement I. Paris.

Roebuck, C. 1953. 'The Economic Development of Ionia.' *CP* 48: 9–16.

– 1955. 'The Early Ionian League.' *CP* 50: 26–40.

– 1959. *Ionian Trade and Colonization*. AIA Monographs on Archaeology and Fine Arts 9. New York.

– 1979. *Economy and Society in the Early Greek World*, with an introduction and bibliography by Carol G. Thomas. Chicago.

– 1986. 'Chios in the Sixth Century BC,' in J. Boardman and C.E. Vaphopoulou-Richardson (eds.), *Chios: A Conference at the Homereion in Chios, 1984*, 81–8. Oxford.

Rolley, C. 1973. 'Bronzes géometriques et orientaux à Dèlos,' in *Études déliennes publiées à l'occasion du centième anniversaire du début des fouilles de l'École française d'Athènes à Délos*, 491–525. *BCH* Supplement I. Paris.

Sanchez, P. 2001. *L'Amphictionie des Pyles et de Delphes: Recherches sur son rôle historique, des origines au IIe siècle de notre ère.* Historia Einzelschrift 148. Stuttgart.

Sancisi-Weerdenburg, H. 2001. '*Yauna* by the Sea and across the Sea,' in I. Malkin (ed.), *Ancient Perceptions of Greek Ethnicity*, 323–46. Cambridge, MA.

Shapiro, H.A. 1992. 'Theseus in Kimonian Athens; the Iconography of Empire.' *Mediterranean Historical Review* 7: 29–49.

Shipley, G. 1987. *A History of Samos, 800–188 BC.* Oxford.

Shipley, G. 2000. *The Greek World after Alexander, 323–30 BC.* London and New York.

Shrimpton, G.S. 1991. *Theopompus the Historian.* Montreal and Kingston.

Shrimpton, G.S. 1997. *History and Memory in Ancient Greece.* Montreal and Kingston.

Shrimpton, G.S. 2001. 'Beyond *The Limits*: New Thoughts on the Origin and Development of Ancient Historical Writing.' *AHB* 15: 50–62.

Stadter, P.A. 1992. 'Herodotus and the Athenian Arche.' *ASNP*, 3rd ser., 22: 787–95.

Stewart, A. 1990. *Greek Sculpture: An Exploration*, vol. 1. New Haven and London.

Stillwell, R., W.L. MacDonald, and M.H. McAllister, eds. 1976. *The Princeton Encyclopedia of Classical Sites.* Princeton.

Svenbro, J. 1988. *Phrasikleia: An Anthropology of Reading in Ancient Greece*, trans. J. Lloyd. Ithaca and London.

Thomas, R. 2000. *Herodotus in Context.* Cambridge.

– 2001. 'Ethnicity, Geneology, and Hellenism in Herodotus,' in I. Malkin (ed.), *Ancient Perceptions of Greek Ethnicity*, 213–33. Cambridge, MA.

Tyrrell, W.B., and F.S. Brown. 1991. *Athenian Myths and Institutions: Words in Action.* Oxford.

van Wees, H. 2002. 'Herodotus and the Past,' in E.J. Bakker, Irene J.F. de Jong, and H. van Wees (eds.), *Brill's Companion to Herodotus*, 321–49. Leiden.

Wise, J. 1998. *Dionysus Writes: The Invention of Theatre in Ancient Greece.* Ithaca and London.

Woodhead, A.G. 1981. 'The Founding Fathers of the Delian Confederacy,' in G.S. Shrimpton and D.J. McCargar (eds.), *Classical Contributions: Studies in Honour of Malcolm Francis McGregor*, 179–90. Locust Valley, NY.

Rescuing Local History: Epigraphy and the Island of Thera

SHEILA AGER

The south Aegean island of Thera (modern Santorini) is famous both for its compelling beauty and for its celebrity in recent decades as the 'Pompeii of the Aegean.'[1] Known in remote antiquity as *Kalliste*, 'most beautiful,' the island's stunning topography and equally sensational archaeology find congruence in the same event: the catastrophic eruption of the Theraian volcano in the Late Bronze Age, an eruption that buried the thriving settlement near the modern village of Akrotiri, and that resulted in the formation of the modern-day caldera and the spectacular cliffs surrounding it.[2] The remarkable archaeological discoveries at Akrotiri, together with the dramatic landscape of the island, have made Santorini a tourist haven, and its blue-domed, white-stuccoed churches (over 250 on this small island) have become a veritable trademark of Greece itself.

Yet the glamour and renown of Santorini, and the intense interest in it on the part of both the tourist industry and scholars of the prehistoric Aegean (not to mention New Age Atlantis enthusiasts), serve only to highlight the poverty of our knowledge about the island in the historical period. Thera occupies the most negligible of places in the ancient historical record. The authors of antiquity – historians, poets, travel writers – mention the island only rarely, and the few notices we do have in the literary record offer only a meagre and tantalizingly fragmentary glimpse of Thera's history.

Epigraphically, however, the island is a place of great wealth and variety, and Thera is the perfect model for the epigraphic recovery of local history. The compensatory role of epigraphy in the absence (total or near-total) of literary evidence has both a temporal and a regional aspect: inscriptions assist both in rescuing the history of obscure regions and in shedding new light on dark periods in the history of better-known places. Some of the most archaic of all Greek inscriptions are to be found on the rocks of Thera, as well as some of the most perplexing (not to mention some of the rudest).[3] The epigraphic contribution to recovering Theraian history is moreover not limited solely to inscriptions found on the island itself. The rare and enigmatic appearance of Thera in the epigraphic record of other states (notably Athens) presents one of the great challenges in reconstructing the local history of Thera. This paper thus seeks to illustrate the role played by epigraphy in establishing at least the rough outlines of Theraian local history: its limitations as well as its contributions, and its interplay with the cryptic literary record.

The History of Thera: The Literary Sources

'The Lovely Island,'[4] as Pindar calls it, figures in two of the poet's victory odes, the earliest recorded literary sources to mention the island of Thera. In *Pythians* 4 and 5, Pindar weaves the story of Thera's colonization from Sparta, and the island's subsequent colonization of Kyrene, into the framework of the odes he wrote to commemorate the chariot victory of Arkesilaos IV, the ruler of Kyrene, at the Pythian Games of 462 BC. The story of these colonial adventures is couched in Pindar's typically allusive and elliptical language, and set in a highly mythical context. In the poet's world, the foundation of Thera is linked to the tale of Jason and Medea through the Argonautic liaison with the women of Lemnos, whose descendants ultimately made their way to Sparta, and thence to Thera.[5] As for the foundation of Kyrene, which took place less than two hundred years before Pindar's own time, that too is linked to the heroic age: Battos/Aristoteles, the Theraian *oikist* who led the colonizing expedition to North Africa, is a descendant of the Argonauts, and in founding Kyrene is fulfilling a prophecy spoken by Medea.[6]

Despite the poetic and mythologizing characteristics of Pindar's narrative, it bears a close resemblance to the chief fifth-century source on Theraian history. Herodotos, himself no stranger to poetic mythology, takes time out from his account of Persian expansionism in North Africa to relate the story of the antecedents of Kyrene (4.145–58). Here too the descendants of the Argonauts find themselves in Sparta, and abandon it in disgruntlement to join the Spartan Theras on his expedition to Kalliste, the island thereafter known as Thera. Generations later, the Theraian *basileus*, Grinnos, is instructed on a visit to the Delphic oracle to found a city in Libya; with tender regard for his own old age, Grinnos points at the more youthful Battos, who happens to be with him, and suggests that he be the one to undertake the task. Nothing is done upon the return of the Theraian embassy from Delphi, and for the next seven years the island receives not a single drop of rain. Inquiring again at Delphi, the Theraians learn that this alarming meteorological phenomenon is a result of the displeasure of the god, and so they decide to move ahead with the colonial effort. After a false start or two, Battos and a hundred or so of his countrymen finally succeed in establishing themselves at Kyrene.[7]

Although there is no reason to doubt the basic truth of Thera's colonization of Kyrene, the precise shape of Herodotos' tale provokes a certain scepticism. Nevertheless, Herodotos gives us the only connected literary narrative of Theraian history we have, however dubious its historical accuracy. Other literary references to Thera are extremely sparse. Thucydides does remark that Thera, like Melos, remained outside the Athenian empire in 431 BC (2.9.4), though he does not, as he does for Melos, offer an account of how Thera came to join that empire. Aristotle observes only that the Thera of his own day was not a democracy, as on that island 'the few, who are *eleutheroi*, rule the many, who are not.'[8]

After the Classical period Thera appears only rarely in any literary source – never again do we find any kind of sustained narrative like that in Herodotos. The one exception (and it is a brief one) is the report of the historian Menekles of Barka, who provides the information that one of the factors provoking the dispatch of the colony to Kyrene had been *stasis* on the island of Thera itself.[9] Furthermore, the majority of the 'sightings' of Thera in post-Classical sources are concentrated very largely on the increasingly mythologized figure of Battos: his connection with the Delphic god, his stammer (and how it was cured by the terror induced by his first encounter with a Libyan lion), his role as the archetypal good king.[10] These accounts add little or nothing to the picture of historical Thera.[11]

The literary sources on Theraian history are thus not only scarce, but considerably mythologized. The only connected narrative of any length that we have focuses on the seventh century. If we were forced to rely solely on literary sources, our reconstruction of Theraian history would be a poor one indeed.

The Corpus of Theraian Inscriptions

In word count alone, the epigraphic sources on Thera outweigh the literary ones. Roughly one thousand Theraian inscriptions survive, from a period extending over one thousand years. Most of them have been found on and around the steep promontory of Mesa Vouno, which thrusts into the sea on the southeast corner of the island and which housed the chief settlement during the historical period. The vast majority of Thera's inscriptions are collected in fascicle 3 of volume xii of the *Inscriptiones Graecae* series, with substantial additions and modifications published in the supplements to the series.[12] The inscriptions of Thera were edited by Friedrich Freiherr Hiller von Gaertringen, 'the Baron,' who excavated Mesa Vouno in the late nineteenth century and whose sculpted image adorns a wall along one of the main streets in the island's chief modern town of Phira. A few Theraian inscriptions have been unearthed subsequent to the publication of the relevant volumes of the *IG* series, but little of startling significance, and the bulk of Theraian inscriptions are to be found in *IG*.[13]

The Theraian inscriptions may be copious in number, but most of them taken individually are very brief. The largest single groupings by type are the grave inscriptions (of both men and women), and the names (chiefly male) and other graffiti inscribed on the rocks of the island.[14] The majority of the grave inscriptions consist of a simple name (or names), inscribed on stones (rough or finely worked) intended to function as grave markers. Some few of these include a line or two of valediction, or an identifying characteristic of the dead person such as an occupation or a family affiliation. Others indicate that the deceased had done something to warrant the granting of public honours at his or her death, such as the popular Theraian practice of literal 'heroization.'[15] Much of the graffiti is of the humble 'Kilroy was here' sort, though in some cases Kilroy was not exactly humble about what he was doing there. The most notorious of the Theraian graffiti are the Archaic inscriptions clustered near the later gymnasium of the ephebes at the southeastern end of the Mesa Vouno site.[16] Several of these inscriptions attest to the sexual energies (if not necessarily the inventiveness) of a number of individuals. One Krimon in particular figures as a repeat performer in this rather uncomfortable open air theatre. In spite of these salacious examples, however, the bulk of Theraian graffiti consists of simple names.[17] Mesa Vouno is an extremely rugged site, and the rocky surfaces of the mountain spine on which the settlement was located must have had the same irresistible appeal as a cinder-block wall.

Religious dedications and offerings also form a large part of the corpus of Theraian inscriptions.[18] Here too the inscriptions often consist simply of the name of a deity scratched into the rock surface. Many of these are to be found in and around the so-called 'agora of the gods' at the southeastern end of the Mesa Vouno site, between the temple of Apollo *Karneios* and the gymnasium of the ephebes.[19] The nature of the script in many cases seems to indicate that the agora of the gods was a sacral area from the earliest period of the settlement.[20] This does not seem to have precluded its use for the sexual antics of Krimon and his friends, who occasionally invoke Apollo (as a witness?) in their graffiti.[21] Perhaps the isolation and liminality of this part of the site (just beyond, the steep cliffs of Mesa Vouno fall directly into the sea) contributed to its use for both sacred and rather earthier purposes.

More elaborate than the austere dedications inscribed at the various small rock niches of Mesa Vouno is the 'Temenos of Artemidoros,' an open-air complex of altars and relief sculptures located along the road leading to the settlement. Artemidoros, who was not a native Theraian but a Pergaian in the service of the Ptolemies, dedicated this sanctuary to a host of deities, among them Zeus, Apollo, Poseidon, Hekate, Priapos, and the Dioskouroi.[22] Artemidoros ultimately settled down permanently on the island, was granted Theraian citizenship, and upon his death was heroized by the Theraians (at the suggestion or command of Delphi).[23] The words and sentiments Artemidoros had inscribed at his Temenos (and elsewhere on Mesa Vouno) offer one of the most vivid portraits we have of an individual inhabitant of Thera and testify to Artemidoros's role in the relations between this little island and the Ptolemaic presence in the Aegean in the mid-third century BC.

The sacred inscriptions of Thera merge with the honorific ones, another important category, as many of the religious dedications were made on behalf of VIPs such as Ptolemaic kings and queens or Roman emperors.[24] Arsinoë II Philadelphos, for instance, is the subject of several votive dedications on Thera, as she was in so many other places within the Ptolemaic sphere.[25] From a period three centuries later come the honours bestowed by the Theraian *dēmos* on the parents of Caligula, Agrippina and Germanicus, identified here with Hestia Boulaia and Zeus Boulaios, and commemorated by statues in the theatre.[26] Moreover, the Theraians were not stingy in bestowing honours on members of their own populace (among whom they eventually counted Artemidoros), both before death and after it via heroization.[27] Men and women alike figure as the subject of these honours, always because of their virtue and their *kalokagathia* (which we might be tempted to translate loosely as 'magnanimity,' given that a certain generosity of the purse-strings probably lies behind some of these commendations).

Least numerous of the Theraian inscriptions – but vital to the reconstruction of various phases of the island's history – are the public decrees and other documents.[28] Compared with Athens, the democratic queen of public epigraphy, Thera (like most other states) has rendered up a grudgingly small number of such public documents, often fragmented, and at times lamentably difficult to interpret.[29] Nor do any of the inscriptions in this group hail from the earlier periods of Theraian history. The earliest, an immensely fragmented inscription that evidently records some sort of judgment, appears (insofar as dating from letter forms can be trusted) to belong to the fourth century, while the first such document offering a continuous legibility – a decree of the people to crown Patroklos, the Ptolemaic admiral – is likely to have been inscribed sometime in the 260s BC, when Patroklos was active in the Aegean.[30] Perhaps the best-preserved of the public decrees of Thera are *IG* xii.3 325 and 326, still in position against the back wall of the Basilike Stoa along the main street of Mesa Vouno.[31] Engraved on twin stelai of the distinctive grey-blue Theraian marble, this pair of inscriptions from the mid-second century AD acquaints us with the members of one of the island's wealthier families, the Kleitosthenes clan, and their benefactions on behalf of the Mesa Vouno community. Other wealthy Theraians are commemorated in the lengthiest of all the island's inscriptions, the so-called 'Will of Epikteta,' a 288-line document wherein the widow Epikteta established a society to pursue the rites now to be accorded to her dead and heroized husband and sons.[32]

The epigraphic legacy of Thera is thus a rich one and goes a considerable distance towards compensating for the lack of literary sources. But there are limitations here too, particularly noticeable when it comes to contemplation of the Classical period. The Archaic- and Classical-era inscriptions contribute to our picture of the social and institutional life of the island, but offer little to flesh out an historical narrative. The expedition to Kyrene – the great adventure in Archaic Theraian history – is invisible in the epigraphic record of Thera itself.[33] With no significant public decrees surviving from before the Hellenistic Age, our picture of Thera's political affairs, external and internal, only gains detail in the latter period. Nevertheless, if Theraian history is shrouded in darkness in the Classical Age – between the literary narrative that sheds some light on her Archaic history and the epigraphic record that illuminates the Hellenistic period – there are still some epigraphic compensations: inscriptions from the world outside Thera itself that are invaluable in reconstructing her lost centuries.[34]

A Tangled Archaic Web: The Correlation of Epigraphic and Literary Sources

One of the most formidable methodological challenges in reconstructing local history through the use of inscriptions is that of determining and disentangling the relationships between the epigraphic sources and the sparse literary sources when the two types appear to overlap. As demonstrated above, the ancient literary record does not go very far to sustain a continuous narrative of Theraian history. Nevertheless, it does offer us the occasional snapshot of events in the island's history, in particular during the Archaic Age. What support does epigraphy offer for the few records we do have of Theraian history?

Two inscriptions are worth mentioning here, the one a brief and puzzling Archaic inscription from Thera itself, the other a much lengthier and on the surface more straightforward inscription from fourth-century Kyrene.[35] The former consists of a flat slab of dark volcanic stone evidently used as a grave marker and bearing several names in Archaic Theraian script. Centred on the horizontal surface of the stone is the word ἀρκ*h*αγέτας. Above it (also on the horizontal surface) appears the name Rheksanor, and below it the two names Prokles and Kleagoras; the stone also bears six other names, most distributed around the shallow vertical sides of the slab. The enigma of this stone lies in the appearance of the central word *archagetas*. Is it a descriptive title somehow to be related to one or more of the men whose names appear on the stone? Or is it simply one more proper name, 'Archagetas'? As a name it would be unusual, unique in fact, at least in the Aegean.[36] But as a title, the word is even more enigmatic.

Herodotos tells us that in the years leading up to the Theraian expedition to Kyrene, Thera had a *basileus*, Grinnos.[37] This term is conventionally translated into English as 'king,' though Robert Drews has pointed out that the Archaic *basileis* of ancient Greece should not be viewed as the kind of exalted monarchs historians of later European history might associate with the word.[38] Whatever the actual status of Grinnos, however, the question here is whether the *archagetas*-stone provides any evidence to support the constitutional picture of an Archaic Theraian *basileia*. The term *archagetas* appears elsewhere with the meaning 'leader, founder' and is often applied to Apollo, in his (Delphi's) role as colonizer.[39] There is one particularly famous literary passage, however, in which the word arguably means 'king,' and it is a context with particular resonance for Thera. In his biographical sketch of Lykourgos, Plutarch quotes the putatively Archaic document known as the Spartan *rhetra*, the only written constitutional document Spartan history offers (*Lykourgos* 6). The *rhetra* refers to officials known as *archagetai*, and Plutarch informs us that the *archagetai* are in fact the *basileis* of Sparta, though nowhere else are the Spartan kings called *archagetai*.[40] It is tempting to see the Theraian *archagetas*-stone as evidence not only for the Spartan ancestry of the island polis, but also as support for Herodotos' picture of Archaic Theraian kingship.[41]

Such a temptation should be met with at least partial resistance. For one thing, it is by no means certain that *archagetas* is *not* in fact a proper name, a grandiose one to match the other pretentious names on the stone. 'Archagetas' could simply have been another member of a (no doubt aristocratic) clan that named its sons for Spartan kings ('Prokles') or gave them heroically descriptive sobriquets (such as Rheksanor, 'breaker of men').[42] Furthermore, even if *archagetas* is a title rather than a name, it is not necessarily in this context a synonym for *basileus;* it might mean 'leader-founder' of a cult, for example.[43] In the end, the *archagetas*-stone remains a riddle, insoluble in the present state of the evidence.

The term appears also in the fourth-century inscription from Thera's colony Kyrene. Here it is less of a puzzle, as it appears to refer simply to Battos and to Apollo in their roles as colonial leader-founders.[44] Nevertheless, the latter document is bewildering enough in other respects and offers a variety of challenges of its own in formulating an understanding of its relationship to the literary record on Theraian history.

The Kyrenean document is an inscription about fifty lines in length, first published in the 1920s.[45] The first half of the inscription records a decree of the people of Kyrene, granting Kyrenean *isopoliteia* to citizens of Kyrene's metropolis, Thera.[46] Such civic privilege is said to be consonant with arrangements made nearly three centuries earlier, at the time of the original colonial foundation. The isopolity decree is to be inscribed on a stele and exhibited in the temple of Apollo *Pythios,* along with the pact sworn by those early Theraian settlers at the time of the original colony.

It is this pact that is the most curious section of the Kyrenean inscription, the portion that raises the most questions about the interplay of epigraphic and literary sources for Theraian history. Labelled the 'oath of the settlers,'[47] this section begins, not with an oath, but with a standard decree formulation (ἔδοξε τᾶι ἐκκλησίαι), followed by what would appear to be the original decision of the Theraian people (in the seventh century BC) to despatch their colony to Libya, and the directives attendant on that decision:

[D]ecreed by the *ekklesia*: Since Apollo spontaneously commanded B[at]|tos and the Theraians to colo[nize] Kyrene, it has been determined by the The[rai|a]ns to send [to Lib]ya Battos, as both *archageta*[s] and *basileus;* as his companions Theraians are to sail. Upon equa[l a|n]d fair terms are they to sail, according to household, and one son is to be enlist|ed; as for the other [citizens] the young men and from the [oth|e]r Theraians the free men, [whoever wishes] is to sail.[48] And if the settlers estab[li]|sh the colony, then any [of the Theraians] saili[ng]| at a later date to Libya shall have a sha[re] in [both citizenship] and offices| and shall be [allo]tted land which is without an owner. But if they do not es[ta]|blish the colony, and they are unable to fo[un]d [the ci]ty|, but *are oppressed by exigency, then (at any time) during the first five years, they are to depa[rt] from the land,*[49] and (return) without fear to Thera, to their own property, and they are to be citize|ns. Anyone who chooses not to sail when the city sends him is liable to the dea[th]| penalty and his property shall be confiscated. The one who wel|comes or conceals him, whether it is a father (protecting) his son or a brother (protecting) his bro|ther, shall suffer the same as the one who is unwilling to sail.[50]

After this string of infinitives and third-person imperatives typical of a decree, the inscription makes a very curious shift into the aorist indicative: it becomes, in effect, an historical narrative rather than the record of a decree *or* an oath.[51] This narrative relates how all the Theraians took an oath – those who left and those who stayed behind, men, women, boys, and girls – and how they sealed this oath with sympathetic magic, making waxen images and dropping them into the fire:

The one who does not abide by these| sworn pacts, but transgresses them, he is to melt and fl|ow away just like the images, himself and his offspring and his pro|perty; but as for those who abide by these sworn agreements, both those who| sail to Libya a[nd] t[hose who re]main on Thera, they will have muc|h good, both for them[selves and their off]spring.[52]

A very extraordinary inscription indeed, and one that cries out for synopsis with Herodotos, our main literary source on the Theraian colonization of Kyrene. The historian tells us that after the command from Delphi, which is ignored for seven years, the Theraians finally send out a scouting party, which establishes a foothold on the island of Plataia (just off the Libyan coast), and then reports back to the homeland:

The Theraians ... told their compatriots, when they reached home, that they had established a settlement on an island off the Libyan coast, and it was thereupon decided to send a party to join the new colony; the party was to represent all the seven villages [*choroi*] in Thera, and brothers were to draw lots to determine which should join it. It was to be under the sole authority of Battus ... [He] and a party of men sailed for Libya in two penteconters; they reached the coast, but, unable to decide what their next move should be, sailed home again to Thera. The islanders, however, refused to allow them to come ashore; they threw things at them as they were making up for the harbour, and shouted that they must put about and go back again; so, as they were compelled, they once more got under way for Libya.[53]

The similarities between the account of Herodotos and the strange passage labelled the *horkion* in the Kyrene decree are striking – but they are not absolute. It is clear that whatever else it is, the *horkion* is not simply a slavish copy of the historian. Both Herodotos and *SEG* ix 3 refer to Battos and the 'spontaneous' command of Apollo; both present the colonial expedition as a decision taken by the Theraian *dēmos* (despite Herodotos' attestation to a contemporary *basileia* on Thera);[54] both state that Battos was to be *basileus* (though Herodotos calls him also *hēgemōn*, while the inscription calls him *archagetas*); and both offer the detail that the colony was to draw its members from amongst the Theraian population on a household-by-household basis. But only Herodotos refers to the Theraian drought (and probable famine), the choice of individual colonists by lot, the representation of the different regions of the island, the total number of colonists, and the abortive attempt to return to Thera. Only the *horkion* refers to the colonists sailing on 'equal and fair terms,' the specification of young (adult) men and 'free men from the rest of Thera,' the promise held out to subsequent arrivals, the possibility of a return to Thera, and the sanctions against those who refused to sail.

These differences are for the most part complementary rather than contradictory: for instance, while only the *horkion* speaks of a possible return to Thera and only Herodotos speaks of an actual return to Thera, the two accounts can easily be reconciled on the assumption that they present different angles of the same story. Let us suppose that the Theraians, under very dire economic circumstances, despatched a portion of their male population under threat of death; that these individuals were to be allowed to return but only after they had made a reasonable effort to make a go of it in Africa; that the would-be colonists at first failed to abide by that agreement and attempted to return before the remaining Theraians were prepared to welcome them back; and that the inhabitants of the island therefore drove their relatives away again. Such a scenario could be supported by the combined testimony of both Herodotos and *SEG* ix 3. A further – and once more, not contradictory – detail could be added to this scenario by the testimony of Menekles. The desperate economic circumstances Thera may have been facing – drought and famine – would have been made all the more grievous if, as Menekles says, the island was also undergoing *stasis* at the time. A picture of civil unrest or outright civil war in Archaic Thera jibes well with the implications of grave hostilities detectable in both Herodotos and the *horkion*, with its unusually grim and powerful oath ceremony.[55]

The assessment of *SEG* ix 3's contribution to an understanding of Theraian history is undeniably complicated by the questionable authenticity of the *horkion*. While there is no reason to doubt the authenticity of the inscription as a veritable fourth-century Kyrenean decree proffering isopolitical rights to the members of the Theraian motherland, the peculiar form and the evident anachronisms embedded in the *horkion* mean that there are many reasons to be cautious, if not downright uncomfortable, about accepting the veracity of the 'archival' material employed to support the rationale of the fourth-century decree. Indeed, this inscription and its application to the reconstruction of an historical event are often cited as the paradigmatic model of the hazards possible epigraphic forgery presents to the historian. Ferri, the very first editor of this inscription, was convinced that the *horkion* was a Theraian invention.[56] Views on the matter range from a cautious acceptance of some or most of the material embedded in the *horkion* as a reasonably legitimate reflection of the substance (if not the actual form) of an authentic seventh-century Theraian decree,[57] to the suggestion that the *horkion* is an elaborate fraud from start to finish, a fourth-century forgery foisted upon its audience for the sake of political propaganda in pursuit of a contemporary agenda.[58] The debate on this matter has been a lively one, and to pursue it further here would be impossible. Suffice it to say that this inscription is without a doubt the most intriguing of all the colonial documents, and the question of its contribution to Theraian history a thought-provoking one.[59]

Discontinuous and Discrete: The Hellenistic Sources

At the opposite end of the spectrum from the tangled web of interdependence presented by the literary and epigraphic sources on the history of Archaic Thera is the picture presented by the sources on the island's history in the Hellenistic Age. Thera, like the Greek world generally, underwent an epigraphic 'boom' in the Hellenistic Age. For the first time, we now have extended inscriptions of a public nature, and also for the first time, we encounter in these inscriptions non-Theraian individuals and bodies recognizable from other historical sources. Nevertheless, those same historical sources were completely unconcerned with the doings of a small Aegean backwater, and while the mighty may appear in the accounts of Thera, Thera makes only slight appearance in the accounts of the mighty. In other words, if the challenge of reconstructing Archaic Theraian history is to determine the interrelationship of the literary and epigraphic sources, the challenge presented by the disjunctive Hellenistic sources is the opposite: there is no correlation at all between the literary and the epigraphic sources (or only a correlation so indirect as to whet rather than satisfy the appetite). The two strands of evidence are truly parallel, and never intersect.

Today the island of Thera is probably most famous (or infamous) for its vulcanism, a geological trait that both destroyed and preserved the Late Cycladic settlement at Akrotiri. Yet this Theraian characteristic does not appear in any recorded historical source until Strabo, in the first century BC.[60] Strabo records that over a period of only four days, volcanic phenomena in the caldera between the main island of Thera and its small companion Therasia resulted in the appearance of a new island (1.3.16). The birth of this island, in all probability the nucleus of modern Palaia Kameni, is attested by a number of other writers, whose combined evidence would seem to place this event in 198/7 BC.[61] A remarkable event, this geological prodigy was interpreted in light of the portent it seemed to have for the mighty figures of the day rather than in consideration of the impact it might have had on the inhabitants of Thera and Therasia themselves. Plutarch reports an oracle in the context of the Second Macedonian War, an oracle that construes the birth of the new island in the Thera complex as an omen of Roman might and its predestined victory over Philip V at Kynoskephalai in 197 BC (*Mor.* 399c–d).[62]

The gigantic geological hiccup of 198/7 BC and a subsequent one in AD 46[63] are the only events involving Thera in the Hellenistic or Roman periods to make their way into the literary record. We can only imagine the impact they had on the people of Thera themselves, as none of the copious inscriptions they have left make any direct references to these events, although we might conjecture that some of the Roman-era inscriptions referring to the rebuilding of public structures imply periodic destruction due to earthquake activity. In the reign of Trajan, three Theraian citizens named Agathopous, Polyouchos, and Aristodamos made contributions to the roofing of the Basilike Stoa and other structures which were evidently in rough shape.[64] Not long after, during the reign of Antoninus Pius, one Flavius Kleitosthenes Claudianus, along with his offspring, also contributed to the restoration of the Stoa, which was evidently once again in a state of collapse and disrepair (as were some of the other public buildings) and in fact is said to have been so 'for a long time now.'[65] One is certainly tempted to speculate either that the Theraians were remarkably poor builders, or that they were constantly bedevilled by the anger of Poseidon. Nevertheless, there is no proof that the destruction implied in these inscriptions was caused by the island's vulcanism. Furthermore, the surviving literary references we do have to continued volcanic activity in the Theraian island complex in the Hellenistic and Roman periods are not made from the point of view of anyone interested in the impact such geological events might have had on the Theraian people themselves, though they are suggestive of a continued uncertainty in the substrate of the Theraians' lives. The island was 'most beautiful,' yes, but it could be treacherous, subjecting its inhabitants to drought, famine, earthquake, and explosive eruption.[66]

Infected with a sense of uncertainty and instability, the Theraians may have been happy to grasp at any security they could get. While no human power could have protected the Theraian people from the violent vagaries of their own island, there were other hazards against which the mighty could provide a bulwark, even if such security came at the cost of Theraian independence. The most remarkable single fact with which the Theraian inscriptions of the Hellenistic – or any – period have acquainted us is that of the Ptolemaic presence on the island.[67] There is no hint of this presence in any of the literary sources, and if it were not for the copious inscriptions of Thera, this vital piece of the jigsaw puzzle of Ptolemaic and Aegean history would be missing. This key interlude in Theraian history is therefore wholly epigraphic and has no literary correlative whatsoever. While we are tremendously fortunate to have these inscriptions, the unfortunate corollary is that in the absence of corresponding literary accounts, we are often lacking contextual meaning and the means to determine the weight that should be assigned to some of the individual epigraphic discoveries.

The inscriptional evidence for Ptolemaic interest in the island does not seem to predate the reign of Ptolemy II. Religious dedications on behalf of Philadelphos' sister-wife Arsinoë II place Thera among the (not small) group of states honouring this remarkable woman, who appears to have died in 270 BC.[68] The earliest surviving public decree of Thera,[69] a decree honouring Patroklos, who served as Ptolemy II's admiral during the Chremonidean War, was probably promulgated in the 260s when Patroklos was busily pursuing Ptolemaic interests in Attica and the Aegean.[70] Patroklos is thanked for his kindness in sending to Thera (at Theraian request) a commission of five judges from Keos to resolve internal disputes on the island. By the second quarter of the third century, therefore, Ptolemy II had established a friendly relationship with Thera: a relationship that either immediately or ultimately involved the stationing of Ptolemaic troops on the island.[71] The Ptolemaic garrison remained on Thera until the mid-second century, when the death of Ptolemy VI in 145 probably necessitated the withdrawal from the Aegean.[72]

The clear benefit of welcoming such a garrison to the Theraian state is evident in one of the island's inscriptions. Thera, like other small littoral communities, was always at risk from pirates, and when a Ptolemaic official posted on the island was responsible for repelling a nocturnal attack, the Theraians gratefully voted public honours to both him and his subordinate officer.[73] What benefit did Thera in turn offer to the Ptolemies? We have only the inscriptions to go on, but they suggest that the island base was important enough to Ptolemaic interests in the Aegean that Thera was not only a posting place for troops but possibly even the home base for the *navarch*, the commander of the Ptolemaic navy in the Aegean. Whether this was so or not has been a matter for debate (the relevant inscription is unfortunately damaged at precisely the crucial point),[74] but at all events it is certain that at least one other Ptolemaic official posted to Thera did have a jurisdiction that extended beyond the island. An Alexandrian by the name of Eirenaios, the son of Nikias, who held the civilian position of *oikonomos* in the reign of Ptolemy VI, evidently exercised his authority not only over Thera, but over the Ptolemaic stations at Methana-Arsinoë on the coast of the Peloponnese, and Itanos on Crete.[75] The Theraian inscriptions thus enable us to flesh out the spotty histories of the Hellenistic period and act as a corrective on Polybios' dismal portrait of Ptolemaic foreign affairs in and after the reign of Ptolemy IV (5.34).

Thera was of course not the only Ptolemaic base in and around the Aegean – there were others such as Methana-Arsinoë in the Peloponnese and Itanos at the eastern extremity of Crete.[76] But Thera does offer one inscription unparalleled at any of these other places. According to yet another dedication made by the assiduous Artemidoros (honouring Ptolemy III, his father, and his grandfather), the Theraians played some role in 'bringing up' Ptolemy III's son, destined to be Ptolemy IV.[77] No doubt the loyal Artemidoros had a part to play in this curious interlude, unattested in any literary source. Did he escort the youthful Ptolemy to the island and maintain a guard over him there? What was the purpose behind this sojourn? Without a literary context it is impossible to say, though one is tempted to speculate (frivolously) that the child was already exhibiting the vicious characteristics with which Polybios later credits him, and that accordingly his parents sent him off to this rather austere Dorian summer camp in an effort to knock him into shape. A frivolous speculation indeed, and not meant very seriously, but the inscription does at least suggest that Thera held a unique place in the overseas possessions of the Ptolemies.

The Limitations of Epigraphy: 'History from Square Brackets'

Between the literary narrative of Archaic Theraian history and the copious epigraphic testimonia of the Hellenistic Age lies the most poorly documented period of Theraian history, the Classical Age. Despite the rather awkward chronology thus imposed on this paper, I have saved for the last this era in the island's history, where there is the greatest need for extrapolation from slight and indirect sources, and likewise the greatest danger of methodological epigraphic pitfalls. Thera does appear – briefly and cryptically – in the epigraphic and the literary records of the fifth and fourth centuries BC, but those appearances are controversial and problematic, and we are forced to rely also on inference from the more general evidence for Aegean history in these centuries.

The Classical Age was of course the era of Athenian power and imperialism, as well as the age of greatest tension between Athens and her enemy Sparta, a tension that embraced and divided the rest of the Greek world in both the fifth and the fourth centuries. Athens had come to see the Aegean as her natural sphere of influence, a state of affairs which placed the small Laconophilic islands of Thera and (far more famously) Melos in a very ticklish situation.[78] Although there are some Classical Age Theraian inscriptions, they are not particularly helpful in reconstructing the history of the island in these centuries. It is in the epigraphic record of other states that we find our few pivotal points of Classical Theraian history. I would therefore like to concentrate here on the extremely terse (and at times purely hypothetical) references to Thera or Theraians in the epigraphic record of Classical Athens.

The most secure and extensive references to Thera in Attic inscriptions are actually the ones least helpful in determining the course of the island's history: sometime perhaps in the fifth century an individual Theraian, Archedamos by name, decorated and inscribed a cave sanctuary on Mt Hymettos in southern Attica,[79] while several fourth-century inscriptions mention 'Theraian garments' among the property recorded by the treasurers of Athena.[80] But the most valuable of the Attic inscriptions (in terms of reconstructing local history) are those that allow us to piece together at least a partial picture of Thera's experience of Athenian imperialism, and these are unfortunately the inscriptions offering the most cursory references to the island.

It was pointed out above that Thucydides tells us that at the beginning of the Peloponnesian War only Thera and Melos remained outside of Athens' maritime 'alliance.'[81] The historian seems to speak a little loosely here, as the Athenian tribute quota lists suggest that not only Thera and Melos but also a few other small Aegean islands were not enrolled in the empire until after the beginning of the war.[82] Perhaps Thucydides has a special reason for bracketing Thera alone with Melos here, but if so, he does not pursue the matter, and we are forced to rely on the evidence of epigraphy to suggest a scenario for Thera's entry into the empire, for join it she did. By 425 at the latest Thera was paying tribute to Athens.[83]

The most commonly accepted date for Thera's entry into the Athenian empire is 430/29, immediately after the war began, based on Thera's putative appearance in the tribute quota list *IG* i^3 281.[84] But here we encounter certain methodological problems associated with epigraphy and reliance on it for reconstruction of history. For one thing, the dates of 430/29 for *IG* i^3 281 and of 429/8 for *IG* i^3 282 are not impervious to challenge. Harold Mattingly has argued vigorously, as part of his general program of contesting a number of conventional dates in Attic epigraphy, that the order of these two lists should be reversed, and that *IG* i^3 282 should be assigned to 427/6 and 281 to the following year.[85] While Mattingly's views have not necessarily gained widespread acceptance, he has not been the only one to query the conventional dating of the tribute quota lists, and it would be methodologically unsound to assume without question that they provide evidence for Thera joining the empire by 430/29.

Making such an unquestioning assumption even more unsound is the nature of Thera's 'appearance' in *IG* i^3 281 and 282. Ernst Badian has held forth on the dangers of 'history from square brackets' – the treatment of *restored* epigraphic text as if it were *received* epigraphic text – and the case of Thera is a good illustration of this particular hazard.[86] Not one letter of the island's name appears in *IG* i^3 281; it is completely restored, under the Islanders' rubric, next to a surviving quota of 300 drachmas.[87] The original editors of *ATL* based this restoration on the belief that they could read traces of Thera's name in the list for the following year (*IG* i^3 282), next to the same quota. The argument is a somewhat slim one and attenuated still more by the fact that *IG* i^3 282 is so damaged as to be extremely hard to read: not one, but two alternate suggestions have been made for *ATL*'s reading of [Θ]ερ[αῖ]οι in *IG* i^3 282.[88]

It would seem then that the first indisputable reference we have to Thera in the Athenian empire comes not from 430/29 but from 426/5: the important decree of Kleonymos on the collection of the tribute.[89] Here the Theraians appear, clearly grouped with the Samians in a special category that suggests that the monies these two states (and perhaps some others) owe (*chremata*) is not regular tribute (*phoros*).[90] It is hard to resist the notion that as far as the Samians are concerned, this is a reference to the war indemnity which we know from other sources they were condemned to pay as a result of their rebellion in 440/39.[91] The grouping of Thera with Samos here may then explain Thucydides' linking of her with Melos in 431. If Thera, like Samos, was condemned to pay a war indemnity to Athens, then it is possible that Thera, like Melos, demurred at the invitation to join the Athenian empire, and that the Athenians met her reticence with a more forcible summons. Thucydides may have had such resistance and insistence in mind when he mentioned Thera and Melos in the same breath, ignoring sundry other small islands who also remained outside the empire in 431, but who were perhaps persuaded to join in a more peaceable fashion.

The second Athenian maritime alliance, like the first one, offers epigraphic food for thought on the subject of Thera, though once again in the form of dainty appetizers rather than a square meal. The literary sources on Athens' fourth-century sea league are meagre (Xenophon does not even mention it), but we are fortunate in having extant the foundation document of the league, the famous stele of Aristoteles.[92] After the statement of purpose and principles governing the foundation and administration of the league, the inscription goes on to list the league members, both those who joined at the time of Aristoteles' motion in 378/7, and those who enlisted in subsequent years. Among those members are what appear to be two democratic factions: the *dēmos* of the Zakynthians and the *dēmos* of the

'–raians.'[93] While it was long held that the vanished ethnic should be restored as 'Kerkyraians,' J.E. Coleman and D.W. Bradeen demonstrated conclusively in the 1960s that such a restoration was epigraphically impossible, and proposed instead [Θη]ραίων.[94] If the Theraians did indeed appear in this fashion on the stele of Aristoteles, this brief notice has significant meaning for the island's history, suggesting as it does that in the fourth century *stasis* erupted once again on the island.

I do not propose to discuss here arguments explored in considerable depth elsewhere.[95] But it is worth bearing in mind, in the context of a discussion of the use of epigraphy to reconstruct Theraian history, the kinds of argumentation that have gone into the matter of the missing letters. Much of it has been based on the principle of *eikos*, of what the inscription is 'likely' to have said, based on historical plausibility. For instance, Coleman and Bradeen had argued that Thera was a credible candidate on the grounds that she, like most other members of the fourth-century sea league, had been a member of Athens' fifth-century naval alliance. Fordyce Mitchel, however, in his criticism of their views, objected that the restoration was *im*plausible on the grounds that the majority of the members of the Delian league did *not* reappear in the second sea league. The arguments on both sides therefore appeal to the principle of *eikos*, in spite of Mitchel's own objection to Coleman and Bradeen's invocation of that principle. Furthermore, while I have argued elsewhere that the restoration of the Theraian *dēmos* to this inscription remains the most attractive proposition, it must be admitted that my own arguments have also had to rely on this same principle.[96]

Conclusion

This paper has taken only a most selective look at the contribution of inscriptions to the reconstruction of Theraian local history and has neglected wholly the important realms of social and religious history. A number of methodological issues have been raised, in response to the challenges posed by the use of epigraphy for the purpose of rescuing lost history, but one issue still remains to be brought forward. It is a problem that appropriately enough has not yet been made explicit, as it is a problem springing from impressions largely left implicit: that is, the subconscious feeling that lost history is lost because, in fact, nothing really *did* happen. While no ancient historian would confess to holding such a belief consciously, it has nevertheless had a subtle impact on past interpretations of a number of inscriptions affecting Theraian history. To give but three examples: the importation of a completely unattested Athenian element into the circumstances surrounding *SEG* ix 3 (because it is otherwise unthinkable that an important state like Kyrene would pursue relations with a tiny and negligible state like Thera);[97] the rejection of '[the *d*]*ēmos* of the [The]raians' as an acceptable restoration in *IG* ii^2 43 (on the grounds that we have no other surviving references to fourth-century Theraian *stasis*, or to Theraian history in general in this period);[98] and the disputed status of the putative Ptolemaic *navarch* of *IG* xii.3 *supplement* 1291 (because a minor island such as Thera should have only a 'minor official' attached to it).[99] While the dangers of reading too *much* into a fragmentary epigraphic record are very real, implicit assumptions such as these are also hazardous, the more so as the tendency to make such assumptions is largely a subconscious one. The well-known 'silences' of Thucydides (on the reassessment of the Athenian tribute in 425) or Xenophon (on the existence of the second sea league) should demonstrate that even the most meticulous of the literary historians may leave gaps, and those gaps may conceal some very real history. Inscriptions, used with caution, help us to bridge those lacunae. Without the evidence of epigraphy, Thera's history would truly be the tale of lost Atlantis.

Notes

1 Doumas 1983.

2 For a summary discussion of this geological event, see Forsyth 1997: 103–16 and 150–6. For the name Kalliste, see Pindar, *Pythian* 4.258; Hdt. 4.147; Apollonios Rh. 4.1758; Kallimachos *ap* Strabo 17.3.21; Pliny, *NH* 4.12; Pausanias 3.15.6 and 7.2.2.

3 Many of the Theraian inscriptions appear to employ very early letter forms (Powell 1991: 13, 129–31, 172). On the other hand, the Theraians do appear to have been rather conservative in their tastes (producing Geometric style pottery, for example, considerably after other regions had moved on: Coldstream 1968: 188, 277). In any case, the dating of these Archaic inscriptions, in the absence of firm chronological controls, is highly problematic (Jeffery 1990: 63–5, 317–19; Johnston *ap* Jeffery 1990: 425, 430; Powell 1991: 55–7, 129–31). Recent examinations of newly discovered grave inscriptions from Thera suggest that earlier estimates of the age of the oldest Theraian inscriptions may have assigned them to an excessively early date; see Sigalas and Matthaiou 1992–8: 386 (*SEG* xlviii [1998] 1065–84).

4 *Pythian* 4.258 (Lattimore's [1976] translation of 'Kalliste').

5 Cf. the account in Apollonios Rh. 4.1756–1764.

6 Kyrene was founded ca. 630 BC.

7 Herodotos also presents an alternative and more romanticized Kyrenean version of the story of Battos himself, in which Battos has some of the characteristics of a folktale hero (4.154–5).

8 *Politics* 1290b8.

9 *FGrHist* 270 F 6 (perhaps second century BC). There is also the hopelessly garbled version of Kyrene's foundation found in Justin (13.7), but unlike Menekles, Justin does not bring anything new to the story (other than confusion).

10 See Arist. fr. 611.16; Kallimachos, *Hymn* 2; Diod. 8.29–30; Ovid, *Fasti* 3.567–78; Silius Italicus, *Punica* 8.57–64; Plut., *Mor* 408a; Pausanias 10.15.4; Justin 13.7; and the *scholia* to Pindar, *Pythians* 4 and 5.

11 The one historical fact that subsequent literary sources do provide is that in 198/7 BC, and again in the Roman period, the island underwent serious renewed volcanic activity, activity that resulted in the birth of the island in the caldera known today as Palaia Kameni (see Forsyth 1992 and further below).

12 *IG* xii.3 (1898); *IG* xii.3 *Supplement* (1904); *IG* xii *Supplement* (1939); all volumes edited by Hiller von Gaertringen. The Theraian inscriptions dominate *IG* xii.3, with four times the number of inscriptions from Melos (also in this volume).

13 Most of the inscriptions discovered since the publication of *IG* have found their way into the *Supplementum Epigraphicum Graecum, Ergon, Archaiologikon Deltion,* etc. Certain non-Theraian inscriptions of tremendous consequence to the history of the island have of course been published in other venues (see further below).

14 Grave inscriptions: *IG* xii.3 762–976, 1266 and *Supplement* 1608–37; *IG* xii *Supplement* 158–62 and 695–700; see also *SEG* xvi, xxv, xxvii, xxviii, xliii, and xlviii. Names and graffiti: *IG* xii.3 536–761 and *Supplement* 1410–1607; *IG* xii *Supplement* 157.

15 For example, *IG* xii.3 864–85 and *Supplement* 1624–5; *SEG* xvi 471. Heroization of the dead appears also to have been a private practice on the island, judging from *IG* xii.3 330, 886–932, 1266, *Supplement* 1626–35, and *SEG* xvi 472–3. See Kurtz and Boardman 1971: 297–302.

16 *IG* xii.3 536–43. See Brongersma 1990; Powell 1991: 172–80.

17 On the inscription of proper names as graffiti, see Thomas 1992: 61. In many cases, the surviving name may have been meant to be something other than a simple 'celebration of the self': potentially unidentified dedications may also at times be lurking among this group. See Powell 1991: 183–4.

18 *IG* xii.3 350–461 and *Supplement* 1307–85; *IG* xii *Supplement* 155–5a.

19 *IG* xii.3 350–409.

20 See Guarducci 1987: 79–80; Jeffery 1990: 318–19; Powell 1991: 129–31.

21 *IG* xii.3 536–7. See Brongersma 1990 and Powell 1991: 172 (who refers to 'the surprising confluence of agonistic dance, *poiesis,* hexametric expression and early alphabetic writing ... interestingly amplified by explicit reference to homosexual *charis* served by excellence in the dance,' perhaps a rather elevated view of the matter).

22 *IG* xii.3 421–2 and *Supplement* 1333–48; Hiller von Gaertringen 1899: 166, 187, 199; 1904: 89–102; Palagia 1992.

23 *IG* xii.3 *Supplement* 1349.

24 *IG* xii.3 462–535 and *Supplement* 1386–1409; *IG* xii *Supplement* 156; *SEG* xvi 470.

25 *IG* xii.3 462, 463, *Supplement* 1386–8, and *IG* xii *Supplement* 156.

26 *IG* xii.3 *Supplement* 1392–3; Hiller von Gaertringen 1904: 128.

27 *IG* xii.3 485, 487, 494, 495, 497–505, 513, 516, 522, 523, 525, 530, and *Supplement* 1402–8. The granting of a crown and citizenship to Artemidoros: *IG* xii.3 *sSupplement* 1343–4.

28 *IG* xii.3 320–9, 331, *Supplement* 1289–96; *SEG* xviii 325; see Rhodes and Lewis 1997: 296–7.

29 On the unique place of Athens in public epigraphy, see Hedrick 1999 and Bodel 2001: 10–13.

30 *IG* xii.3 *Supplement* 1289; *IG* xii.3 320.

31 Hiller von Gaertringen 1899: 217–37; 1904: 112–13, 129.

32 *IG* xii.3 330.

33 One possible meagre exception is the appearance of the word *Bakalos* on a late Archaic Theraian gravestone, which may represent the genitive of a name common in Kyrene (Bakal), apparently adopted there from the Libyans (*IG* xii.3 812; Masson 1967; *LGPN I* 98; Johnston *ap* Jeffery 1990: 470). This individual may represent a sort of post-colonial 'reflux' (as may 'Barbaks,' *IG* xii.3 543).

34 Of these, the most significant are *IG* i^3 68 and 71, *IG* ii^2 43, and *SEG* ix 3 (see below); among other external inscriptions of interest are *IG* i^3 977–80, *IG* ii^2 179, and *SEG* ix 2.

35 *IG* xii.3 762 (ca. 650–600 BC?; Guarducci 1987: 80; Jeffery 1990: 323); *SEG* ix 3 (370–360 BC?; Lalonde 1987: 162; Dobias-Lalou 1994: 244).

36 *LGPN I* express doubt as to the Theraian Archagetas being a personal name; cf. however *SEG* xxxviii 322 (an 'Archagetas' from Epidauros).

37 The name Grinnos is also an unusual one, and does not appear elsewhere in the Aegean; it is, however, attested in later Theraian inscriptions as a name used by one of the more influential families on the island, that of Epikteta (*IG* xii.3 330; see also 1032). Grinnos' embassy to Delphi may have taken place about 640 BC, not too far distant in time from the *archagetas* inscription.

38 Drews 1983.

39 Galites 1960; Jeffery 1961: 144.

40 Carlier (1984: 312), however, argues for an occasional synonymity of *archagetas* and *basileus* in tragedy.

41 Hiller von Gaertringen 1932.

42 Guarducci 1939–40. The name Prokles appears in other Theraian inscriptions (*IG* xii.3 335A and *Supp.* 1444), as well as in a very early inscription from Kyrenaika (*SEG* xlv 2170). Cf. the Roman-era Theraian who claimed direct descent from the kings of Lakedaimon (*IG* xii.3 868).

43 Vollgraff 1951: 17–19; Jeffery 1976: 186.

44 *SEG* ix 3, lines 11 and 26.

45 Ferri 1925: 19ff., II (and Wilamowitz, [*ap*. Ferri, pp. 34ff.]); a superior edition was published by Oliverio 1928: 222ff., 2. See also (*inter al.*) Ferrabino 1928; Dovatur 1928; *SEG* ix 3; Chamoux 1953: 105–8; Graham 1960; Jeffery 1961; Seibert 1963: 9ff.; Graham 1964: 224ff.; Oliver 1966; Yailenko 1973; Gawantka 1975: 101–11; Dušanić 1978; Fornara 1983: 18; Crawford and Whitehead 1983: 16; Rhodes 1986: 25–8; Pugliese Carratelli 1987; Meiggs-Lewis no. 5; Chaniotis 1988: 238, 264, 273; Dobias-Lalou 1994.

46 Probably to any Theraians who came to settle in Kyrene, rather than simply to Theraian metics currently resident in Kyrene; see Ager 2001: 105, and the sources cited there.

47 Lines 24–51, preceded by the heading: ὅρκιον τῶν οἰκιστήρων.

48 τός τε ἄλλος [πολιάτας] τοὺς ἡβῶντας καὶ τῶν [ἄλ|λ]ων Θηραίων ἐλευθέρος [ὅ κα λῆι] πλέν· (Dobias-Lalou 1994). Previous editions were largely unable to fill this lacuna.

49 Or 'if they are oppressed by exigency for a period of five years, then they are to depart from the land.' The meaning of the phrase is not entirely clear, and Jeffery exemplifies well the lack of clarity, arguing in 1961 that it meant the colonists were to be able to return to Thera only after a period of five years, and in 1976 (52–3, 58) that the colonists were to be able to return to Thera *within* the first five years.

50 Lines 24–40; the translation is based on the text of Dobias-Lalou.

51 Lines 40ff.

52 Lines 46–51; thus, only the last few lines of the inscription actually contain something that could be described as an 'oath,' and even so, these lines represent only the sanctioning formula.

53 Hdt. 4.153 and 156 (translation A. de Sélincourt 1954). Herodotos' account of the actual sequence of events suffers from both conflation and doublets, but it is not necessary to analyse or systematize his sequencing here; what is of interest are the discrete details he reports.

54 ἔδοξε τᾶι ἐκκλησίαι (*SEG* ix 3); Θηραίοισι δὲ ἕαδε (Hdt. 4.153).

55 See Faraone 1993 for a discussion of the weighty nature (and authenticity) of the sympathetic magic ritual described in the *horkion*; see also Harris 1996: 66.

56 Ferri 1925: 23–4.

57 Graham 1960 (cf. Robert *REG* 1961: 839); Jeffery 1961; Seibert 1963; Oliver 1966; Yailenko 1973; Murray 1980: 114–15; Crawford-Whitehead 1983; Rhodes 1986; Meiggs-Lewis: 7–9; Rhodes and Lewis 1997: 297; Malkin 2003.

58 Ferri 1925 (and Wilamowitz *ap* Ferri); Ferrabino 1928; Dovatur 1928; Chamoux 1953; Dušanić 1978; Walter 1993: 141. The weakness of some of the sceptical views of the *horkion* is that those who express such scepticism have thus far

been unable to present a convincing argument as to the purpose of such a forgery or whom it was meant to benefit; for criticism of the views of Ferrabino and Dušanić in particular, see Ager 2001: 105–7.

59 On the possible implication of *SEG* ix 3 for the history of Thera in the *fourth* century, see Ager 2001.

60 If we except the slight possibility that Apollonios, who may be prefigured by Pindar (in talking about Thera's own birth from the clod of earth thrown into the sea by the hero Euphemos), is referring poetically to a folk memory of unstable geology (Apollonios Rh. 4.1756–64; cf. Pindar, *Pythian* 4).

61 See Forsyth 1992 for a discussion of the sources and a reconstruction of the geologic event.

62 Cf. Justin 30.4.4.

63 Late antiquity reports yet another major eruption in AD 726.

64 *IG* xii.3 324.

65 *IG* xii.3 325–6.

66 Efforts to avert the anger of heaven (so apt to display itself through natural disaster) through appeasement may have inspired the Rhodian dedication of a shrine to Poseidon *Asphaleios* on the new island that appeared in 197 BC, and even the medieval name of Thera (Santorini = St *Eirene*; Georgacas 1970: 361).

67 See Bagnall 1976: 123–34; van't Dack 1973 and 1981.

68 See above, n. 25; on the (disputed) date of Arsinoë's death, see Cadell 1998. Other dedications on behalf of Ptolemaic rulers: *IG* xii.3 464–8, *Supplement* 1389–91.

69 Aside from the extremely fragmented *IG* xii.3 *Supplement* 1289, perhaps from the fourth century.

70 *IG* xii.3 320. On Ptolemaic activity in Attica at this time, see McCredie 1966, especially 107–15.

71 Epigraphic evidence for Ptolemaic officials and garrison on Thera: *IG* xii.3 327, 466, 467, *Supplement* 1291, 1296, 1390, 1391; *SEG* xviii 325; note also the Artemidoros inscriptions. On the Mesa Vouno structures associated with the Ptolemaic garrison (the Ptolemaic gymnasium and command post), see Hiller von Gaertringen 1899: 204–17; 1904: 105–6.

72 Huß 2001: 603–4.

73 *IG* xii.3 *Supplement* 1291 (and cf. *IG* xii.3 328); see Ager 1998.

74 *IG* xii.3 *Supplement* 1291: [–]χος καὶ στραταγὸς τᾶς πόλιος. Bagnall (1976: 132–4) supports the reading [ναύαρ]χος, and the view that the chief Ptolemaic naval commander was stationed on Thera, while van't Dack (1973 and 1981) argues in favour of the less elevated [φρούραρ]χος. Witschel (1997: 20) agrees with Bagnall.

75 *IG* xii.3 466 and *Supplement* 1390; Bagnall 1976: 130–1; Huß 2001: 579.

76 Methana: Bagnall 1976: 135–6, Cohen 1995: 124–5; Itanos: Spyridakis 1970;

Bagnall 1976: 120–3. It was a Theraian inscription (*IG* xii.3 466 and *Supplement* 1390) that assisted in the identification of Methana as Arsinoë (Hiller von Gaertringen 1925–6: 69–70).

77 *IG* xii.3 464.

78 The Melians, like the Theraians, claimed descent from Sparta (Thucydides 5.84, and the 'Melian Dialogue' passim); that Thera cherished her tie with Sparta (whatever its real nature) even into the period of the Roman empire – and that Sparta in turn fostered that affection – is suggested by such sources as *IG* xii.3 868 and Pausanias 3.15.8.

79 *IG* i^3 977–980; Weller and Dunham 1903; Connor 1988. It is by no means certain that these inscriptions belong to the fifth century.

80 *IG* ii^2 1413, 1415, 1421; cf. *sch.* Ar. *Lys.* 150, Ath. 10.424, Pollux, *Onom.* 4.118, 7.48, 7.77.

81 Thuc. 2.9. 4; cf. Diod. 12.42.

82 Thera's closest neighbour, Anaphe, for example, does not appear in the tribute lists until 428/7 (*IG* i^3 283); Kimolos, Sikinos, Pholegandros – and Melos – were assessed for the first time in 425 (*IG* i^3 71). See Piérart 1984: 165 and Seaman 1997: 414.

83 *IG* i^3 71.

84 The editors of *ATL* (followed by Lewis *ap IG* i^3 281) assigned this list to 430/29. See Sperling 1973: 63; Kagan 1974: 198; Meiggs 1975: 322.

85 Mattingly 1978 (1996).

86 Badian 1989; see also Bodel 2001: 52–5.

87 Column ii, l. 54; a quota of 300 drachmas presupposes a tribute payment of three talents.

88 [H]EΦ[A]Ị[Σ]Ṭ[IEΣ] (Mattingly 1978 [1996]: 434); [ΣI]ΦṆ[I]OI (Piérart 1984: 164–5).

89 *IG* i^3 68; Samons 2000: 184–7.

90 Lines 21–5.

91 Thuc. 1.117.3. See Meiggs 1975: 192–3; Mattingly 1978 (1996: 431); Piérart 1984: 163; Shipley 1987: 118, 294–6; Meiggs-Lewis: 187.

92 *IG* ii^2 43; Cargill 1981: 16–27.

93 Lines 97–8: [–]ραίων [ὁ δ]ῆμος.

94 Coleman and Bradeen 1967.

95 See Coleman and Bradeen 1967; Mitchel 1984; Cargill 1981 and 1996; Ager 2001.

96 Ager 2001.

97 Ferrabino 1928; Dušanić 1978.

98 Mitchel 1984.

99 Merker 1970: 153–4.

References

Ager, S. 1998. 'Thera and the Pirates: An Ancient Case of the Stockholm Syndrome?' *AHB* 12: 83–95.

– 2001. '4th Century Thera and the Second Athenian Sea League.' *Ancient World* 32: 99–119.

Badian, E. 1989. 'History from "Square Brackets."' *ZPE* 79: 59–70.

Bagnall, R.S. 1976. *The Administration of the Ptolemaic Possessions outside Egypt.* Leiden.

Bodel, J., ed. 2001. *Epigraphic Evidence: Ancient History from Inscriptions.* London and New York.

Brongersma, E. 1990. 'The Thera Inscriptions – Ritual or Slander?' *Journal of Homosexuality* 20: 31–40.

Cadell, H. 1998. 'À quelle date Arsinoé II Philadelphe est-elle décédée?' in H. Melaerts, (ed.), *Le culte de souverain dans l'Égypte ptolémaïque au IIIe siècle avant notre ère,* 1–3. Leuven.

Cargill, J. 1981. *The Second Athenian League.* Berkeley.

– 1996. 'The Decree of Aristoteles: Some Epigraphical Details.' *Ancient World* 27: 39–51.

Carlier, P. 1984. *La royauté en Grèce avant Alexandre.* Strasbourg.

Chamoux, F. 1953. *Cyrène sous la monarchie des Battiades.* Paris.

Chaniotis, A. 1988. *Historie und Historiker in den griechischen Inschriften.* Stuttgart.

Cohen, G.M. 1995. *The Hellenistic Settlements in Europe, the Islands, and Asia Minor.* Berkeley, Los Angeles, and Oxford.

Coldstream, J.N. 1968. *Greek Geometric Pottery.* London.

Coleman, J.E., and D.W. Bradeen. 1967. 'Thera on I.G., II^2, 43.' *Hesperia* 36: 102–4.

Connor, W.R. 1988. 'Seized by the Nymphs: Nympholepsy and Symbolic Expression in Classical Greece.' *ClAnt* 7: 155–89.

Crawford, M., and D. Whitehead. 1983. *Archaic and Classical Greece.* Cambridge.

de Sélincourt, A., trans. 1954 (1972) . *Herodotus: The Histories.* Revised, with introduction and notes by A.R. Burn. New York.

Dobias-Lalou, C. 1994 (1995). '*SEG* IX, 3: un document composite ou inclassable?' *Verbum* 3/4: 243–56.

Doumas, C. 1983. *Thera: Pompeii of the Ancient Aegean.* London.

Dovatur, A. 1928. 'Le serment des fondateurs de Cyrène.' *Comptes rendus de l'Académie des Sciences de l'URSS*: 233–6 (in Russian).

Drews, R. 1983. *Basileus: The Evidence for Kingship in Geometric Greece.* Yale.

Dušanić, S. 1978. 'The ὅρκιον τῶν οἰκιστήρων and Fourth-Century Cyrene.' *Chiron* 8: 55–76.

Faraone, C. 1993. 'Molten Wax, Spilt Wine and Mutilated Animals: Sympathetic Magic in Near Eastern and Early Greek Oath Ceremonies.' *JHS* 113: 60–80.
Ferrabino, A. 1928. 'La stele dei patti.' *RFIC* 56: 250–4.
Ferri, S. 1925. 'Alcune iscrizioni di Cirene.' *APAW* 5: 3–40.
Fornara, C.W. 1983. *Archaic Times to the End of the Peloponnesian War*². Cambridge.
Forsyth, P.Y. 1992. 'After the Big Bang: Eruptive Activity in the Caldera of Greco-Roman Thera.' *GRBS* 33: 191–204.
– 1997. *Thera in the Bronze Age*. New York.
Galites, G.A. 1960. ''Αρχηγὸς-'Αρχηγέτης dans la littérature et la religion grecque.' *Athena* 64: 17–138.
Gawantka, W. 1975. *Isopolitie*. Munich.
Georgacas, D.J. 1970. 'On the Names of the Santorini Island Group.' *Beiträge zur Namenforschung* 5: 341–70.
Graham, A.J. 1960. 'The Authenticity of the ΟΡΚΙΟΝ ΤΩΝ ΟΙΚΙΣΤΗΡΩΝ of Cyrene.' *JHS* 80: 94–111.
– 1964. *Colony and Mother City in Ancient Greece*. New York.
Guarducci, M. 1939–40. 'Fu Prokles re di Thera?' *ASAA* 1–2: 41–5.
– 1987. *L'epigrafia greca dalle origini al tardo impero*. Rome.
Harris, W.V. 1996. 'Writing and Literacy in the Archaic Greek City,' in J. Strubbe et al. (eds.), ΕΝΕΡΓΕΙΑ, 57–77. Amsterdam.
Hedrick, C.W. 1999. 'Democracy and the Athenian Epigraphical Habit.' *Hesperia* 68: 387–439.
Hiller von Gaertringen, F., et al. 1899. *Thera i: Die Insel Thera in Altertum und Gegenwart*. Berlin.
– 1904. *Thera iii: Untersuchungen, Vermessungen und Ausgrabungen in den Jahren 1895–1902*. Berlin.
Hiller von Gaertringen, F. 1925–26. ''Επιγραφαι ἐκ τοῦ ἱεροῦ τῆς 'Επιδαῦρου.' *AE* 1925–6: 67–86.
– 1932. 'König Prokles von Thera.' *JdI* 47: 127–34.
Huß, W. 2001. *Ägypten in hellenistischer Zeit, 332–30 v. Chr.* Munich.
Jeffery, L.H. 1961. 'The Pact of the First Settlers at Cyrene.' *Historia* 10: 139–47.
– 1976. *Archaic Greece*. London.
– 1990. *The Local Scripts of Archaic Greece*². Oxford (includes new supplement by A.W. Johnston, 423–81).
Kagan, D. 1974. *The Archidamian War*. Ithaca.
Kurtz, D.C., and J. Boardman. 1971. *Greek Burial Customs*. London.
Lalonde, A. 1987. *Cyrène et la Libye hellénistique*. Paris.
Lattimore, R. 1976. *The Odes of Pindar*. Chicago.
Malkin, I. 2003. '"Tradition" in Herodotus: The Foundation of Cyrene,' in P. Derow and R. Parker (eds.), *Herodotus and His World*, 153–70. Oxford.

Masson, O. 1967. 'Remarques sur deux inscriptions de Cyrène et de Théra.' *RPh* 1967: 225–31.

Mattingly, H.B. 1978. 'The Tribute Quota Lists from 430 to 425 BC.' *CQ* 28: 83–8 (reprinted with corrections in Mattingly 1996: 427–34).

– 1996. *The Athenian Empire Restored*. Ann Arbor.

McCredie, J.R. 1966. *Fortified Military Camps in Attica*. Princeton.

Meiggs, R. 1975 (1972). *The Athenian Empire*. Oxford (reprint of 1972 edition with corrections).

Merker, I.L. 1970. 'The Ptolemaic Officials and the League of the Islanders.' *Historia* 19: 141–60.

Mitchel, F.W. 1984. 'The Rasura of *IG* II^2 43: Jason, the Pheraian Demos and the Athenian League.' *Ancient World* 9: 39–58.

Murray, O. 1980. *Early Greece*. Glasgow.

Oliver, J.H. 1966. 'Herodotus 4.153 and *SEG* IX 3.' *GRBS* 7: 25–9.

Oliverio, G. 1928. 'Iscrizioni di Cirene.' *RFIC* 56: 183–239.

Palagia, O. 1992. 'Cult and Allegory: The Life Story of Artemidoros of Perge,' in J.M. Sanders (ed.), *Philolakon: Lakonian Studies in Honour of Hector Catling*, 171–7. London.

Piérart, M. 1984. 'Deux notes sur la politique d'Athènes en mer Égée (428–425).' *BCH* 108: 161–76.

Powell, B.B. 1991. *Homer and the Origin of the Greek Alphabet*. Cambridge.

Pugliese Carratelli, G. 1987. 'ΚΥΡΗΝΑΙΚΑ.' *QAL* 12: 25–32.

Rhodes, P.J. 1986. *The Greek City-States*. London.

Rhodes, P.J., and D.M. Lewis. 1997. *The Decrees of the Greek States*. Oxford.

Samons, L.J. 2000. *Empire of the Owl: Athenian Imperial Finance*. Stuttgart.

Seaman, M.G. 1997. 'The Athenian Expedition to Melos in 416 BC.' *Historia* 46: 385–418.

Seibert, J. 1963. *Metropolis und Apoikie: historische Beiträge zur Geschichte ihrer gegenseitigen Beziehungen*. Diss. Würzburg.

Shipley, G. 1987. *A History of Samos, 800–188 BC*. Oxford.

Sigalas, C., and A. Matthaiou. 1992–98. ''Επιγραφὲς Θήρας.' *Horos* 10–12: 385–402.

Sperling, J.W. 1973. *Thera and Therasia*. Athens.

Spyridakis, S. 1970. *Ptolemaic Itanos and Hellenistic Crete*. Berkeley and Los Angeles.

Thomas, R. 1992. *Literacy and Orality in Ancient Greece*. Cambridge.

van't Dack, E. 1973. 'Les commandants de place lagides à Théra.' *Ancient Society* 4: 71–90.

– 1981. 'Le problème des commandants de place lagides à Théra réexaminé,' in E. Bresciani et al. (eds.), *Scritti in onore di Orsolina Montevecchi*, 419–29. Bologna.

Vollgraff, W. 1951. *L'inhumation en terre sacrée dans l'antiquité grecque*. Paris.

Walter, U. 1993. *An der Polis teilhaben: Bürgerstaat und Zugehörigkeit im archaischen Griechenland*. Stuttgart.

Weller, C.H., M.E. Dunham, et al. 1903. 'The Cave at Vari.' *AJA* 7: 263–349.

Witschel, C. 1997. 'Beobachtungen zur Stadtentwicklung von Thera in hellenistischer und römischer Zeit,' in W. Hoepfner et al. (eds.), *Das dorische Thera v: Stadtgeschichte und Kultstätten am nördlichen Stadtrand*, 17–46. Berlin.

Yailenko, V.P. 1973. 'Greek Colonisation in Archaic Times, from Epigraphical Sources.' *Vestnik drevnei istorii* 2: 43–69 (in Russian, with a brief summary in English).

INDEX OF SOURCES

INDEX OF NAMES

INDEX OF PLACES

GENERAL INDEX

PHOENIX SUPPLEMENTARY VOLUMES

1 *Studies in Honour of Gilbert Norwood* edited by Mary E. White

2 *Arbiter of Elegance: A Study of the Life and Works of C. Petronius* Gilbert Bagnani

3 *Sophocles the Playwright* S.M. Adams

4 *A Greek Critic: Demetrius on Style* G.M.A. Grube

5 *Coastal Demes of Attika: A Study of the Policy of Kleisthenes* C.W.J. Eliot

6 *Eros and Psyche: Studies in Plato, Plotinus, and Origen* John M. Rist

7 *Pythagoras and Early Pythagoreanism* J.A. Philip

8 *Plato's Psychology* T.M. Robinson

9 *Greek Fortifications* F.E. Winter

10 *Comparative Studies in Republican Latin Imagery* Elaine Fantham

11 *The Orators in Cicero's 'Brutus': Prosopography and Chronology* G.V. Sumner

12 *'Caput' and Colonate: Towards a History of Late Roman Taxation* Walter Goffart

13 *A Concordance to the Works of Ammianus Marcellinus* Geoffrey Archbold

14 *Fallax opus: Poet and Reader in the Elegies of Propertius* John Warden

15 *Pindar's 'Olympian One': A Commentary* Douglas E. Gerber

16 *Greek and Roman Mechanical Water-Lifting Devices: The History of a Technology* John Peter Oleson

17 *The Manuscript Tradition of Propertius* James L. Butrica

18 Parmenides of Elea *Fragments: A Text and Translation with an Introduction* edited by David Gallop

19 *The Phonological Interpretation of Ancient Greek: A Pandialectical Analysis* Vít Bubeník

20 *Studies in the Textual Tradition of Terence* John N. Grant

21 *The Nature of Early Greek Lyric: Three Preliminary Studies* R.L. Fowler

22 Heraclitus *Fragments: A Text and Translation with Commentary* edited by T.M. Robinson

23 *The Historical Method of Herodotus* Donald Lateiner

24 *Near Eastern Royalty and Rome, 100–30 BC* Richard D. Sullivan

25 *The Mind of Aristotle: A Study in Philosophical Growth* John M. Rist

26 *Trials in the Late Roman Republic, 149 BC to 50 BC* Michael Alexander

27 *Monumental Tombs of the Hellenistic Age: A Study of Selected Tombs from the Pre-Classical to the Early Imperial Era* Janos Fedak

28 *The Local Magistrates of Roman Spain* Leonard A. Curchin

29 Empedocles *The Poem of Empedocles: A Test and Translation with an Introduction* edited by Brad Inwood

30 Xenephanes of Colophon *Fragments: A Text and Translation with a Commentary* J.H. Lesher

31 *Festivals and Legends: The Formation of Greek Cities in the Light of Public Ritual* Noel Robertson

32 *Reading and Variant in Petronius: Studies in the French Humanists and Their Manuscript Sources* Wade Richardson

33 *The Excavations of San Giovanni di Ruoti, Volume 1: The Villas and Their Environment* Alastair M. Small and Robert J. Buck

34 *Catullus Edited with a Textual and Interpretative Commentary* D.F.S. Thomson

35 *The Excavations of San Giovanni di Ruoti, Volume 2: The Small Finds* C.J. Simpson, with contributions by R. Reece and J.J. Rossiter

36 The Atomists: Leucippus and Democritus *Fragments: A Text and Translation with a Commentary* C.C.W. Taylor

37 *Imagination of a Monarchy: Studies in Ptolemaic Propoganda* R.A. Hazzard

38 *Aristotle's Theory of the Unity of Science* Malcolm Wilson

39 Empedocles *The Poem of Empedocles: A Text and Translation with an Introduction, Revised Edition* edited by Brad Inwood

40 *The Excavations of San Giovanni di Ruoti, Volume 3: The Faunal and Plant Remains* M.R. McKinnon, with contributions by A. Eastham, S.G. Monckton, D.S. Reese, and D.G. Steele

41 *Justin and Pompeius Trogus: A Study of the Language of Justin's 'Epitome' of Trogus* J.C. Yardley

42 *Studies in Hellenistic Architecture* F.E. Winter

43 *Mortuary Landscapes of North Africa* edited by David L. Stone and Lea M. Stirling

44 Anaxagoras of Clazomenae *A Text and Translation with Notes and Essays* edited by Patricia Curd

45 *Virginity Revisited: Configurations of the Unpossessed Body* edited by Bonnie MacLachlan and Judith Fletcher

46 *Roman Dress and the Fabrics of Roman Culture* edited by Jonathan Edmondson and Alison Keith

47 *Epigraphy and the Greek Historian* edited by Craig Cooper

48 *In the Image of the Ancestors: Narratives of Kinship in Flavian Epic* Neil W. Bernstein

www.ingramcontent.com/pod-product-compliance
Lightning Source LLC
LaVergne TN
LVHW090808070826
844660LV00022B/1114
* 9 7 8 1 4 4 2 6 5 2 4 8 4 *